Motor Vehicle Science
Part 1

Motor Vehicle Science

Part 1

P. W. Kett

LONDON   NEW YORK

CHAPMAN AND HALL

First published 1982 by
Chapman and Hall Ltd
11 New Fetter Lane, London EC4P 4EE
Published in the USA by
Chapman and Hall
in association with Methuen, Inc.
733 Third Avenue, New York NY 10017

ISBN 0 412 23590 0 (cased)
ISBN 0 412 22100 4 (paperback)

Printed in Great Britain
at the University Press, Cambridge

British Library Cataloguing in Publication Data

Kett, P. W.

  Motor vehicle science.
  Part 1
  1. Automobiles — Design and construction
  I. Title
  629.2   TL145

  ISBN 0-412-23590-0
  ISBN 0-412-22100-4 Pbk

Library of Congress Cataloging in Publication Data

Kett, P. W.

  Motor vehicle science.

  Includes index.
  1. Motor vehicles. I. Title.
  TL146.K47   629.2   81-11336

  ISBN 0-412-23590-0 (v. 1) AACR2
  ISBN 0-412-22100-4 (pbk. : v. 1)

To my wife I dedicate this book. Her forbearance,
help and understanding over the past two years made
the book possible.

Contents

Preface   xi

Nomenclature   xiii

1. Materials (A1)   1
  1.1 Stress and strain   1
  1.2 Hooke's Law and Young's Modulus   4
  1.3 Testing of materials: load—extension graphs   8
  Exercises 1.1   19

2. Heat   22
  2.1 Linear and cubical expansion (B2)   22
  Exercises 2.1   27
  2.2 Sensible heat and latent heat (B3)   28
  2.3 Specific heat capacity   30
  2.4 Boiling point of liquids   33
  Exercises 2.2   34
  2.5 Elementary thermodynamics (B4)   35
  Exercises 2.3   42
  2.6 Compression ratios (B5)   43
  Exercises 2.4   48
  2.7 Engine power and efficiency (B6)   49
  Exercises 2.5   52
  2.8 Internal combustion engine cycles   52
  2.9 Imep, bmep and mechanical efficiency   56
  Exercises 2.6   61
  2.10 Engine torque and brake power   61
  2.11 Fuel consumption and thermal efficiency   65
  Exercises 2.7   69
  2.12 Engine testing and characteristic curves   71
  2.13 Conservation of energy   74
  2.14 Indicated power and mechanical efficiency   74
  Exercises 2.8   77
  Exercises 2.9   79

2.15 Fuel consumption and thermal efficiency   85
2.16 Ignition tests   86
2.17 Heat balance tests   89
Exercises 2.10   95
2.18 Fuels used in IC engines (B7)   97

3. Dynamics   104
3.1 Velocity and acceleration (C8)   104
Exercises 3.1   110
3.2 Free falling and projected bodies   111
Exercises 3.2   121
3.3 Angular and linear motion (C9)   121
Exercises 3.3   126
3.4 Friction and bearings (C10)   128
Exercises 3.4   133
3.5 Clutches   133
Exercises 3.5   138
3.6 Brakes   139
Exercises 3.6   153

4. Lubrication (D11)   155
4.1 Principles of bearings and their uses   155
4.2 Ball and roller bearings   157
4.3 Properties of lubricating oils   164

5. Statics   169
5.1 Triangle and polygon of forces (E13)   169
5.2 Piston, connecting rod and cylinder wall forces   175
5.3 Torque at the crankshaft   176
5.4 Piston displacement   179
5.5 Wheel balance   181
Exercises 5.1   188
5.6 Principle of moments (E14)   190
5.7 Centre of gravity   195
Exercises 5.2   204
5.8 Reaction of beam supports (E15)   205
5.9 Bending moments and shearing forces   210
Exercises 5.3   226
5.10 Springs and torsion bars (E16)   228
Exercises 5.4   238
5.11 Transmission and steering components (E17)   238
Exercises 5.5   262

6. Electricity (F18)   265
   6.1 The secondary cell   265
   6.2 Battery developments   269
   Exercises 6.1   270

7. Miscellaneous exercises   271
   7.1 Materials   271
   7.2 Heat   272
   7.3 Dynamics   274
   7.4 Statics   276

Answers to Exercises   278

Index   287

The alpha-numeric code which appears after the entries refers to the
TEC U77/413 and 415 Motor Vehicle Science II and III Model Programmes
of Study.

Preface

A motor vehicle technician has to attain high technological skills to enable him or her to diagnose faults and service modern transport vehicles and their components.

Science is a branch of study concerned with the systematic investigation of observed facts, and forms an important foundation on which to build sound engineering practice. Such a background will stimulate personal development by increasing confidence and intellectual ability. This is the first of two books planned to cover the TEC U77/413 and 415 Motor Vehicle Science II and III Model programmes of study. Part 1 is intended to cover the requirements of Motor Vehicle Science II. The fundamental principles of engineering science have been applied to the motor vehicle in a systematic and progressive manner to enable the reader to follow most of the work on his or her initiative. The book is aimed mainly at the student who is attending a recognized college course leading to a Technician qualification. The importance of the college lecturer and his individual method of teaching the subject remains of prime importance to the student. The book is designed to become a valid source of information to assist the student both in and out of the classroom environment to attain his or her objective.

Numerous fully worked and exercise examples are given. Plenty of practice in solving problems is an excellent way to gain knowledge of the subject, and improve confidence in preparation for an examination.

The signs and symbols used in this book will be repeated where applicable in Part 2, thus the reader can become conversant with them and recognize their meaning immediately. All the SI symbols and abbreviations used are the official ones.

Filby   P.W.K.
Norfolk

Nomenclature

The following is a list of abbreviations and symbols used in the book.

A	area (m^2)
a	acceleration (m/s^2)
ACW	anti-clockwise
BDC	bottom dead centre
bhp	brake horse power
BM	bending moment (N m)
bmep	break mean effective pressure (N/m^2)
c	specific heat capacity ($J/(kg\ °C)$) or ($J/(kg\ K)$)
CF	centrifugal force (N)
CG	centre of gravity
CI	compression ignition
CP	circular pitch
CSA	cross-sectional area (m^2)
CV	calorific or heat value (J/kg)
CW	clockwise
D	diameter (m)
d	diameter (m) or relative density (no units)
DOM	direction of motion
DOR	direction of rotation
DP	diametrical pitch
DVN	driven
DVR	driver
E	Young's Modulus (Modulus of Elasticity) (N/m^2) or equilibrant force (N)
e	tensile or compressive strain, or transmission efficiency
F	force (N)
f	stress (N/m^2) or final drive ratio
FR	force ratio (or mechanical advantage)
g	acceleration due to gravity (usually taken as $9.81\ m/s^2$)
GR	gear ratio
h	height (m) or hub reduction ratio

hp	horse power
ihp	indicated horse power
imep	indicated mean effective pressure (p_m) (N/m^2, Pa)
L	length (m)
l	latent heat (J/kg)
L of P	limit of proportionality
LCV	lower calorific value
m	mass (kg)
mc	master cylinder
ME	mechanical efficiency (%)
MP	module pitch
MR	movement ratio
N	revolutions per minute (rev/min)
n	number (e.g. pistons) or reduction ratio
NTP (or STP)	normal (or standard) temperature and pressure
P	power (W)
p	pressure (Pa, N/m^2)
PC	pitch circle
PCD	pitch circle diameter (m)
R	reaction (or resultant force) (N) or radius (m)
r	compression ratio (CR)
S	distance or displacement (m) or piston speed (m/s)
SF	shearing force (N)
SFC	specific fuel consumption (kg/(kW h) or 1/(kW h))
STP	see NTP
TE	tractive effort
T	temperature ($^\circ$C, K) or torque (N m) or number of gear teeth
t	time (s, h)
TDC	top dead centre
u	initial velocity (m/s)
V	volume (m^3) or velocity (m/s)
v	velocity or final velocity (m/s)
wc	wheel cylinder (hydraulic)
W (or w)	weight or load (kg)
x	extension (m)

Greek letters

α	coefficient of linear expansion (per $^\circ$C)
η	efficiency (%)
μ	coefficient of friction

ρ	density
ϕ, θ	angles (rad, $^\circ$)
ω	angular velocity (rad/s)

Subscripts

B	big end
b	bearing or braking
c	connecting rod or clearance or crown
D	drag
d	drum
e	expanded
F	front
f	fusion or friction
I	inlet
i	indicated or inner
L	leading
m	mean or mechancial
N	normal or nearside
O	outlet or offside
o	outer
p	piston
R	road or rear
r	radial
s	swept or servo or shoe
T	trailing
t	total or tangential
w	cylinder wall

1
Materials (A1)

1.1 STRESS AND STRAIN

Materials under stress

The materials used to construct motor vehicles and other structures have
forces acting upon them during their normal use which produce slight
deformation or change of shape, and it is said that these components have
been strained or put under stress. The strength of a material is its resistance
to strain. The application of an external load or force on a piece of material
will be resisted by an internal resisting force, and under these conditions the
material is considered to be under stress, and any alteration in shape is called
strain. Care must be taken to use stress and strain in the right context. The
types of stress are tensile, compressive, single and double shear, bending and
torsional stress.

Tensile stress

This is the stress set up in a material when its internal forces are resisting axial
loading or force which is tending to pull or stretch the material. Any
extension which takes place is termed tensile strain (see Fig. 1.1).

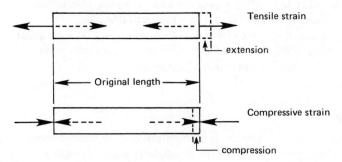

Fig. 1.1 Tensile and compressive strain.

Compressive stress

When the internal forces are resisting a compressive load the material is under compressive stress, and any deformation or reduction in length is termed compressive strain (see Fig. 1.1).

Shear stress

This is the internal resistance a material possesses to a cutting or sliding process where external forces are trying to slide one section of the material past another. When the material of the rivets shown in Fig. 1.2 is under shear forces rivet (a) will shear across plane *xx* which is single shear, but rivet (b) has to be sheared across planes *xx* and *yy* which is double shear.

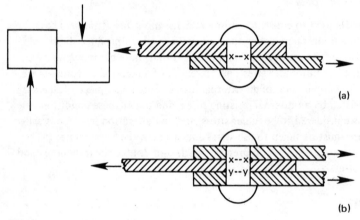

Fig. 1.2 (a) Single shear and (b) double shear.

Bending or flexing

The internal resistance to bending is quite complex. If a piece of material is subjected to bending forces (see Fig. 1.3) the top section is under a compressive stress and the bottom section under tensile stress. At some point there is a layer of material which is under neither tensile nor compressive stress and is therefore neutral and is termed the neutral plane of bending or the neutral axis.

Torsional stress

When a material is twisted it is under torsional stress and the internal forces are resisting the tendency to shear due to the applied torque or twisting moment (see Fig. 1.4).

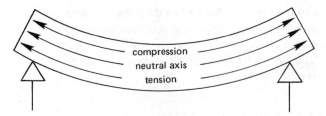

Fig. 1.3 Bending or flexing.

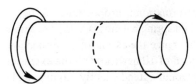

Fig. 1.4 Torsional stress.

Tensile strain

When a material is under tensile stress tensile strain will result, and the ratio

$$\frac{\text{extension}}{\text{original length}} = \frac{x}{L} = e = \text{tensile strain}$$

As the extension and the original length must be in the same units they cancel out, hence strain has no units.

Compressive strain

Under a compressive load a material will undergo a slight reduction in length, and the ratio

$$\frac{\text{alteration in length}}{\text{original length}} = \frac{x}{L} = e = \text{compressive strain}$$

Under compressive strain a material tends to buckle or distort especially if its length is greater than its cross-sectional dimensions. If the compressive load is not a true axial one, bending or buckling may take place as the stress is combined compression and bending.

Elasticity

All the materials used in motor vehicle construction possess some form of elasticity, which is the ability to stretch or compress slightly under load, but return immediately to their original shape when the straining forces are removed. This phenomena is only possible within certain limits known as the elastic range. Beyond the elastic range the material will lose its elastic properties and become what is termed plastic, thus becoming permanently deformed or what is called strained.

1.2 HOOKE'S LAW AND YOUNG'S MODULUS

Hooke's Law

Within the elastic limit the deflection or deformation is proportional to the applied load. A helical open coiled spring in a spring balance is a good example. When the spring is loaded within its working range the extension is proportional to the load applied. For example, if for a load of 10 newtons (N) the extension was 0.8 mm, for a load of 20 N the spring would extend exactly 1.6 mm, and 3.2 mm for a 40 N load. Thus extension is proportional to load. The results of a valve spring under compressive loads (Fig. 1.5) show a straight line graph passing through the origin which is the characteristic of proportionality. The important feature of the ratio stress/strain within the elastic limit termed

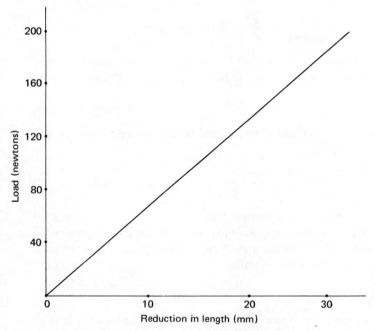

Fig. 1.5 Helical valve spring compression test.

'limit of proportionality' (L of P) is known as the Elastic Law or Hooke's Law.

Modulus of Elasticity or Young's Modulus

Hooke's Law states: *the strain produced in a material is directly proportional to the stress producing it.* Thus the ratio (stress/strain) is a constant. This constant is known as the Modulus of Elasticity or Young's Modulus (E).

Units for E and stress are: N/m^2, kN/m^2, MN/m^2, and GN/m^2. Note that: $1 \ m^2 = mm^2 \times 10^6$ thus $1 \ MN/m^2 = 1 \ N/mm^2$.

$$\text{stress} = \frac{\text{load}}{\text{area}} = \frac{W}{A} \ N/m^2, \text{ or } kN/m^2, MN/m^2 \text{ (which equals } N/mm^2\text{)}$$

Stress plotted against strain produces a straight line graph passing through the origin (Fig. 1.6) when the limits of proportionality are not exceeded, and the slope of the graph represents the ratio

$$\frac{\text{stress}}{\text{strain}} = \frac{f}{e}$$

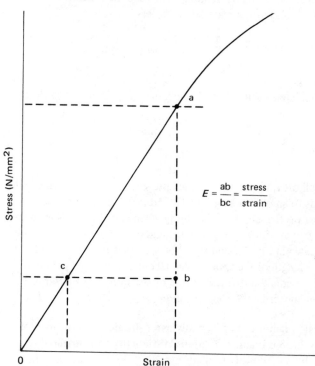

Fig. 1.6 Young's Modulus (see example).

and in Fig. 1.6 represents

$$\frac{ab}{bc} = E \text{ or Young's Modulus}$$

An error is sometimes made regarding E and what it represents. Young's Modulus does not indicate the strength of the material, only its degree of elasticity. A good example is to compare the tensile strength and value of E for mild steel with that of a nickel–chrome steel.

mild steel:	tensile strength	455 MN/m²,	$E = 203$ GN/m²
nickel–chrome steel:	tensile strength	1068 MN/m²,	$E = 200$ GN/m²

Tensile strength

Tensile strength represents the maximum stress which the material can sustain before fracture, and is obtained by dividing the maximum load by the original cross-sectional area (CSA) of the material under test.

$$\text{tensile strength} = \frac{\text{maximum load}}{\text{original CSA}}$$

Units are as for stress.

Some worked examples will help to understand the principles and the units involved.

Worked examples

Helical spring

A helical brake pull-off spring is 12 cm in length when carrying a load of 8 N. The spring extends to an overall length of 13.25 cm when 13 N load is applied. Determine (a) the length of the spring when a load of 15 N is applied to it, (b) the free length of the spring, (c) the load per cm length.

The graph is drawn in Fig. 1.7 and it will be seen that the answer to (a) is 13.75 cm; the free length of the spring (b) is 10 cm and the load per cm (c) is 4 N/cm, which represents the stiffness or rate of the spring. The latter is dealt with in the section concerning *Springs* (Section 5.10).

A steel suspension radius rod of 2 cm diameter sustains a tensile load of 26 kN when the vehicle is braking. The tensile strength of the material is 467 MN/m² and the modulus of elasticity $E = 205$ GN/m². Calculate the safe tensile load if a factor of safety 5 is employed, and the extension on a

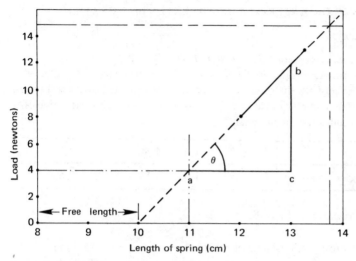

Fig. 1.7 Hooke's Law (see example).

one metre length of the material.

$$\text{safe working stress} = \frac{\text{tensile strength}}{\text{factor of safety}} = \frac{467}{5} = 93.4 \text{ MN/m}^2$$

$$\text{stress} = \frac{\text{load}}{\text{area}} = f = \frac{W}{A}$$

thus tensile load $= W = f \times A$

$$= \frac{93.4 \times \pi \times 20^2}{4 \times 10^3}$$

$$= 29.34 \text{ kN}$$

$$\text{strain} = e = \frac{f}{E}$$

thus $e = \dfrac{93.4}{205 \times 10^3} = 0.000\ 455$ (no units)

also

$$\text{strain} = \frac{\text{extension}}{\text{gauge or test piece length}} = \frac{x}{L} = e$$

thus x mm $= e \times L = 0.000\ 455 \times 1000$

$$= 0.455 \text{ mm extension}$$

♦♦♦

1.3 TESTING OF MATERIALS: LOAD–EXTENSION GRAPHS

Worked examples

Load versus extension for rubber material
A length of rubber 4.5 mm in diameter is subjected to tension and the loads applied together with the resulting extension were recorded over a test length of 12 cm. Plot a graph of load versus extension and determine the value of Young's Modulus for the material.

Load (N)	0	0.5	1.0	1.5	2.0	2.5	3.0
Mean extension (cm)	0	0.525	1.05	1.55	2.075	2.6	3.1

The graph is shown in Fig. 1.8.

$$\text{cross-sectional area of rubber} = \frac{\pi d^2}{4} = \frac{\pi \times 4.5^2}{4} = 15.9 \text{ mm}^2$$

$$\text{stress} = f = \frac{\text{load}}{\text{area}} = \frac{W}{A} = \frac{2}{15.9} = 0.125\ 78 \text{ N/mm}^2 \text{ or MN/m}^2$$

$$\text{strain} = e = \frac{\text{extension}}{\text{original length}} = \frac{x}{L} = \frac{2.075}{12} = 0.173 \text{ (no units)}$$

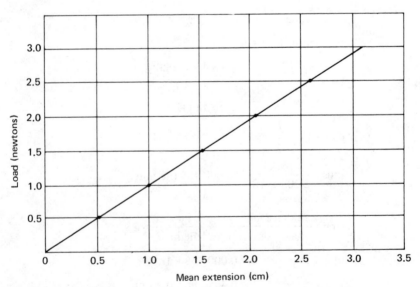

Fig. 1.8 Load versus extension for rubber.

$$\text{Young's Modulus} = E = \frac{\text{stress}}{\text{strain}} = \frac{f}{e} = \frac{0.125\ 78}{0.173} = 0.727 \text{ N/mm}^2$$

The value of the modulus for rubber is a variable one and depends on the age of the material and the temperature.

◆◆◆

Tensile test on a steel wire

A tensile test was carried out on a 2 m length of steel wire 0.6 mm in diameter. From the recorded data plot a load versus extension graph and determine Young's Modulus for the material.

Load (N)	0	5	10	15	20	25	30
Extension (cm)	0	0.173	0.346	0.519	0.692	0.866	1.039

The graph is shown in Fig. 1.9.

$$\text{cross-sectional area of wire} = \frac{\pi \times 0.6^2}{4} = 0.283 \text{ mm}^2$$

$$\text{stress} = f = \frac{W}{A} = \frac{30}{0.283} = 106 \text{ MN/m}^2$$

$$\text{strain} = \frac{x}{L} = \frac{1.039}{2 \times 10^3} = 0.000\ 519$$

$$E = \frac{f}{e} = \frac{106}{0.000\ 519} = 204\ 423 \text{ N/mm}^2 \text{ or MN/m}^2$$

$$= 204 \text{ GN/m}^2$$

◆◆◆

Tensile test on annealed copper wire

An annealed copper wire of 0.7 mm diameter was tested for extension over a gauge length of 2 m when subjected to a series of loads. The results were plotted as load versus extension (see Fig. 1.10). Fracture took place at a load of 78 N. Record your conclusions of the results and determine the tensile strength of the material.

The graph is a curve thus there is no definite period of elasticity and Hooke's Law does not apply. The material is very ductile as seen from the extension, and this would produce a reduction in the cross-sectional area (CSA) of the wire throughout the test. The degree of annealing will influence the ductility.

$$\text{tensile strength} = \frac{\text{load at fracture}}{\text{original CSA}} = \frac{78 \times 4}{\pi \times 0.7^2}$$

$$= 202 \text{ N/mm}^2 \text{ or MN/m}^2$$

◆◆◆

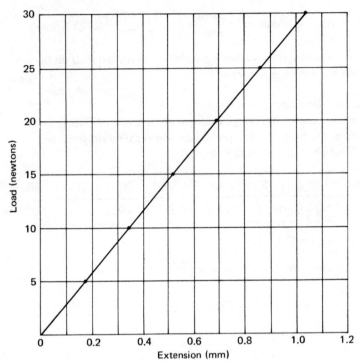

Fig. 1.9 Load versus extension for steel wire.

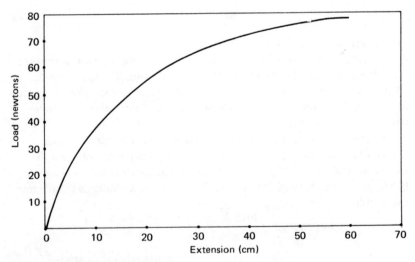

Fig. 1.10 Load versus extension for annealed copper wire.

Testing of materials

The mechanical properties of the materials used in motor vehicle construction must be known and understood by the design teams to enable the best materials for particular components to be selected. The likely stresses which the components will have to endure have been researched and reasonable factors of safety determined. There are a number of tests available to determine the mechanical properties of a material such as tensile and compression, impact and hardness tests, and others including fatigue tests.

The most common tests are tensile, hardness, impact and shear, and, for items such as half shafts and torsion bars, torsional shear tests. Cast iron and other brittle metals are compression tested. Bending tests are given to spring steel and sheet metal; the latter, used in vehicle bodywork, has to withstand considerable bending to various shapes and angles without surface cracking or failure.

A tensile test

This is a vital test for material such as steel which is to undergo tensile forces during its normal working function. Some of the information which may be required from such a test is as follows:
(a) elastic limit and Modulus of Elasticity
(b) yield point
(c) proof stress
(d) breaking stress
(e) elongation
(f) reduction in area

The test piece or specimen

British Standards lay down specification for the manufacture of test pieces. A diagram of a round test piece is shown in Fig. 1.11. The gauge length is

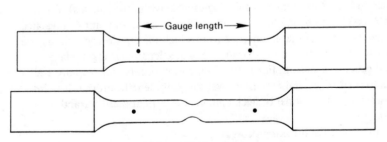

waist formed before fracture

Fig. 1.11 Mild steel tensile test piece.

marked on the test section of the specimen which has been carefully machined to a good standard of surface finish with smooth radii at the reduction section. The larger ends are engaged by the test machine's vice grips.

To facilitate calculations, the diameter of the test section is made a dimension that will give a round figure for the cross-sectional area. 11.285 mm diameter provides a cross-sectional area (CSA) of 100 mm^2, a 5.65 mm diameter gives a CSA of 25 mm^2, 7.98 mm a CSA of 50 mm^2 and 15.96 mm a CSA of 200 mm^2.

The test specimen is placed between the machine's vice grips, indicating dials set to zero and the load applied gradually increased until fracture occurs. As heat is created in the test piece where the elongation and waisting occurs, the test should remain slow but continuous to give the correct physical qualities. If the test were stopped during elongation and the test piece cooled down this would slightly affect the physical qualities of the material.

Mild steel load – extension graph (Fig. 1.12)

Mild steel has been chosen as this material shows more clearly such points as elastic limit, yield point, etc. The graph has been slightly exaggerated to show more clearly the points 1, 2 and 3.

The elastic portion O1 is a straight line passing through the origin, and shows that during this stage the material is behaving according to Hooke's Law. The value for E, Young's Modulus, is obtained from the slope of this part of the graph. The point 1 is the limit of proportionality and the working stress is a percentage of O1 depending upon the factor of safety employed. From point 1 there is a sudden change in the ratio load/extension until point 2 is reached. (The distance between points 1 and 2 is very, very small even for mild steel, and for higher carbon steels it would be impossible to segregate them.) Point 2 is the elastic limit and from this point the material will not return to its original length on removal of the load. Point 3 is the yield point: the material is now becoming more plastic and yields or gives without an increase in load (this yield is not distinguishable with other metals). From point 3 load has to be applied to cause further strain until point 4 is reached, which is the point of maximum load from which the tensile strength may be calculated. From 3 to 4 an extension over gauge length has taken place, termed general extension. From 4 to 5 extension occurs more rapidly and marks the end of general extension over the gauge length. From this point the formation of the waist or neck commences until at point 5 fracture occurs.

At this point the breaking stress is

$$\frac{\text{load at 5}}{\text{area of waist}}$$

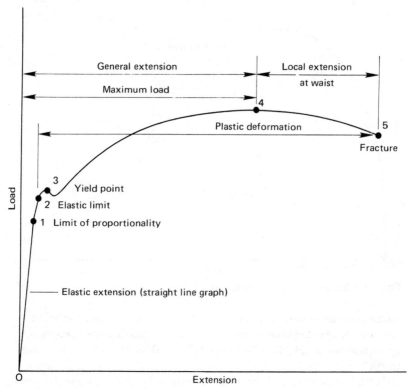

Fig. 1.12 Tensile test on mild steed.

and is the greatest stress to which the specimen is subjected. The nominal fracture or breaking stress is the ratio

$$\frac{\text{load at fracture}}{\text{original CSA}}$$

The *true* fracture or breaking stress is the ratio

$$\frac{\text{load at fracture}}{\text{CSA at fracture}}.$$

As the CSA at fracture is considerably reduced, but the load in each case is the same figure, the true or actual fracture stress is considerably higher than the nominal.

Proof stress

Many materials such as brass, copper and other alloys do not show a yield point during a tensile test (see Fig. 1.13) but designers require a guide to the

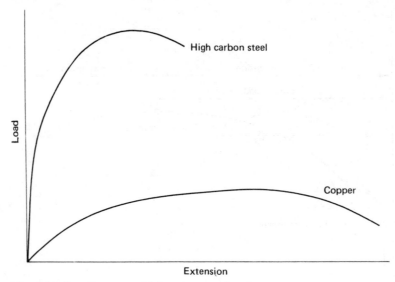

Fig. 1.13 Tensile test on high carbon steel and copper.

elastic qualities of some alloys which they are considering using so proof tests are instigated. This represents the stress at which a certain permanent elongation has taken place and is usually 0.1%, 0.2% and 0.5% of the gauge length.

A load versus extension graph for the material is plotted in Fig. 1.14 and 0.1% proof stress is determined by drawing the tangent Oa and then drawing bc parallel to Oa and c is the point at which the extension is 0.1% of the gauge length. Proof stress is also shown for 0.2% and 0.5%.

Worked examples

Mild steel tensile test

A 16 mm diameter mild steel test piece having a gauge length of 8 cm produced the following results during a tensile test:

load at the limit of proportionality	= 65.2 kN
extension at the limit of proportionality	= 0.13 mm
load at yield point	= 89 kN
maximum load	= 128.6 kN
load at fracture	= 78 kN
extension at fracture	= 23.5 mm
diameter at fracture	= 9.95 mm

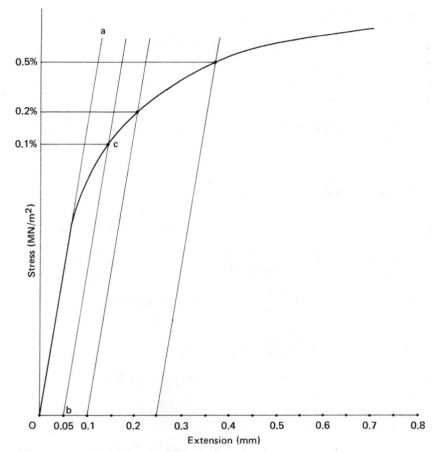

Fig. 1.14 Proof stress graph. Gauge length of specimen, 50 mm.
        0.1% of 50 mm = 0.05 mm
        0.2% of 50 mm = 0.1 mm
        0.5% of 50 mm = 0.25 mm

Determine: (a) the stress at the limit of proportionality; (b) Young's modulus of elasticity; (c) the yield stress; (d) the tensile strength; (e) the breaking stress; (f) the percentage of elongation; (g) the percentage reduction in the area.

(a) stress at limit of proportionality $= \dfrac{\text{load at limit of proportionality}}{\text{original cross-sectional area}}$

$$= \frac{65.2 \times 10^3}{200}$$

$$= 326 \text{ N/mm}^2 \text{ or MN/m}^2$$

(b) strain at limit of proportionality

$$= \frac{\text{extension at limit of proportionality}}{\text{original gauge length}}$$

$$= \frac{0.13}{80} = 0.001\ 625$$

Young's Modulus $E = \frac{\text{stress}}{\text{strain}} = \frac{326}{0.001\ 625 \times 10^3}$

$$= 200.6\ \text{GN/m}^2$$

(c) yield stress $= \dfrac{\text{load at yield point}}{\text{original CSA}} = \dfrac{89 \times 10^3}{200}$

$$= 445\ \text{N/mm}^2 \text{ or } \text{MN/m}^2$$

(d) tensile strength $= \dfrac{\text{maximum load}}{\text{original CSA}}$

$$= \frac{128.6 \times 10^3}{200} = 643\ \text{N/mm}^2 \text{ or } \text{MN/m}^2$$

(e) breaking stress $= \dfrac{\text{load at fracture}}{\text{original CSA}} = \dfrac{78 \times 10^3}{200}$

$$= 390\ \text{N/mm}^2 \text{ or } \text{MN/m}^2$$

(f) percentage elongation $= \dfrac{\text{extension at fracture}}{\text{original gauge length}} \times 100$

$$= \frac{23.5}{80} \times 100 = 29.37\%$$

(g) percentage reduction in area $= \dfrac{\text{original CSA} - \text{CSA at fracture}}{\text{original CSA}} \times 100$

$$= \frac{200 - (\pi \times 9.95^2)/4}{200} \times 100$$

$$= 61.12\% \qquad \qquad \blacklozenge\blacklozenge\blacklozenge$$

Tensile test
The results below were obtained during a tensile test on a steel specimen of
11.285 mm diameter and 50 mm gauge length.

Load (kN)	2.75	8.25	13.75	19.25	24.75	30.25	33.6	36.4	38	39.2
Extension (μm)	5.5	19.8	33	47.3	60.5	73.7	89.6	96.3	108	168

The maximum load during the test was 49.8 kN. Final diameter of test piece at waist, 7.56 mm; and final gauge length, 69.6 mm.
Determine: (a) Stress at limit of proportionality when load is 33.6 kN;
(b) Young's Modulus E; (c) Tensile strength; (d) Percentage of reduction in area of test piece; (e) Percentage of elongation.

(a) cross-sectional area (CSA) of test piece $= \dfrac{\pi \times 11.285^2}{4} = 100 \text{ mm}^2$

stress at limit of proportionality $= \dfrac{\text{load at L of P}}{\text{original CSA}} = \dfrac{33.6 \times 10^3}{100}$

$$= 336 \text{ N/mm}^2 \text{ or MN/m}^2$$

(b) strain at limit of proportionality $= \dfrac{\text{extension at L of P}}{\text{original gauge length}}$

$$= \dfrac{89.6}{50 \times 10^3} = 0.001\ 792$$

Young's Modulus $E = \dfrac{\text{stress at L of P}}{\text{strain at L of P}} = \dfrac{336}{0.001\ 792}$

$$= 187\ 500 \text{ N/mm}^2 \text{ or MN/m}^2$$

$$= 187.5 \text{ GN/m}^2$$

(c) tensile strength $= \dfrac{\text{maximum load}}{\text{original CSA}} = \dfrac{49.8 \times 10^3}{100}$

$$= 498 \text{ N/mm}^2 \text{ or MN/m}^2$$

(d) reduction in area (%) = original area − final area

$$= 100 - \dfrac{\pi \times 7.56^2}{4}$$

$$= 100 - 44.88$$

$$= 55.12\% \text{ reduction in area}$$

(e) elongation = final length − original length

$$= 69.6 - 50$$

$$= 19.6 \text{ mm}$$

and $\dfrac{19.6}{50} \times 100 = 39.2\%$ elongation.

◆◆◆

Proof stress (see Fig. 1.15)
A 15.96 mm diameter test piece having a gauge length of 80 mm was
manufactured from a partially heat treated aluminium alloy to be used for
an engine connecting rod. The material was subjected to a tensile test and
the results are recorded below.

Strain (%)	0	0.05	0.1	0.15	0.2	0.3	0.35
Load (kN)	0	4.7	8.55	10.65	12.1	14.2	14.9

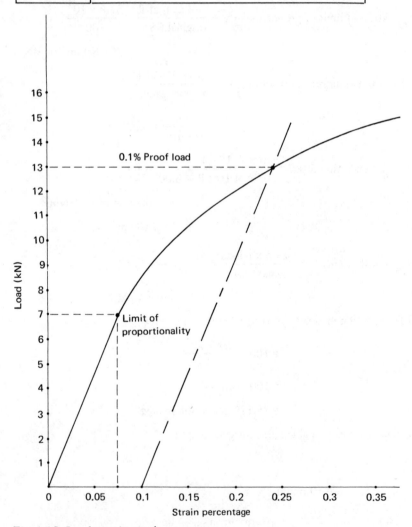

Fig. 1.15 Load–strain graph.

The limit of proportionality (L of P) occurred at a load of 7 kN. Draw the load versus percentage extension graph and determine the following:
(a) the 0.1% proof stress MN/m^2; (b) the modulus of elasticity GN/m^2;
(c) the tensile strength when the maximum load was 37 kN.

(a) From Fig. 1.15, the 0.1% proof is 13 kN

thus 0.1% proof stress $= \dfrac{0.1\% \text{ proof load}}{\text{original CSA}} = \dfrac{13 \times 10^3}{200} = 65 \text{ MN/m}^2$

(b) stress $= \dfrac{\text{load at L of P}}{\text{original CSA}} = \dfrac{7 \times 10^3}{200}$

$= 35 \text{ N/mm}^2 \text{ or MN/m}^2$

strain at L of P $= \dfrac{\text{strain \%}}{100} = \dfrac{0.075}{100}$

$= 0.000\ 75 \text{ (no units)}$

Young's Modulus of Elasticity $E = \dfrac{\text{stress}}{\text{strain}} = \dfrac{35}{0.000\ 75 \times 10^3}$

$= 46.6 \text{ GN/m}^2$

(c) tensile strength $= \dfrac{\text{maximum load}}{\text{original CSA}} = \dfrac{37 \times 10^3}{200}$

$= 185 \text{ MN/m}^2$

♦♦♦

EXERCISES 1.1

Materials (A1)

1. A spring is stretched within its elastic limit to 2.8 cm by a load of 28 N. By how much will it stretch for a load of only 4 N?

2. A helical open coiled compression spring is 9 cm in length when under a compressive load of 20 N, and reaches a length of 11 cm when the load is reduced to 8 N. What is the length of the spring when the load is 11 N, and the overall length when no load is applied?

3. State Hooke's Law and describe an experiment which had the objective of verifying the law.

4. A piece of steel 17 mm in diameter is subjected to a tensile load of 26 kN on the length of 30 cm. Young's Modulus for the material is 208 GN/m^2. Determine the extension over the test length.

5. An engine valve spring has a length of 10 cm when a compressive force of 32 N acts upon it, and the length is reduced to 8.4 cm when 58 N load is applied. What force is required to produce a length of 9 cm, and what is the spring's free length?

6. A mild steel brake rod of 9 mm diameter sustains a tensile load of 300 N. The tensile strength of the material is 453 MN/m^2 and the modulus of elasticity 203 GN/m^2. Calculate the maximum safe tensile load for the rod if the safety factor is 6, and the extension on a 2 m length of the rod when under the maximum safe tensile load.

7. A wire of 0.6 mm diameter and 220 cm in length is stretched 2.1 mm under a load of 54 N. Find the value of Young's Modulus of elasticity for the material.

8. A heavy duty tow bar 3 m in length has a cross-sectional area of 14.44 cm^2. Calculate the maximum pull it can sustain if the extension is not to exceed 0.4 mm (Young's Modulus 200 GN/m^2).

9. A helical coiled spring has an overall free length of 20 cm. When a load of 6 kN is applied the spring compresses to 15 cm. What length will the spring become under a loading of 9.5 kN and what is the stiffness of the spring?

10. A tensile test on 2 m of wire 8 mm^2 in cross-sectional area caused an extension of 0.08 mm under a load of 45 N. Calculate the stress in the material, the strain and the modulus of elasticity.

11. The following data was recorded during a tensile test on a steel specimen of 11.284 mm diameter and gauge length 50 mm. The length at the point of fracture was 66 mm, and the diameter 7.1 mm. The load at the yield point was 52 kN and 88 kN was the maximum recorded load. Calculate: (a) the percentage reduction in area, (b) the percentage elongation, (c) the stress at yield point, and (d) the tensile strength.

12. The load versus extension figures from a tensile test on an alloy steel test piece of 80 mm gauge length and 200 mm^2 cross-sectional area are given below. Plot the results and determine the 0.1% and 0.2% proof stress.

Load (kN)	0	9.96	19.92	32.88	35.87	37.86	39.8
Extension (mm)	0	0.076	0.15	0.23	0.254	0.3	0.635

13. Sketch a load versus extension diagram for a mild steel specimen tested to destruction by tensile forces. Some exaggeration is permitted to emphasize the important changes.

14. A tensile test carried out on a mild steel test piece of 11.284 mm diameter and gauge length 50 mm had the following data recorded: the load at yield point was 48.5 kN and extension 0.13 mm; maximum load recorded was 64.5 kN; diameter at fracture 6.94 mm.
Calculate (a) the yield point stress, (b) the Modulus of Elasticity, (c) the percentage reduction in area, (d) the percentage elongation, and (e) the tensile strength of the material.

15. Sketch a load versus extension graph for a very ductile material under tension. Compare it with that of an elastic material.

2
Heat

2.1 LINEAR AND CUBICAL EXPANSION (B2)

Thermal and linear expansion

Thermal expansion is the ability of many materials to expand when heated, and then contract again when cooled. The degree of expansion depends upon the temperature rise and the type of material. Steel has a lower expansion than aluminium alloy, therefore if new pistons are to be fitted they may be placed in very hot water for a short period and on removal the steel gudgeon pins may be pushed out quite easily. The procedure can be repeated when the pins are to be replaced. Starter rings are heated uniformly and then placed on the machined section of the flywheel, and as the ring cools it will create a highly compressive force radially thus gripping the flywheel tightly. Refrigeration or liquefied gas such as liquid nitrogen is frequently used to fit such items as valve guides, bushes, cylinder liners, etc. When placed or lightly pushed into position they expand as they return to room temperature and thus fit tightly as if they had been driven or pressed in with an interference fit requiring considerable force.

The coefficient of linear expansion (α) of a material is the fractional increase in length per unit of length when the temperature of the material is raised through one degree centigrade. Therefore

$$\alpha = \frac{\text{change of length or expansion}}{\text{original length} \times \text{temperature change } (^\circ C)}$$

and providing the same units of length are used throughout, the ratio will be valid (see Table 2.1).

Worked examples

An aluminium piston 118 mm diameter at a room temperature of $15^\circ C$ has its temperature increased to $325^\circ C$ under normal working conditions. What

Table 2.1 *Coefficient of linear expansion*

Material	per °C
mercury	0.000 0599
aluminium	0.000 0221
brass	0.000 0189
copper	0.000 0171
steel	0.000 0119
iron	0.000 0117
cast iron	0.000 0112
invar	0.000 0010

will be its working diameter? (coefficient of linear expansion for aluminium 0.000 0221 per °C)

$$\text{expansion} = \text{original diameter} \times \alpha \times \text{temperature change}$$

$$= 118 \times 0.000\ 022 \times (325 - 15)$$

$$= 0.804\ 76 \text{ mm}$$

working diameter = 118.804 76 mm   ◆◆◆

The length between centres of a steel connecting rod is 142.3 mm at 17°C. The rod is heated to 230°C for the fitting of the small end bush. What increase in length takes place during this process. (α for steel = 0.000 0119 per °C)

$$\text{expansion} = \text{original length} \times \alpha \times \text{temperature change}$$

$$= 142.3 \times 0.000\ 011\ 9 \times (230 - 17)$$

$$= 0.36 \text{ mm increase in the original length}$$

length during process = 142.66 mm   ◆◆◆

A steel flywheel has a diameter of 361.25 mm at room temperature 16°C. The starter ring to be fitted has an internal diameter of 361.05 mm at the same room temperature. If the ring is heated to 271°C will it expand sufficiently to be placed on the flywheel? (α for steel 0.000 0119 per °C)

$$\text{expansion} = \text{original diameter} \times \alpha \times \text{temperature change}$$

$$= 361.05 \times 0.000\ 0119 \times (271 - 16)$$

$$= 1.0955 \text{ mm}$$

therefore diameter under heating process = 361.05 + 1.0955

$$= 362.1455 \text{ mm}$$

thus there is 362.1455 − 361.25 = 0.8955 mm clearance   ◆◆◆

A cast iron cylinder block is bored out to 96.84 mm diameter at a room temperature of 16°C, and the steel cylinder liners to be fitted measure 96.93 mm outside diameter at the same temperature. To what temperature must the liners be cooled by liquid nitrogen to enable the liners to be pressed in by gloved hand?

contraction = original diameter x α x temperature change

therefore   temperature change = $\dfrac{\text{contraction}}{\text{original diameter} \times \alpha}$

$$(X°C - 16) = \frac{96.93 - 96.84}{96.93 \times 0.000\ 0119} = \frac{0.09}{0.001\ 153} = 78$$

$$(X°C - 16) = 78$$

therefore liners must be cooled to minus (78 − 16) = −62°C

♦♦♦

Superficial expansion (area)

Consider a square plate having sides 1 m in length being heated through 1°C. Expansion will take place and the area will increase. Let a represent the expansion on each side (see Fig. 2.1).

$$\text{new area} = (1 + a) \times (1 + a)\ \text{m}^2$$
$$= 1 + 2a + a^2$$

Since expansion is very small, a^2 is very small. For steel it represents 0.000 000 014. In practical terms the new area equals $2a$ or 2α. Thus the coefficient of superficial expansion is twice the coefficient of linear expansion.

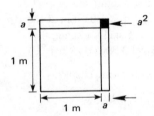

Fig. 2.1 Superficial expansion.

Cubical expansion (volume)

If a cube having sides of 1 m in length is heated through 1°C each side becomes $(1 + a)$

$$\text{new volume of cube} = (1 + a) \times (1 + a) \times (1 + a)$$
$$= 1 + 3a + 3a^2 + a^3$$
$$= 1 + 3a \text{ approximately}$$

thus in practice new volume equals $3a$ or 3α. The coefficient of cubical expansion is three times the coefficient of linear expansion.

Worked examples

Superficial and cubical expansion
A block of steel 11 cm x 4 cm x 27 cm is at a temperature of 17°C. The block is heated for a heat treatment process to 700° C. By how much does its volume increase?

$$V_e = 3 \times \alpha [V(T_2 - T_1)]$$
$$= 3 \times 0.000\ 0119\ [11 \times 4 \times 27(700 - 17)]$$
$$= 28.96 \text{ cm}^3 \qquad \blacklozenge\blacklozenge\blacklozenge$$

A copper plate 20 cm in diameter at a temperature of 15°C is heated to 310°C. By how much does the area increase? (α for copper = 0.000 0171)

$$\text{area} = \frac{\pi \times 20^2}{4} = 314 \text{ cm}^2$$
$$\text{superficial expansion} = A_e = 2 \times \alpha [A(T_2 - T_1)]$$
$$= 2 \times 0.000\ 0171\ [314(310 - 15)]$$
$$= 3.168 \text{ cm}^2 \qquad \blacklozenge\blacklozenge\blacklozenge$$

Superficial expansion
An aluminium alloy piston having a coefficient of expansion of 0.000 0221 and a cast iron piston 0.000 0112 have identical diameters of 106 mm measured at room temperature of 16°C. What is the difference in their diameters when they are at a working temperature of 312°C?

$$\text{area of pistons at } 16°C = \frac{\pi d^2}{4} = \frac{\pi \times 106^2}{4} = 8824.73 \text{ mm}^2$$

superficial expansion of aluminium alloy piston (A)

$$= 2\alpha A(T_2 - T_1)$$
$$= 2 \times 0.000\ 0221 \times 8824.73 \times (312 - 16)$$
$$= 115.46 \text{ mm}^2$$

superficial expansion of cast iron piston (B)

$$= 2 \times 0.000\ 0112 \times 8824.73 \times 296$$
$$= 58.51\ \text{mm}^2$$

working area of piston (A) = 8824.73 + 115.46 = 8940.2 mm^2

working area of piston (B) = 8824.73 + 58.51 =   8883.24 mm^2

working diameter of piston (A) = $d = \sqrt{(4 \times \text{area}/\pi)} = \sqrt{(4 \times 8940.2/\pi)}$

$$= 106.69\ \text{mm}$$

working diameter of piston (B) = $d = \sqrt{(4 \times 8883.24/\pi)}$

$$= 106.35\ \text{mm}$$

then
$$106.69 - 106.35 = 0.34\ \text{mm}$$

which is the difference in the diameters of the aluminium alloy and cast iron pistons at the same working temperature.   ◆◆◆

Engine pistons

In the early era of motor vehicles cast iron was used for pistons as they were cheap to produce, casting techniques were well known, their strength and wear characteristics very good and the low degree of expansion enabled low clearances to be employed and piston slap was rarely experienced. As engine speeds and angular acceleration of the crankshaft had to be increased, the inertia loads due to the heavy pistons necessitated the use of aluminium alloy pistons which, despite their thickness to give them strength, are almost half the weight of their cast iron counterpart.

The higher rates of expansion with the aluminium alloy pistons require greater 'cold' clearances, but certain minerals reduce the coefficient of expansion. The following is a specification for such a piston material where the chief ingredient is silicon.

copper	0.5–1.3 wt%
magnesium	0.8–1.5 wt%
silicon	11–13.0 wt%
iron	0.8 wt%
manganese	0.5 wt%
nickel	0.7–3.0 wt%
zinc	0.1 wt%
lead	0.1 wt%
tin	0.1 wt%
aluminium to make up 100%	

The worked example in this chapter shows the superficial expansion between aluminium alloy and cast iron pistons of the same diameter.

One of the necessary functions of a piston is the dissipation of the combustion heat, thus because aluminium alloy pistons have a specific heat capacity of 880 to 920 J/(kg °C) as compared to cast iron of 500 to 555 J/(kg °C), the improved thermal conductivity of the aluminium alloy piston crown enables higher compression ratios to be used without the production of overheating, pinking and detonation.

EXERCISES 2.1

Linear and cubical expansion (B2)

1. An aluminium alloy connecting rod is 22 cm in length between centres at a temperature of 17°C. At what temperature will its length be increased by 0.08 mm if the coefficient of linear expansion of the material is 0.000 022?

2. A cast iron exhaust manifold measures 0.826 m between the two extreme bolt hole centres at a temperature of 19°C. If the manifold is free to expand, what change in the measurement would take place when the manifold reaches 370°C (the coefficient of linear expansion for the material is 0.000 0112)?

3. A steel exhaust pipe fitted to an engine test bench is 8.54 m in length at a temperature of 14°C. On engine test the exhaust temperature increases to 376°C. By how much has the exhaust pipe increased in length?

4. The bore of a gudgeon pin boss in an aluminium alloy piston is 20 mm in diameter at a temperature of 17°C and the steel gudgeon pin is 20.012 mm at the same temperature. The pin is to be a hand push fit. To what temperature must the piston be raised to fit the pin?

5. A cylinder bore of a CI engine is 112 mm in diameter and the top of the aluminium alloy piston has a clearance of 2 mm when at a temperature of 16°C. Find the clearance that will be available when the piston reaches a working temperature of 330°C.

6. A copper plate 20 cm in diameter at a temperature of 15°C is heated to 310°C. By how much does the area increase? (coefficient of linear expansion for copper 0.000 0171)

7. An engine piston at a temperature of 298°C has a diameter at the top land of 87 mm. Superficial expansion from a room temperature of 15°C was 109 mm². Determine the diameter at room temperature.

8. The tappet clearance of an engine is set at 0.38 mm at an ambient temperature of 15°C and the steel push rod 23 cm in length reaches a

temperature of 208°C when operating under working conditions. Determine the tappet clearance after allowing 60% reduction for the expansion of the other engine components.

9. A CI engine piston of aluminium alloy has a diameter of 115 mm when the temperature is 18°C. Calculate the increase in diameter when the piston temperature rises to 370°C.

10. A block of copper measuring 10 mm x 4 mm x 25 mm at room temperature of 16°C is heated to 180°C. Find the cubical expansion if the coefficient for copper is 0.000 017.

2.2 SENSIBLE HEAT AND LATENT HEAT (B3)

Sensible heat is sometimes referred to as heat which can be detected by touch or can be sensed by the use of a thermometer.

Latent heat

Latent heat is the heat energy required to change a substance into a liquid or a liquid into a gas or vice versa. When the change of state is taking place the temperature of the substance does not change, although heat is still being applied or reduced depending upon what change of state is taking place. An example is the boiling of water. Steam is formed, but the water remains at the boiling temperature although heat is still being added. This supply of heat is termed latent heat.

Latent heat of vaporization

Consider the petrol and air mixture when heated as it passes through the heated induction manifold. A percentage of the petrol vaporizes thus changing its state, but at the same time this conversion absorbs heat from the manifold, and this amount of heat energy would be termed the latent heat of vaporization.

Latent heat of fusion

This is the amount of heat energy when a unit mass of a solid substance liquifies or vice versa.

To help to explain the above terms and processes, consider a quantity of ice placed in a suitable container, being heated slowly and the temperature recorded at regular intervals of time. A graph can be drawn (see Fig. 2.2) which shows sensible heat, latent heat of fusion and vaporization. The first period, A to B, is sensible heat supplied to the ice and its temperature is rising

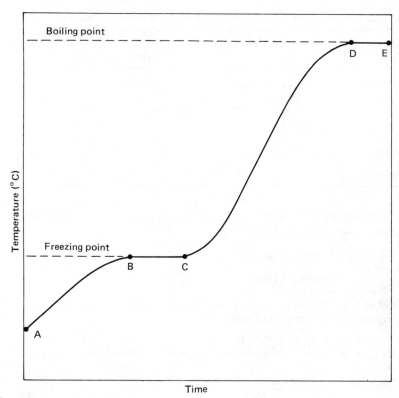

Fig. 2.2 Change of state graph for ice.

uniformly. At the melting point the temperature remains steady while the change is taking place (latent heat of fusion) but latent heat is being absorbed so preventing a change in temperature, BC on graph. From C to D sensible heat is being supplied and the temperature of the water is rising uniformly until the water boils, thus any further heat supplied simply vaporizes the water at constant temperature and is termed latent heat of vaporization (D to E).

Latent heat units are J/kg, kJ/kg and MJ/kg. Table 2.2 gives values for some of the more common materials or substances.

Worked examples

A piece of copper having a mass of 3.2 kg at room termperature of 16°C is to be melted, which requires a temperature of 1080°C. Its latent heat of fusion

Table 2.2 *Values of latent heat of fusion for some common materials*

Material	Latent heat of fusion (kJ/kg)
aluminium	402
ice	334
nickel	306
iron	268
copper	205
zinc	100
tin	60
mercury	11.7

is 205 kJ/kg and specific heat capacity 380 J/(kg °C). How much heat energy is required to melt the piece of copper?

$$MJ = \text{sensible heat} + \text{latent heat of fusion}$$

$$= m \times c \times (T_2 - T_1) + m \times l_f$$

where m = mass of copper; c = specific heat capacity; $T_2 - T_1$ = temperature change; and l_f = latent heat of fusion. Thus

$$MJ = \frac{[3.2 \times 380 \times (1080 - 16)] + (3.2 \times 205 \times 10^3)}{10^6}$$

$$= 797.7 \text{ MJ}$$

◆◆◆

A quantity of aluminium alloy pistons is to be melted down which requires a temperature of 660°C. The specific heat capacity for this alloy is 905 J/(kg °C), and the latent heat of fusion 399 kJ/kg. The total mass of the alloy is 45 kg at a room temperature of 15°C. What quantity of heat energy is required to melt all the pistons?

$$MJ = \text{sensible heat} + \text{latent heat of fusion}$$

$$= m \times c \times (T_2 - T_1) + (m \times l_f)$$

$$= \frac{[45 \times 905 \times (660 - 15)] + (45 \times 399 \times 10^3)}{10^6} = \frac{20\ 582\ 625}{10^6}$$

$$= 20.58 \text{ MJ}$$

◆◆◆

2.3 SPECIFIC HEAT CAPACITY

The amount of heat required to raise the temperature of a unit mass of a substance 1°C is termed the specific heat capacity (c) of that substance. Lead for instance only requires 130 joules of heat energy to raise the temperature of 1 kg 1°C, but 1 kg of water requires 4180 joules to raise it 1° C.

The heat required to raise the temperature of X kg mass of a substance by y°C is as follows:

joules = mass of substance x specific heat capacity x temperature change

$$J = m \times c \times (T_2 - T_1)$$

where m = mass of substance, c = specific heat capacity [J/(kg °C)], T_1 = initial temperature (°C) and T_2 = final temperature (°C). Specific heat capacities for some common substances are shown in Table 2.3.

Table 2.3 *Specific heat capacities for some common substances*

Material	Specific heat capacity [J/(kg°C)]
water	4180
alcohol	2500
petrol	1800
oil	1670
aluminium	880
cast iron	500
steel	485
wrought iron	470
brass	395
copper	380
lead	130

Heat transfer

Heat can only flow from a hotter to a cooler body. For example if a hot piece of steel is quenched in cool oil and left for a period, both the oil and the steel will become the same temperature, thus:

heat lost by the steel = heat energy gained by the oil

An example will demonstrate this equation:

Worked examples

A mass of steel is heated to 500°C and then quenched in a tank containing 10 kg of oil at a room temperature of 15°C. The final temperature of both oil and steel is 51°C. Neglecting other losses determine the mass of the steel. (*c* for oil and steel to be taken from Table 2.3)

heat lost by steel = heat gained by the oil

m of steel x c x temperature change = m of oil x c x temperature change.

Thus:

$$\text{mass of steel kg} = \frac{\text{kg of oil} \times c \times (T_2 - T_1)}{c \text{ of steel} \times (T_3 - T_2)}$$

$$= \frac{10 \times 1670 \times (51 - 15)}{485 \times (500 - 51)}$$

$$= 2.761 \text{ kg} \qquad \blacklozenge\blacklozenge\blacklozenge$$

A steel crankshaft of 32.3 kg mass is heated during manufacture from 17°C to 732°C. How much heat energy does this represent? (c for steel 485 J/(kg °C))

$$\text{kJ} = \frac{\text{mass of steel} \times c \times \text{temperature change}}{10^3}$$

$$= \frac{32.3 \times 485 \, (732 - 17)}{10^3}$$

$$= 11\,200 \text{ kJ} \qquad \blacklozenge\blacklozenge\blacklozenge$$

An engine circulates its cooling water at the rate of 26 l/min. The difference in temperature between the cool and hot areas in the system is 2.7°C. Neglecting other losses, how much heat energy is passing to the water per minute, and what would this represent in lost power? [c of water 4180 J/(/kg °C)]

Note: 1 litre of water = 1 kg

$$\text{kJ} = \frac{\text{mass of water} \times c \times \text{temperature change}}{10^3}$$

$$= \frac{26 \times 4180 \times 2.7}{10^3}$$

$$= 293.4 \text{ kJ/min}$$

$$\text{kW} = \frac{\text{kJ/min}}{60} = \frac{293.4}{60}$$

$$= 4.89 \text{ kW power lost to cooling system} \qquad \blacklozenge\blacklozenge\blacklozenge$$

A steel casting having a mass of 52 kg is heated to a temperature of 530°C and then immersed in 380 litres of oil which is at a temperature of 26°C. If the specific heat capacity of the oil is 1660 J/(kg °C) and 485 J/(kg °C) for the steel, what is the final temperature of the oil? (relative density of the oil 0.89)

Heat lost by steel = heat gained by oil

mass of steel x *c* x temperature change = mass of oil x *c* x temperature change

$$52 \times 485 \times (530 - T_2) = 380 \times 0.89 \times 1660 \times (T_2 - 26)$$

$$\frac{(52 \times 485 \times 530) + (380 \times 0.89 \times 1660 \times 26)}{(380 \times 0.89 \times 1660) + (52 \times 485)} = T_2$$

$$T_2 = 47.67°C$$

♦♦♦

2.4 BOILING POINT OF LIQUIDS

When a liquid is heated, vaporization takes place, and if confined to a closed vessel, vapour pressure will be formed. When the vapour pressure equals the pressure acting upon the liquid, boiling takes place. Thus pressure within the vessel must advance or retard the temperature at which boiling takes place. Raising the internal pressure will delay or retard the boiling point and the temperature will be higher; and a low internal pressure will advance the boiling point which will take place at a lower temperature (see Table 2.4 for some common boiling points at 760 mm Hg).

Table 2.4

Liquid	Boiling point at 760 mm mercury (°C)
Ether	36
Alcohol	78
Water	100
Mercury	35
Petrol	180−195
Methanol	66

Water will boil at 80°C when the pressure is about half an atmosphere, thus atmospheric changes affect the boiling point. Some days it could be 99.5°C and others perhaps 100.5°C, thus the higher fixed point of a thermometer is standardized as boiling at 100°C at atmospheric pressure of 760 mm mercury or 101.325 kN/m^2 at sea level. Vehicles operating at very high levels, besides having volumetric or breathing problems, may develop overheating and boiling due to the lower atmospheric pressure. Pressurized cooling systems are in use today, operating between 122 kN/m^2 and 246 kN/m^2, which enable higher boiling points to be employed. This has the direct result of reducing water losses and at the same time improving engine thermal efficiency as gas or charge heat losses are reduced. The venting of braking and cooling systems is necessary to allow for the cubical or volumetric expansion of the liquid as its working temperature rises. Change in volume = 3α x original volume x temperature change

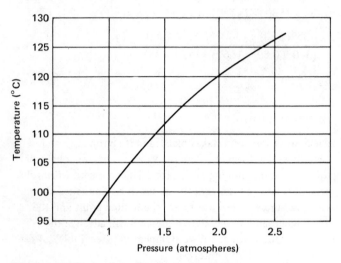

Fig. 2.3 Boiling point of water under pressure.

EXERCISES 2.2

Specific heat capacity, etc. (B3)

1. A test-bench cooling system has a flow of 8 l/min. The inlet and outlet temperatures are 14.8°C and 54.5°C respectively. If the specific heat capacity of water is 4180 J/(kg °C) what power is lost to the coolant if radiation and other losses are neglected?

2. Oil passing through a cooler at the rate of 7.6 l/min represents a heat exchange of 162.5 kJ/min. The inlet temperature of the oil is 93°C, relative density 0.9 and the specific heat capacity 1676 J/(kg °C). Find the outlet temperature of the oil.

3. A steel forging after machining has a mass of 106 kg. It is heated to 676°C and then immersed in 167 l of oil having a specific heat capacity of 1680 J/(kg °C) and temperature of 45°C. Calculate the final temperature of the oil and steel forging (*c* for steel 485 J/(kg°C)).

4. The water coolant flowing in an engine test bench system had an inlet

temperature of 13.6°C and outlet 62°C. The power lost to the coolant in the form of heat energy was 35 kW. Determine the rate of flow of the water coolant in 1/min (*c* for water 4180 J/(kg°C)).

5. A cast iron exhaust heated induction manifold has to operate at a temperature of 102°C. Find the quantity of heat required with a manifold mass of 1.79 kg and temperature of 15° C (*c* for cast iron 500 J/(kg °C)).

2.5 ELEMENTARY THERMODYNAMICS (B4)

Introduction

The petrol vapour and induced air of the petrol engine, and the compressed air and the fuel oil injected into it with the compression ignition (CI) engine may be considered as gases.

The gaseous content within the engine cylinder is compressed and expanded resulting in a percentage of the gas energy being converted into work via the engine piston, connecting rod and crankshaft. The laws that govern gases must be studied in order to understand the properties of a gas, such as pressure, temperature and volume, and their behaviour under certain conditions.

Volume (V)

In a piston engine this would be the space above the piston at the top of its stroke (TDC) and is termed the clearance volume (V_c) or the whole or part of the volume swept by the piston (V_s). Volumes may be given in litres, cubic centimetres (cm^3) or cubic metres (m^3).

Pressure (p)

The pressures used in gas equations must always be in absolute pressure (abs), i.e. gauge + atmospheric pressure. Standard atmospheric pressure = 760 mm of mercury or 101.325 kN/m^2. The bar is sometimes used and 100 kN/m^2 = 1 bar. Thus a gas showing a gauge pressure of 500 kN/m^2 = 500 + 101.325 = 601.325 kN/m^2 abs. The pascal (Pa) is now used to represent a unit of pressure. 1 pascal (Pa) = 1 N/m^2.

Temperature (T)

If the gas in the tube (Fig. 2.4) undergoes a change of temperature of 1°C increase or decrease, the volume will change by 1/273 increase or decrease. If the temperature of the gas were lowered to −273 °C the gas volume in theory would be zero (the gas in fact would liquefy and freeze solid before −273°C

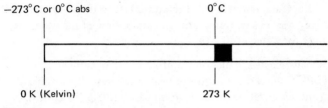

Fig. 2.4

was reached). The temperature $-273°$C or 0 K (Kelvin) is termed the absolute zero of temperature. In thermodynamics the Kelvin scale of temperature is used (temperature K = $°$C + 273).

Boyle's Law

If the temperature of a mass of gas remains constant, then during compression or expansion the product of the absolute pressure and volume will always remain constant (pV = a constant). In Fig. 2.5 the value of the three properties in (a) will equal those in (b) and those in (c), thus

$$\frac{p_1 V_1}{T_1} = \frac{p_2 V_2}{T_1} = \frac{p_3 V_3}{T_1} \text{ and } p_1 V_1 = p_2 V_2 = p_3 V_3$$

and $$\frac{V_1}{V_2} = \frac{p_2}{p_1} = \frac{p_3}{p_2} \text{, etc.}$$

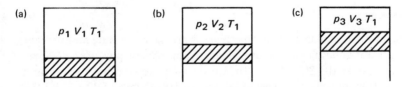

Fig. 2.5

If the absolute pressure of a given mass of gas is doubled, its volume will be halved, and doubling the volume will halve the pressure. When the pressure p is plotted against the volume, a curve (termed a rectangular hyperbola) is produced as shown Fig. 2.6 (a), but if the pressure p is plotted against the reciprocal of the volume ($1/V$) the result is a straight line passing through the origin, Fig. 2.6(b), and shows that the pressure is inversely proportional to V, or directly proportional to $1/V$.

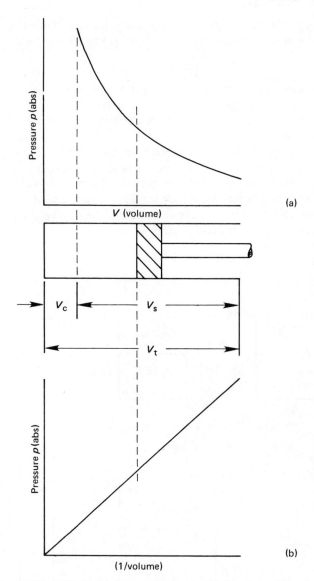

Fig. 2.6 V_c is the clearance volume, V_s the swept volume and V_t the total volume.

Charles' Law

This law states that the volume of a mass of gas changes by 1/273 of its volume at 0°C for every increase or decrease of 1°C providing the pressure remains constant. C and D (Fig. 2.7) are any two points on the volume graph, and AE and AF are the equivalent temperatures T_1 and T_2, thus CE = V_1 and DF = V_2 and $V_1 T_1 = V_2 T_2$ and $V_1/V_2 = T_1/T_2$.

At constant pressure the volume is directly proportional to the absolute temperature, or the ratio between any two volumes is the same as the ratio between any two absolute temperatures. Charles' law also states that at constant volume, the pressure of a given mass of gas is directly proportional to its absolute temperature.

The graph, Fig. 2.8, is similar to the volume graph and shows that the same relationship exists between the pressure of the gas and its absolute temperature as between the volume and the absolute temperature. The pressure will increase in exactly the same way that the volume increased under constant pressure. The ratio between any two pressures is the same as the ratio between the two corresponding absolute temperatures. Thus

$$\frac{p_1}{T_1} = \frac{p_2}{T_2}$$

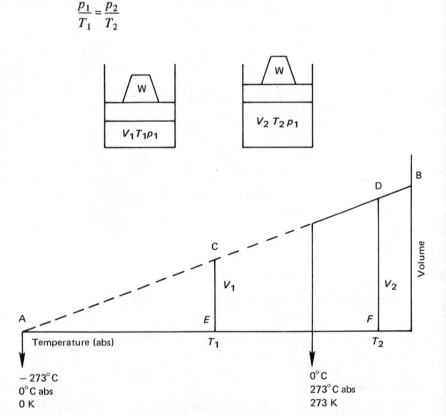

Fig. 2.7

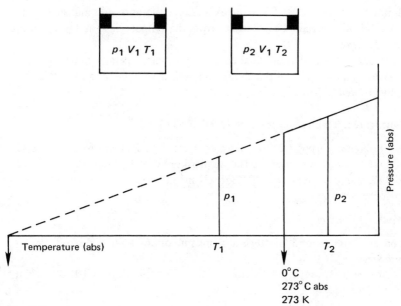

Fig. 2.8

and the ratio

$$\frac{p_1}{p_2} = \frac{T_1}{T_2}$$

The gas equation

The gas in an engine cylinder is compressed, burnt and expanded under conditions which are neither truly those of Charles' or Boyle's Laws, but a combination of each. In practice all three quantities — pressure, volume and temperature — change their values, and pV/T = a constant and is termed the gas equation.

$$\frac{p_1 V_1}{T_1} = \frac{p_2 V_2}{T_2} = \frac{p_3 V_3}{T_3}$$

Quite a variety of calculations concerning the changes in the conditions of a gas may be performed using the above queation, providing absolute pressures and temperatures are always used.

Isothermal and adiabatic expansion or compression

Expansion or compression of gases within an engine cylinder under isothermal conditions indicates that the temperature of the gases remains constant during the engine cycle. Adiabatic expansion or compression indicates that no heat is lost or gained by the gases from the cylinder head and walls during the engine cycle.

In practice a modern internal combustion engine operates more closely to adiabatic conditions, and the above equations have to be modified (this is fully covered in Part 2).

Normal temperature and pressure (NTP or STP)

For reference purposes or to make a comparison, a standard for both pressure and temperature is necessary. The standard or normal temperature is $0°C$ or 273 K. Standard pressure is 101.325 kN/m² (1.013 25 bar) or 760 mm of mercury.

Worked examples

Convert a volume of 3.9 l of gas at a pressure of 860 kN/m² abs and temperature 20°C to NTP.

$p_1 = 860$ kN/m²; $V_1 = 3.9$ l; $T_1 = 20 + 273 = 293$ K; $p_2 = 101.325$ kN/m²; $T_2 = 273$ K; $V_2 = ?$

$$\frac{p_1 V_1}{T_1} = \frac{p_2 V_2}{T_2}$$

thus
$$V_2 = \frac{p_1 V_1 T_2}{T_1 p_2}$$

$$= \frac{860 \times 3.9 \times 273}{293 \times 101.325}$$

$$= 30.842 \text{ l}$$

Note: Expansion had to take place to reduce both the pressure and temperature.   ♦♦♦

A combustion chamber contains 0.3 m³ of gas at a pressure of 105 kN/m² abs and temperature of 32°C. At the completion of compression the volume becomes 0.002 m³ and gas temperature 298°C. Calculate the new absolute pressure.

$$\frac{p_1 V_1}{T_1} = \frac{p_2 V_2}{T_2}$$

thus p_2 MN/m² $= \dfrac{p_1 V_1 T_2}{T_1 V_2} = \dfrac{105 \times 0.3 \times 571}{305 \times 0.002 \times 10^3}$

$$= 29.48 \text{ MN/m}^2 \text{ abs}$$ ♦♦♦

(a) Four cubic metres of air at 103 kN/m² abs pressure and 17°C temperature are compressed according to Boyle's Law, reaching a pressure of 586 kN/m² abs. Determine the final volume of the air.

(b) If the air is now heated to 320°C while the pressure remains constant, calculate the new volume.

$$\text{(a)} \quad p_1 V_1 = p_2 V_2 \text{ and } V_2 = \frac{p_1 V_1}{p_2} = \frac{103 \times 4}{586} = 0.7 \text{ m}^3$$

$$\text{(b)} \quad \text{by Charles' Law } V_3 = \frac{V_2 T_3}{T_2} = \frac{0.7 \times (320 + 273)}{(17 + 273)} = 1.43 \text{ m}^3$$

using gas equation $\dfrac{p_1 V_1}{T_1} = \dfrac{p_3 V_3}{T_3}$

$$\text{thus } V_3 = \frac{p_1 V_1 T_3}{T_1 p_3} = \frac{103 \times 4 \times 593}{290 \times 586} = 1.43 \text{ m}^3 \qquad \blacklozenge\blacklozenge\blacklozenge$$

The temperature of the air in a vehicle's tyre is 15°C and the pressure 198 kN/m². Assuming the tyre volume remains unchanged when the air pressure has increased to 206 kN/m² after a road journey, determine the temperature change.

$$\frac{p_1}{T_1} = \frac{p_2}{T_2}$$

$$\text{therefore } T_2 = \frac{p_2 T_1}{p_1} = \frac{(206 + 101.3) \times (15 + 273)}{(198 + 101.3)}$$

$$= 296 \text{ K or } 23°\text{C}$$

Temperature change = $23 - 15 = 8°\text{C}$ $\qquad \blacklozenge\blacklozenge\blacklozenge$

The gas in an engine cylinder of 82 mm diameter and stroke is at a temperature of 165°C and 102 kN/m² absolute pressure. The clearance volume per cylinder is 70 cm³. Determine the temperature of the gas when the piston reaches top dead centre (TDC) if the pressure at this point is 780 kN/m² abs.

$p_1 = 102 \text{ kN/m}^2; p_2 = 780 \text{ kN/m}^2; V_1 = ?; V_2 = 70 \text{ cm}^3;$
$T_1 = 165 + 273 = 438 \text{ K}; T_2 = ?$

$$\text{swept volume of cylinder } V_s = \frac{\pi d^2}{4} \times L = \frac{\pi \times 8.2^2 \times 8.2}{4} = 433 \text{ cm}^3$$

total volume $V_1 = V_s + V_c = 433 + 70 = 503 \text{ cm}^3$

$$\text{compression ratio } r = \frac{V_1}{V_2} = \frac{503}{70} = 7.185{:}1$$

$$\frac{p_1 V_1}{T_1} = \frac{p_2 V_2}{T_2}$$

therefore $T_2 = \dfrac{p_2 V_2 T_1}{p_1 V_1} = \dfrac{780 \times 1 \times 438}{102 \times 7.185}$

$$= 466.16 \text{ K}$$

$$= 193.16°\text{C} \qquad \blacklozenge\blacklozenge\blacklozenge$$

The air pressure in a diesel engine cylinder at bottom dead centre (BDC) is 1.06 bar at a temperature of 27°C. At the end of the compression stroke the air pressure has risen to 63 bar and the temperature to 667°C. Calculate the engines compression ratio.

$p_1 = 1.06$ bar; $p_2 = 63$ bar; $T_1 = 27 + 273 = 300$ K; $T_2 = 667 + 273 = 940$ K

$$\frac{p_1 V_1}{T_1} = \frac{p_2 V_2}{T_2}$$

and $\dfrac{V_1}{V_2} = r = \dfrac{p_2 T_1}{T_2 p_1} = \dfrac{63 \times 300}{940 \times 1.06} = 18.96{:}1 \qquad \blacklozenge\blacklozenge\blacklozenge$

EXERCISES 2.3

Elementary thermodynamics (B4)

1. The air tank of a compressed air braking system is found to be at a gauge pressure of 369 kN/m² and temperature of 16°C. The compressor then raises the air pressure to 760 kN/m². What is the new air temperature?

2. The temperature of a car tyre was 10°C and the pressure 173 kN/m². After road testing the tyre pressure had increased to 196 kN/m². Assuming the tyre volume remains unchanged, calculate the new temperature.

3. A CI engine has a cylinder bore diameter of 135 mm and stroke 120 mm. The clearance volume is 116 cm³. The air pressure at the beginning of compression is 102 kN/m² abs and temperature 38°C. The pressure reaches 4870 kN/m² abs at the end of compression. Calculate the temperature.

4. A four-cylinder engine of 3000 cm³ swept capacity has a clearance volume per cylinder of 55 cm³. The pressure of the charge before compression is 108 kN/m² abs and temperature 17°C. At the end of compression the temperature has increased to 612°C. Calculate the final pressure.

5. A compressor is operating at an air pressure of 103 kN/m² abs and temperature 18°C at the commencement of its compression stroke. At the end of compression the pressure and temperature have become 1760 kN/m² abs and 132°C respectively. Determine the volume ratio of the compressor.

6. If a quantity of gas at a pressure of 717 mm of mercury and temperature 16°C occupies a volume of 360 ml, what volume would it occupy under standard temperature and pressure conditions?

7. The air pressure in a CI engine cylinder is 1.22 bar and temperature 23°C. The compression ratio is 19:1. At the end of compression the pressure reaches 73 bar. Calculate the air temperature.

8. An air compressor tank contains 5.58 m³ of air at a pressure of 565 kN/m² abs. If this volume of air was allowed to expand until the pressure was 105 kN/m² abs, what would be its volume, assuming there is no temperature change?

9. The gas in an engine cylinder of 76 mm diameter and 84 mm stroke is at a temperature of 170°C and 107 kN/m² abs pressure. The clearance volume is 68 cm³. Find the temperature of the gas when the piston reaches top dead centre if the pressure is then 757 kN/m² abs.

10. The pressure, volume and temperature of a quantity of gas are 120 kN/m² abs, 1.2 m³ and 260°C respectively. The final volume is 3.9 m³ and temperature 72°C. Calculate the final gas pressure.

11. The air in a car tyre is found to be at a pressure of 193 kN/m² and temperature 30°C after a fast journey on a motorway. Later it was found that the temperature had fallen to 19°C. Assuming the tyre volume remained constant what would the new tyre pressure read? Why should care be taken regarding tyre pressures for motorway travel?

2.6 COMPRESSION RATIOS (B5)

Compression ratios: full swept volume (See Fig. 2.9)

When the piston is at the bottom of its stroke (crank at bottom dead centre BDC) the volume available for the gas charge is the sum of the clearance and swept volumes: $V_c + V_s$. Thus the compression ratio (r) has a value equal to the total volume divided by the clearance volume, V_t/V_c. Thus

$$r = \frac{\text{clearance} + \text{swept volume}}{\text{clearance volume}} = \frac{V_c + V_s}{V_c} = 1 + \frac{V_s}{V_c}$$

and $\qquad r - 1 = \dfrac{V_s}{V_c}$

therefore $V_s = (r - 1) \times V_c$

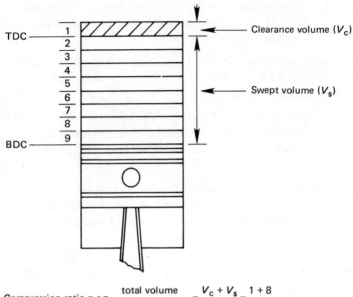

$$\text{Compression ratio} = r = \frac{\text{total volume}}{\text{clearance volume}} = \frac{V_c + V_s}{V_c} = \frac{1 + 8}{1}$$

$$= 9 : 1$$

$$\frac{V_c + V_s}{V_c} = \frac{V_c}{V_c} + \frac{V_s}{V_c} = 1 + \frac{V_s}{V_c}$$

Fig. 2.9 Compression ratio: full swept volume.

Worked example

The compression ratio of an engine is 7.6:1. If the clearance volume is 62 cm^3, determine the swept capacity.

Method 1

$$r = \frac{V_c + V_s}{V_c} = 1 + \frac{V_s}{V_c}$$

thus $(r - 1) \times V_c = V_s$

$(7.6 - 1) \times 62 = 409.2$ cm^3

Method 2

$$r \times V_c - V_c = V_s$$

$7.6 \times 62 - 62 = 409.2$ cm^3

♦♦♦

Compression ratios: Part swept volume

No real compression of the charge can take place until both valves are closed. Therefore a more realistic figure for the compression ratio for use in engine test and research work is to base the swept volume on that which is available after the closing of the inlet valve. It is sometimes necessary to calculate the compression ratio when a certain percentage of the compression stroke has been completed. Fig. 2.10 shows a piston in such a position. Thus

$$V_3 = V_c + (\% \text{ of } V_s \text{ uncompleted})$$

$$= V_c + \% (r - 1)$$

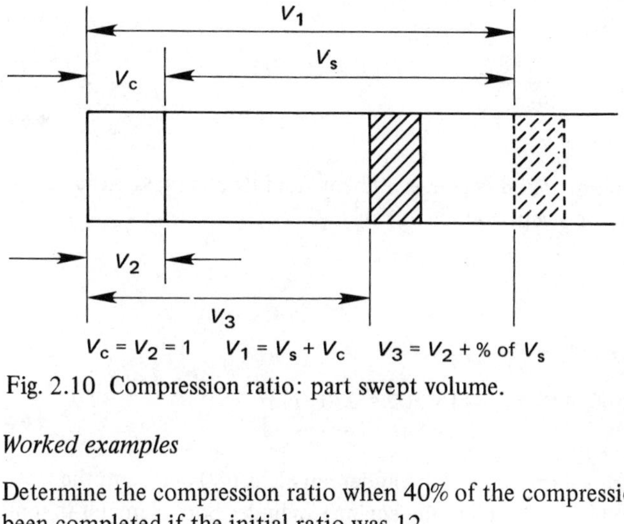

$$V_c = V_2 = 1 \qquad V_1 = V_s + V_c \qquad V_3 = V_2 + \% \text{ of } V_s$$

Fig. 2.10 Compression ratio: part swept volume.

Worked examples

Determine the compression ratio when 40% of the compression stroke has been completed if the initial ratio was 12.

$$V_c = 1 \text{ and } V_s = r - 1$$

$$= 12 - 1$$

$$= 11$$

$$V_3 = V_c + \% \text{ of } V_s$$

$$= 1 + 0.6 \times 11$$

$$= 7.6$$

where % of V_s is the % of the uncompleted compression stroke therefore

$$\text{new ratio} = \frac{V_3}{V_2} = \frac{7.6}{1}$$

$$= 7.6$$

♦♦♦

An engine having a bore and stroke of 110 mm and 100 mm, respectively, has a clearance volume of 86 cm^3. Calculate (a) the theoretical compression ratio, and (b) the ratio based on the closing point of the inlet valve when piston moved 17 mm from BDC.

(a)   volume swept $V_s = \dfrac{\pi d^2}{4} \times L = \dfrac{\pi \times 11^2 \times 10}{4} = 950$ cm^3

compression ratio $r = \dfrac{V_c + V_s}{V_c} = \dfrac{86 + 950}{86} = 12.0$

(b)   new $V_s = \dfrac{\pi \times 11^2 \times 8.3}{4} = 788$ cm^3

thus $r = \dfrac{86 + 788}{86} = 10.16$

◆◆◆

If the clearance volume of an engine is 302 cm^3 and its compression ratio 8.62:1, determine the swept volume in cm^3.

$$r = \frac{V_s}{V_c} + 1$$

thus $(r - 1) \times V_c = V_s$

hence $V_s = (8.62 - 1) \times 302 = 2301$ cm^3

◆◆◆

The total clearance volume for a six-cylinder engine is 680 cm^3, and the compression ratio 8.2:1. Calculate the engine's cylinder bore diameter in mm if the stroke is 98 mm.

$$V_s = (r - 1) \times V_c$$

thus $V_s = (8.2 - 1) \times 680 = 4896$ m^3

$$\frac{\pi \times d^2 \times L \times 6}{4} = 4896 \text{ cm}^3 \text{ total swept volume}$$

where d is in cm.

Therefore d(cm) $= \sqrt{\left(\dfrac{V_s + 4}{\pi \times L \times 6}\right)} = \sqrt{\left(\dfrac{4896 \times 4}{\pi \times 9.8 \times 6}\right)}$

$= 10.29$ cm

$= 102.9$ mm diameter

◆◆◆

The compression ratio of an oil engine is 17:1. Determine the compression ratios when only (a) 10%, (b) 30%, (c) 50%, and (d) 80% of the compression stroke is completed.

Study the text together with Figs. 2.9 and 2.10. It will be seen that $V_s = (r - 1)$, $V_c = 1 = V_2$, and $V_3 = V_c + \%$ of V_s. Thus $V_3 = 1 + \%(r - 1)$ where the percentage represents the *uncompleted* percentage of the compression stroke.

$$\text{Compression ratio} = r = \frac{V_s + V_c}{V_c} = \frac{V_1}{V_2} + 1$$

and where a percentage of the compression stroke is completed

$$r = \frac{V_3}{V_2} = \frac{V_3}{1}$$

(a)   10% of compression stroke completed: $V_3 = 1 + \%(r - 1)$
$$= 1 + 0.9(17 - 1) = 15.4$$
thus $r = 15.4{:}1.$

(b)   30% of compression stroke completed: $V_3 = 1 + 0.7(17 - 1) = 12.2$
thus $r = 12.2{:}1$

(c)   50% of compression stroke completed: $V_3 = 1 + 0.5(17 - 1) = 9$
thus $r = 9{:}1$

(d)   80% of compression stroke completed: $V_3 = 1 + 0.2(17 - 1) = 4.2$
thus $r = 4.2{:}1$ ◆◆◆

Determination of engine compression ratio by experiment

The compression ratio of an engine can be found practically, with simple equipment: a quantity of thin oil, syringe and measuring vessel marked in millilitres or cm^3, and some grease. For this experiment a side-valve four-stroke motor cycle engine is ideal. Ensure that the engine is firmly held and level. With the cylinder head removed, turn the engine to top dead centre (TDC) position with both valves closed. Lightly grease round the piston and valves. Grease the cylinder head gasket and bolt down the cylinder head.

Through the sparking plug orifice, fill up the clearance volume with oil from the measuring vessel. Note the amount of oil used, then syringe the oil from the engine. Turn the engine to bottom dead centre (BDC) and seal with grease. From the vessel fill up the cylinder to piston TDC position. Note the amount of oil used, then remove the oil with the syringe. The compression ratio can now be calculated as:

$$\frac{V_c + V_s}{V_c}$$

It is instructive to determine at this point what is sometimes referred to as the actual swept volume of the engine. This is the volume swept by the piston after the closing of the inlet valve. The reasoning is that no compression of the charge can take place until all valves are closed. Turn the engine in the direction of rotation (DOR) until the inlet valve just closes. Make sure the tappets are correctly adjusted, carefully seal the piston with grease and fill up as before from the measuring vessel. Note the amount used.

$$\text{actual compression ratio} = \frac{\text{actual } V_s + V_c}{V_c}$$

While such an engine is available it is instructive to measure the piston travel against crankshaft degrees. With the head removed, the piston exactly at TDC and a degree protractor on the crankshaft set at zero degrees turn the crankshaft exactly 90° from TDC and measure the piston travel from TDC. Note reading. Measure the full stroke of the piston from TDC to BDC. You will find that the piston travelled more than half the stroke in the first 90° which shows that the piston travel is not harmonic. See section on engine balance (Part 2).

EXERCISES 2.4

Compression ratios (B5)

1. The total clearance volume of a six cylinder engine is 680 cm^3 and the compression ratio 8.2:1. Determine the cylinder bore diameter in mm if the stroke is 98 mm.

2. The bore and stroke of an engine are 62 mm and 56 mm, respectively. The clearance volume is 21 cm^3. Find the engine's compression ratio when the piston is commencing its compression stroke, and when 30% of the stroke is completed.

3. The compression ratio of a CI oil engine is 17.8:1 and the clearance volume per cylinder 47 cm^3. Calculate the compression ratio when 58% of the compression stroke is completed.

4. The compression ratio of an engine having a clearance volume per cylinder of 62 cm^3 is 9.37:1 when 40% of the compression stroke is completed. Find the compression ratio of the engine.

5. An engine having a cylinder bore of 88 mm diameter and a stroke of 110 mm has a clearance volume of 74 cm^3. Calculate: (a) the compression ratio when the piston is at bottom dead centre; (b) when 40% of the compression stroke is completed.

6. The total clearance volume of a four cylinder engine is 155 cm^3, and the compression ratio 7.8:1. Determine the cylinder bore diameter in mm if the engine stroke is 68 mm.

7. An engine having a bore and stroke of 110 mm and 100 mm respectively has a clearance volume per cylinder of 86 cm^3. Calculate the engine compression ratio (a) when the piston is at bottom dead centre, and (b) when the piston has moved 20 mm on the compression stroke.

8. A six cylinder engine of 3 litres swept volume and a clearance volume per cylinder of 44.17 cm^3. The cylinder bore diameter is 80 mm. Find the compression ratio of this engine and the stroke in mm.

2.7 ENGINE POWER AND EFFICIENCY (B6)

In the early part of this century steam, gas and spark ignition engines, having a low speed of rotation, had the power developed within the engine cylinder [indicated horse power (ihp)] obtained through the medium of a drum-type engine indicator fitted and connected to the engine cylinder. A friction brake or dynamometer enabled the torque and power developed at the crankshaft or flywheel to be evaluated, and the power was termed the brake horse power (bhp). Using Imperial units of the time:

$$\text{indicated horse power (ihp)} = \frac{p_m LAnN}{33\ 000} \quad \text{(2 stroke cycle)}$$

$$= \frac{p_m LAnN}{66\ 000} \quad \text{(4 stroke cycle)}$$

where p_m = indicated mean effective pressure (imep)(lbf/in^2)

L = length of piston stroke (feet)

A = area of a piston crown or engine cylinder (in^2)

n = number of cylinders

N = revolutions per minute (rev/min)

If the mechanical efficiency of the engine was known the bhp could be calculated from the ihp. Thus if η_m = mechanical efficiency (η is the Greek letter used for efficiency) then

$$\text{ihp} = \frac{p_m LAnN}{66\ 000} \qquad \text{4 stroke cycle}$$

$$\text{and bhp} = \frac{\eta_m p_m LAnN}{66\ 000} \qquad \text{4 stroke cycle}$$

The pressure/volume diagram produced by a drum indicator for slow speed engines formed the basis for early engine research. A pV diagram is given Fig. 2.14 and a full description of the drum indicator is given in Part 2.

As motor vehicles became more popular a form of taxation was introduced called the RAC Treasury Horse Power Rating (Hp $= D^2 n/2.5$). This formula was based on the following data: mechanical efficiency of 75%, imep of 90 lbf/in^2, mean maximum piston speed of 1000 feet per minute. When this data is introduced into the bhp formula, then:

$$\text{bhp} = \frac{\eta_m p_m LAnN}{66\ 000} = \frac{\eta_m p_m L\pi D^2 nN}{66\ 000 \times 4}$$

mean or average piston speed is $2LN$ ft/min, therefore:

$$\text{bhp} = \frac{75 \times 90 \times 1000 \times \pi \times D^2 n}{100 \times 66\ 000 \times 2 \times 4} = \frac{D^2 n}{2.5}$$

For a very few years the power output of a motor car engine approximated fairly closely to the above formula, but the engine manufacturers wanted to improve engine performance but still retain low taxation for the motorist. Thus engines were designed consisting of small diameter pistons, but with long strokes to increase the cylinder capacity or swept volume. High revolutions per minute (power is the rate of doing work) resulted in high mean piston speeds with very high acceleration factors creating large inertia loads. It is beyond the scope of this book to give further details, but the reader would be wise to research this interesting subject. Before the Second World War car engines and the like produced at least three or four times the RAC hp rating.

Worked examples

A four cylinder car engine manufactured in the early 1920s had a cylinder bore diameter of 2.4 inches. A similarly dimensioned engine produced in 1940 had a power output 3.6 times that of the RAC hp rating. Determine the RAC hp rating of the engines and the power output of the later unit.

$$\text{RAC hp rating} = \frac{D^2 n}{2.5} = \frac{2.4^2 \times 4}{2.5} = 9.216 \text{ hp}$$

$$9.216 \times 3.6 \quad = 33 \text{ hp} \qquad\qquad \blacklozenge\blacklozenge\blacklozenge$$

A four cylinder four stroke engine manufactured in 1938 had a 2.76 inch cylinder bore diameter and 3.6 inch stroke. At an engine speed of 2700 rev/min a bhp of 36.6 was developed. Determine the bmep and the RAC hp rating.

$$\text{bhp} = \frac{\text{bmep } LAnN}{66\ 000}$$

$$\text{bmep} = \frac{\text{bhp} \times 66\ 000}{LAnN} = \frac{\text{bhp} \times 66\ 000 \times 4 \times 12}{L\pi D^2 nN} \quad (note: L \text{ must be in feet})$$

$$= \frac{36.6 \times 66\ 000 \times 4 \times 12}{3.6 \times \pi \times 2.76^2 \times 4 \times 2700}$$

$$= 124.6 \text{ lbf/in}^2$$

$$\text{RAC hp rating} = \frac{D^2 n}{2.5} = \frac{2.76^2 \times 4}{2.5} = 12.188 \text{ hp}$$

◆◆◆

A four-stroke cycle engine built in 1937 had four cylinders giving a total swept capacity of 91.5 in³. The compression ratio was 8.3:1 and the maximum power developed 50 bhp at 4000 rev/min. A maximum bmep of 127 lbf/in² was produced at 2000 rev/min.
Determine: (a) the bmep at maximum power, (b) the maximum engine torque, (c) the total clearance volume (in³), (d) the engine stroke if it is 1.2 times greater than the bore diameter, (e) the RAC hp rating.

(a) $$\text{bmep} = \frac{\text{bhp} \times 66\ 000 \times 12}{LAnN} \quad (note: LAn \text{ is the total swept volume})$$

$$= \frac{50 \times 66\ 000 \times 12}{91.5 \times 4000}$$

$$= 108 \text{ lbf/in}^2$$

(b) $T2\pi$ = bmep × $LAn/2$

$$T = \frac{127 \times 91.5}{4 \times \pi \times 12}$$

$$= 77 \text{ lbf ft}$$

(c) $r = \dfrac{V_s}{V_c} + 1$ and $V_c = \dfrac{V_s}{r-1} = \dfrac{91.5}{8.3 - 1} = 12.53 \text{ in}^3$

(d) $\dfrac{L\pi D^2 n}{4}$ = total swept volume in³

where L and D are in inches as $L = 1.2D$ therefore $1.2D \times D^2 = 1.2D^3$

$$\frac{1.2D^3 n}{4} = 91.5 \text{ in}^3$$

and

$$D = \sqrt[3]{\left(\frac{91.5 \times 4}{1.2 \times 4}\right)}$$

$$= = 4.24 \text{ in}$$

therefore

$$L = 1.2\,D$$

$$= 1.2 \times 4.24$$

$$= 5.088 \text{ in}$$

(e)   RAC hp rating $= \dfrac{D^2 n}{2.5} = \dfrac{4.24^2 \times 4}{2.5} = 28.76 \text{ hp}$

◆◆◆

EXERCISES 2.5

1. A six cylinder engine of 2.5 inch diameter bore developed 48 bhp when manufactured in 1939. By how much was this power greater than the RAC hp rating?

2. A single cylinder four-stroke motorcycle engine manufactured in 1924 had a bore and stroke of 2.75 in and 3.85 in, respectively. A bmep of 128 lbf/in^2 at 3800 rev/min was developed. Determine the bhp and RAC hp rating.

3. A six cylinder high performance four-stroke engine of the pre-War era had a total swept volume of 230 in^3 and a compression ratio of 9:1. A maximum of 235 bhp was developed at 5500 rev/min, and maximum torque was 242 lb ft. Determine: (a) the maximum bmep, (b) the bmep at maximum power, (c) the clearance volume of one cylinder in^3, (d) the engine stroke if it is 1.3 times greater than the cylinder bore diameter, (e) the RAC hp rating.

2.8 INTERNAL COMBUSTION ENGINE CYCLES

In the spark ignition and compression ignition piston type engines the energy contained in the fuel is converted to mechanical energy by burning the fuel with air behind a piston within the engine cylinder. The process is termed a thermodynamic operation.

The sequence of events are briefly explained as follows:

1. The introduction of a charge of air into the engine cylinder (induction stroke) which includes the petrol, gas or paraffin in the case of the spark ignition engine, and air only for the diesel or CI oil engine.

2. Compression of the charge during the compression stroke creating a rise in temperature. Fuel injected at end of compression with the CI engine.

3. The combustion of the fuel in the charge of air produces a large addition of heat.

4. The expansion or power stroke producing torque and power at the crankshaft.

5. Heat is rejected via exhaust valve and port to the atmosphere.

Three internal combustion cycles – the constant volume, constant pressure and the dual cycle – are briefly described. Further information together with details of efficiencies are given in Part 2.

Constant volume cycle (Fig. 2.11)

The line BC represents a rise in pressure at constant volume following ignition at B. AB and CD are compression and expansion curves, respectively, and they are created under adiabatic conditions. DA represents the sudden fall of pressure and temperature at constant volume as heat is rejected as the exhaust valve opens. If the gaseous mixture is air only in the cycle, the thermal efficiency so determined would be called the *Air Standard Efficiency* (see Part 2).

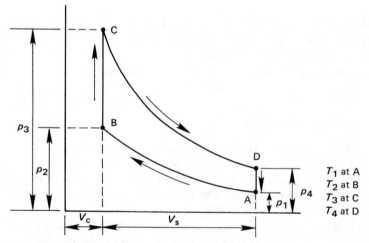

Fig. 2.11 Constant volume cycle.

Constant pressure cycle (Fig. 2.12)

To enable high compression ratios to be used with improved thermal efficiency, air only is compressed and its temperature rises above the ignition

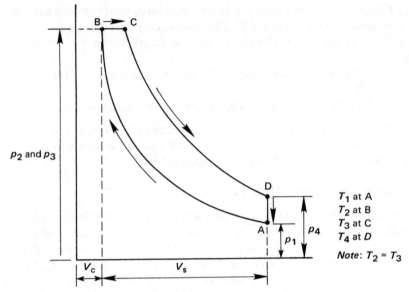

Fig. 2.12 Constant pressure cycle.

temperature of the fuel oil that is injected into this hot compressed air. AB is the compression curve, and CD the expansion curve, both theoretically adiabatic, but BC is combustion at constant pressure, and DA represents pressure and temperature fall under constant volume conditions.

The dual combustion cycle (Fig. 2.13)

The original diesel engines operating on the constant pressure cycle had the fuel oil injected by a blast of highly compressed air, hence the term *air blast injection*. Modern high speed compression–ignition oil engines have their fuel injected by mechanical/hydraulic means via injection pumps. This type of injection is referred to as solid injection.

At full load most of the fuel is burnt under constant volume conditions, and only a small amount under constant pressure conditions during what is termed *the direct burning period*, hence the name dual cycle. The higher pressures produce better torque figures and vastly improved power-to-weight ratios. The area of the diagram represents the work done, and from the three diagrams it can be seen that the petrol engine operating on the constant volume cycle would produce the greater work if its compression ratio could be raised to create pressures such as those available with the CI engine.

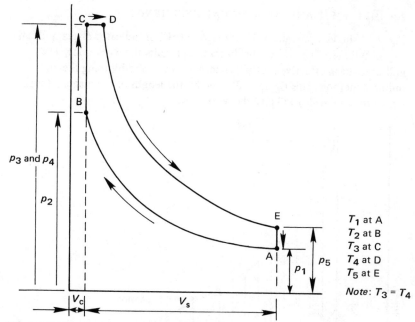

Fig. 2.13 The dual combustion cycle.

Work done in an engine cylinder

Exactly how the torque is developed at the crankshaft due to gas pressures within the cylinder is not always appreciated, hence the following description: The mean or average gas pressure multiplied by the piston crown area gives the average force acting on the piston crown. Take an average pressure of 700 kN/m² and a piston diameter of 80 mm. If p = pressure (kN/m²) and A = area (m²) = $\pi D^2/4$ then

$$\text{average force kN} = p \times A = p \times \frac{\pi D^2}{4}$$

$$= \frac{700 \times \pi \times 0.08^2}{4}$$

$$= 3.519 \text{ kN}$$

work done = force × distance moved in direction of the force

$$= p \times A \times L$$

where L is the engine stroke 110 mm

$$= 3.518 \times 10^3 \times 0.11$$

$$= 386.98 \text{ N m or J}$$

2.9 IMEP, BMEP AND MECHANICAL EFFICIENCY

Fig. 2.14 shows a pressure/volume diagram (pV) or indicator diagram for an engine cylinder. The area of the diagram represents the work done. The indicated mean effective pressure (imep) can be found by using the mid-ordinate method. This figure multiplied by the length of the diagram (engine stroke to same scale) will give the work done.

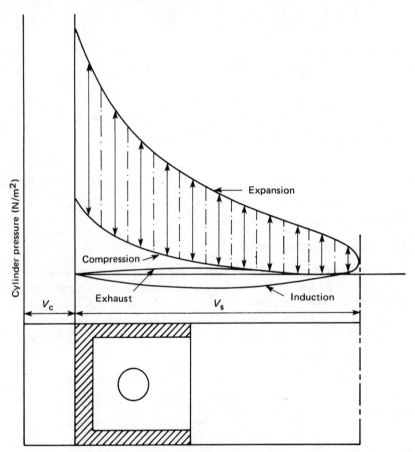

Fig. 2.14 Cylinder pressure or indicated diagram. V_c is the clearance volume and V_s the swept volume. Thus $V_c + V_s$ = total volume.

Indicated mean effective pressure (imep)

This is the average pressure acting on the power stroke which creates the same amount of work as the varying pressure within the engine cylinder acting behind the piston. Imep units are N/m^2, kN/m^2, and the pascal (N/m^2) could be used.

Indicated power (P_i)

This is the power that would be available at the crankshaft if a mechanical efficiency of 100% was possible. The term 'indicated' is derived from the use of engine indicators and their diagrams from which indicated power could be calculated.

$$\text{indicated power } (P_i) = \frac{\text{imep} \times LAn(N/2)}{60} \text{ N m/s, W or kW}$$
(4-stroke cycle)

where imep = average or mean indicated pressure (N/m^2 or kN/m^2)

A = area of a piston crown (m^2)

n = number of engine cylinders

L = piston or engine stroke (m)

$N/2$ = number of firing impulses per cylinder per minute
(4-stroke cycle)

$nN/2$ = number of firing impulses per minute (4-stroke cycle)

nN = number of firing impulses per minute (2-stroke cycle)

LAn = total swept volume of engine, or engine capacity (m^3 or cm^3)

Worked example

Firing impulses
A six cylinder four-stroke cycle engine is making 4800 rev/min. How many firing impulses: (a) per one revolution; (b) per minute; and (c) repeating (a) and (b) as for a two-stroke cycle engine?

(a) Power impulses per revolution $= \dfrac{n}{2} = \dfrac{6}{2} = 3$

(b) power impulses per minute $= \dfrac{nN}{2} = \dfrac{6 \times 4800}{2} = 14\ 400$

(c) power impulses per revolution $= n = 6$

power impulses per minute $= nN = 6 \times 4800 = 28\ 800$

♦♦♦

A check for the indicated power formula:

imep x An = total average force per revolution (N or kN)

imep x AnL = total work done per revolution (N m or J, kN m or kJ)

imep x $AnLN$ = total work done per minute (N m or J, kN m or kJ)

$\dfrac{\text{imep x } AnLN}{60}$ = total work done per second (2-stroke cycle) (N m/s or watts (W), kN m/s or kW)

Brake mean effective pressure (bmep)

Bmep is the proportion of the imep which is available to perform external work at the engine crankshaft. Bmep is calculated from the brake power, and is smaller than the imep by the amount of pressure required to overcome the engine's frictional and pumping losses. It is the average force that is applied to every square metre of piston area (force per unit of area). Engines of differing design and capacity can be compared accurately for performance from their ability to develop good bmep figures. Bmep units are N/m^2 or kN/m^2.

Mechanical efficiency

The ratio

$$\frac{\text{bmep}}{\text{imep}} \quad \text{or} \quad \frac{\text{brake power}}{\text{indicated power}} = \text{mechanical efficiency, } \eta_m$$

thus

$$\eta_m \times \text{imep} = \text{bmep}$$

and $\eta_m \times$ indicated power = brake power

therefore

$$\text{indicated power } P_i = \frac{\text{imep } LAnN}{60} \text{ 2-stroke cycle}$$

and $$\text{brake power } P_b = \frac{\eta_m \times \text{imep } LAnN}{60} \text{ W or kW}$$

$$= \frac{\text{bmep} \times LAnN}{60} \text{ W or kW}$$

Worked examples

An engine has a pressure of 686 kN/m^2 acting upon its 76 mm diameter

piston, the stroke of which is 85 mm. Calculate the work done during one
power stroke neglecting friction losses.

$$\text{work done} = p \times A \times L = p \times \frac{\pi D^2}{4} \times L$$

$$= \frac{686 \times 10^3 \times \pi \times 0.076^2 \times 0.085}{4}$$

$$= 264.52 \text{ N m or J} \qquad \blacklozenge\blacklozenge\blacklozenge$$

A four-stroke cycle engine has a swept capacity of 0.003 m³. If the bmep
figure is 742 kN/m² at 4230 rev/min, find the brake power of the engine.

$$\text{brake power} = \frac{\text{bmep} \times LAnN}{2 \times 60} = \frac{742 \times 0.003 \times 4230}{120}$$

$$= 78.466 \text{ kW} \qquad \blacklozenge\blacklozenge\blacklozenge$$

If the mechanical efficiency of the above engine is 76%, what are the bmep
and indicated power figures?

$$\eta_m \times \text{imep} = \text{bmep}$$

therefore $\text{imep} = \dfrac{\text{bmep}}{\eta_m} = \dfrac{742}{0.76} = 976.3 \text{ kN/m}^2$

$$P_i = \frac{P_b}{\eta_m} = \frac{78.466}{0.76} = 103.24 \text{ kW} \qquad \blacklozenge\blacklozenge\blacklozenge$$

An engine develops 32 kW power at 2400 rev/min. This four cylinder four-
stroke engine has a swept capacity of 0.002 m³. The stroke/bore ratio is 1.4.
Determine the bmep and the dimensions of the engine bore and stroke.

$$\text{kW} = \frac{\text{bmep } LAnN}{60 \times 2}$$

and $\text{bmep kN/m}^2 = \dfrac{\text{kW} \times 60 \times 2}{LAnN} = \dfrac{32 \times 120}{0.002 \times 2400}$

$$= 800 \text{ kN/m}^2.$$

Total swept volume $V_s = LAn = \dfrac{L \times \pi D^2 n}{4}$

and $L = 1.4 \times D$

$$V_s = 0.002 \times 10^6 = \frac{1.4 \times D^3 \pi n}{4} \text{ cm}^3$$

Note: 1.4 x *D* was substituted for *L*.

Therefore $D^3 = \dfrac{0.002 \times 10^6 \times 4}{1.4 \times \pi \times 4} = 454.72$

and $D = \sqrt[3]{(454.72)}$

              $= 7.689$ cm or 76.69 mm

and $L = 1.4 \times D = 1.4 \times 76.99$

              $= 107.79$ mm

              bmep $= 800$ kN/m^2

              bore diameter $= 76.69$ mm

              stroke $= 107.36$ mm   ◆◆◆

A single cylinder motorcycle engine has a cylinder bore diameter of 82 mm and a stroke of 86 mm. When the bmep is 806 kN/m^2, what work is completed on the power stroke?

$\qquad$ work done (J) = average force N x distance moved by piston (m)

$\qquad\qquad$ = bmep (kN/m^2) x area of piston (m^2) x stroke (m)

$\qquad\qquad$ = bmep (kN/m^2) x 10^3 x $\dfrac{\pi D^2}{4} \times L$

$\qquad\qquad$ = $(808 \times 10^3 \times \pi \times 0.082^2 \times 0.086)/4$

$\qquad\qquad$ = 367 N m or J   ◆◆◆

An engine having a compression ratio *r* of 9.5:1 has a clearance volume V_c of 58 cm^3 and a stroke of 102 mm. If the bmep is 796 kN/m^2, determine the work done per power stroke.

$$r = \frac{V_c + V_s}{V_c} = 1 + \frac{V_s}{V_c} \text{ thus } (r-1) \times V_c = V_s$$

hence $(9.5 - 1) \times 58 = 493$ cm^3

and $V_s = \dfrac{\pi D^2}{4} \times L$ therefore $D^2 = \dfrac{V_s \times 4}{\pi \times L}$

$\qquad\qquad$ thus $D = \sqrt{\left(\dfrac{V_s \times 4}{\pi \times L}\right)}$

$\qquad\qquad\qquad$ $= \sqrt{\left(\dfrac{493 \times 4}{10^6 \times \pi \times 0.102}\right)}$

$\qquad\qquad\qquad$ $= 0.0784$ m or 78.4 mm

work done (J) = bmep (kN/m^2) x piston area (m^2) x stroke (m)

$$= (796 \times 10^3 \times \pi \times 0.0784^2 \times 0.102)/4$$

$$= 392 \text{ N m or J}$$

◆◆◆

EXERCISES 2.6

Engine bmep and power (B6)

1. A six cylinder four-stroke engine developing 168 kW brake power with a bmep of 834 kN/m^2 at 2000 rev/min, has a stroke/bore ratio of 1.25. Calculate the engine bore and stroke in millimetres.

2. The total swept volume of a six cylinder four-stroke engine is 0.002 65 m^3. Power of 76.4 kW is being delivered at 5200 rev/min. Determine the bmep in bar.

3. A four cylinder four-stroke engine having a total swept volume of 0.0028 m^3 is producing a bmep of 6.45 bar abs at 4360 rev/min. Calculate the brake power in kilowatts.

4. The swept volume of a six cylinder engine operating on the four-stroke cycle is 0.002 m^3, and it develops a torque of 111.2 N m. Calculate the bmep.

5. A twin cylinder two-stroke diesel engine develops 14 kW at 2800 rev/min. The area of a piston crown is 0.007 85 m^2 and the stroke 0.15 m. Calculate the average force created on one piston when on power stroke, and the work done.

6. The compression ratio of a single cylinder motorcycle engine is 9.6:1. The clearance volume is 45 cm^3 and stroke 76 mm. When the bmep is 846 kN/m^2 determine the average work done on a power stroke.

2.10 ENGINE TORQUE AND BRAKE POWER

Engine torque (T)

Torque (T) is a turning moment (N m) and is dependent on the pressure produced within the engine cylinders, the piston crown area upon which the effective pressure (bmep) is applied, and the crankshaft angle or effective radius which, like the gas pressure, is a varying one. Engine capacity thus plays a large part in torque production. Doubling an engine's capacity (swept volume V_s) will almost double the engine torque. Engine torque plays an important role in vehicle performance as will be seen later.

When engine testing with a dynamometer, the load lifted is situated at the end of the dynamometer torque arm:

thus torque $T = w \times R$ N m.

The work done in one revolution is calculated as follows (see Fig. 2.15). If the brake load w was moved through one revolution or $360°$ with a radius or torque arm of R m, the work done in one revolution

$$= w \times 2\pi R \text{ N m or J}$$

$$= T2\pi \text{ as } w \times R = T \text{ N m}$$

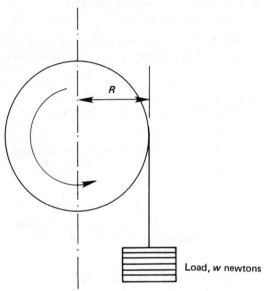

Load, w newtons

Fig. 2.15

Brake power (P_b)

This is the power developed at the crankshaft or flywheel. The term *brake* originated from the method used to determine an engine's power output by measuring the torque using some form of friction dynamometer. In early days of engine design the flywheel was often used for the brake dynamometer. Often quoted brake power figures do not indicate whether they are gross or net.

An engine connected to a modern test bench is generally without such items as a cooling fan, coolant pump and radiator, dynamo and clutch unit and is connected to the large test bench exhaust system. Thus some 10–15%

more power is often possible under these conditions (gross power) compared to the 'under the bonnet' performance (net power).

On the Continent, the DIN rating is used, which confirms the engine's performance with all its accessories as fitted to the chassis together with corrections for normal temperature and pressure.

In the USA the SAE rating method is adopted which in effect is the gross engine output.

Power is the rate of doing work, therefore:

brake power (P_b) = work done in one revolution x revolutions per second

$$= T \times 2\pi \times \frac{N}{60} = \frac{T2\pi N}{60} \text{ watts (W) or kilowatts (kW)}$$

Work done was previously stated as equal to $\dfrac{\text{bmep} \times LAn}{2}$ (4-stroke engine)

or $\qquad\qquad\qquad\qquad$ = bmep x LAn (2-stroke engine).

therefore $\quad T2\pi = \dfrac{\text{bmep} \times LAn}{2}$ (4-stroke engine)

and = bmep x LAn (2-stroke engine)

also brake power $P_b = \dfrac{T2\pi N}{60} = \dfrac{\text{bmep} \times LAnN}{60 \times 2}$ (4-stroke engine)

and $\qquad$ bmep $= \dfrac{T4\pi}{LAn}$

For indicated power, substitute imep for bmep in above formulae.

Torque and the crankshaft angle

Work is also accomplished when the torque is applied through an angle. Distance xy (Fig. 2.16) is equal to $r\theta$ where θ is the angle through which the crankshaft moves, in radians.

$$\text{torque} = \text{force} \times \text{radius}$$

$$= F \times r$$

$$\text{work done} = F \times \text{distance } xy$$

$$= F \times r\theta$$

$$= T \times \theta$$

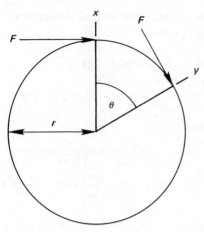

Fig. 2.16

Power is the rate of doing work $= \dfrac{\text{work done}}{\text{time taken}}$ joules/second or watts

$$= \frac{\text{force x distance}}{\text{time taken (t seconds)}}$$

$$= \frac{F \times xy}{t} = \frac{F \times r\theta}{t} = \frac{T \times \theta}{t} = T\omega$$

Note: θ/t = angular velocity in radians/second $= \omega = 2\pi N/60 = \pi N/30$ where N = engine rev/min.

   Note: The use of the radian for torque etc., is not required until Part 2.

Worked examples

An engine develops 26 kW of power at 3800 rev/min. Determine the engine torque.

$$\text{kW} = \frac{T 2\pi N}{60 \times 10^3}$$

therefore $T \,\text{N m} = \dfrac{\text{kW} \times 60 \times 10^3}{2 \times \pi \times N}$

$$= \frac{26 \times 60 \times 10^3}{2 \times \pi \times 3800}$$

$$= 65.33 \text{ N m torque}$$

◆◆◆

A two-stroke engine is developing a torque of 210 N m at 1600 rev/min. Calculate the power in kW.

$$\text{kW} = \frac{T2\pi N}{60 \times 10^3} = \frac{210 \times 2 \times \pi \times 1600}{60 \times 10^3} = 35.18 \text{ kW}$$

♦♦♦

A four-stroke cycle oil engine develops a torque of 200 N m which produces 62 kW of power. At which rev/min was the engine operating?

$$\text{kW} = \frac{T2\pi N}{60 \times 10^3}$$

and

$$N = \frac{\text{kW} \times 60 \times 10^3}{T \times 2 \times \pi} = \frac{62 \times 60 \times 10^3}{200 \times 2 \times \pi}$$

$$= 2960 \text{ rev/min}$$

♦♦♦

A two-stroke engine developing a bmep of 740 kN/m^2 has a total swept capacity of 2800 cm^3. Determine (a) the engine torque, and (b) the work done in one revolution.

(a) $T2\pi = \text{bmep } LAn$

and

$$T(\text{N m}) = \frac{\text{bmep } LAn}{2\pi} = \frac{740 \times 10^3}{2 \times \pi} \times \frac{2800}{10^6} = 329.76 \text{ N m}$$

(b) work done in one revolution $= T2\pi = 329.76 \times 2 \times \pi = 2072$ N m

or bmep $\times LAn = 740 \times 10^3 \times \dfrac{2800}{10^6} = 2072$ joules or N m

♦♦♦

2.11 FUEL CONSUMPTION AND THERMAL EFFICIENCY

The fuel an engine consumes can be measured by volume or by mass. By volume the units are cm^3/min, litres per second, minute or hour (1000 cm^3 = 1 litre). By mass the units are kg per second, minute or hour (1 litre of water = 1 kg)

litres x relative density of the fuel = kg of fuel

Specific fuel consumption

Specific fuel consumption represents the mass or volume of fuel an engine consumes per hour while it produces 1 kW of power. It is an indication of the engine's thermal or heat efficiency and is one of the most important engine characteristics. Comparisons can be made between engines of widely different capacities and characteristics, providing similar fuel and test conditions are arranged for each test.

A mirrored reflection of the specific consumption curve shows the shape of the engine's thermal efficiency curve. The lowest point on the consumption curve becomes the highest point on the thermal efficiency curve.

If specific consumption = kg/(kW h) or l/(kW h) (h = hour)

then $\dfrac{\text{kg/h}}{\text{kW}}$ = kg/(kW h) and kg/(kW h) x kW = kg/h,

and likewise $\dfrac{\text{l/h}}{\text{kW}}$ = l/(kW h)

thus l/(kW h) x kW = l/h

The above equations will be found useful when calculating thermal efficiency and similar problems.

Note: It is important when checking and/or comparing performance graphs to note the scale which is used in each case. A comparatively flat specific consumption curve can be made to look quite different if the scale was opened up. Fig. 2.17 shows graphs of the engine performance curves mentioned above which are dealt with in some detail later, and in Part 2.

Thermal efficiency

The efficiency of an engine in converting the heat energy contained in the liquid fuel into mechanical energy is termed its thermal efficiency. A study of the results taken from heat balance tests shows clearly that internal combustion engines are inefficient at this conversion. The petrol engine is particularly inefficient and at its best may reach 25% efficiency.

$$\text{brake thermal efficiency} = \frac{\text{output (heat units)}}{\text{input (heat units)}} = \frac{\text{brake power}}{\text{fuel power}} = \frac{P_b}{\text{kg/s} \times \text{CV}}$$

where CV is the calorific or heat value of 1 kg of the fuel (J/kg, kJ/kg or MJ/kg).

$$\text{brake thermal efficiency } \eta = \frac{P_b \times 60 \times 60}{\text{kg/h} \times \text{CV}}$$

$$= \frac{P_b \times 3600}{\text{l/h} \times d \times \text{CV}}$$

where d is the relative density of the fuel.

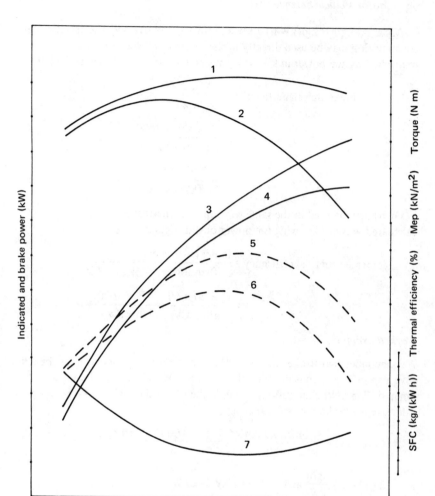

Engine speed (rev/min)

1 Imep
2 Bmep and torque
3 Indicated power
4 Brake power
5 Indicated thermal efficiency
6 Brake thermal efficiency
7 Specific fuel consumption

Fig. 2.17 Graphs of engine performance curves.

Note: As kg/h = kg/(kW h) x kW and l/h = l/(kW h) x kW, the specific fuel consumption may be used directly in the thermal efficiency formulae multiplied by the power in kW. The powers will cancel out as shown below:

$$\text{brake thermal efficiency} = \frac{\text{kW} \times 3600}{\text{kg/h} \times \text{CV}}$$

$$= \frac{\text{kW} \times 3600}{\text{kg/(kW h)} \times \text{kW} \times \text{CV}}$$

$$= \frac{3600}{\text{kg/(kW h)} \times \text{CV}}$$

l/(kW h) may be used in the same way, and the thermal efficiency may be calculated without knowing the power output figures.

$$\text{indicated thermal efficiency} = \frac{\text{indicated power}}{\text{fuel power}} = \frac{P_i}{\text{kg/s} \times \text{CV}}$$

$$= \frac{P_i \times 60 \times 60}{\text{kg/h} \times \text{CV}} = \frac{P_i \times 3600}{\text{l/h} \times d \times \text{CV}}$$

Worked examples

A six cylinder two-stroke engine of 4100 cm^3 swept capacity on a test bench gave a specific fuel consumption of 0.366 kg/(kW h) when developing a bmep of 758 kN/m^2 at 1500 rev/min. If the CV of the fuel was 44.5 MJ/kg calculate the brake thermal efficiency.

$$\text{brake power} = \frac{\text{bmep} \times LAnN}{60} = \frac{758 \times 0.0041 \times 1500}{60} = 77.7 \text{ kW}$$

$$\text{kg/kW h} = \frac{\text{kg/h}}{\text{kW}} \text{ and kg/h} = \text{kg/kW h} \times \text{kW}$$

$$= 0.366 \times 77.7$$

$$= 28.44 \text{ kg/h}$$

$$\text{brake thermal efficiency} = \frac{P_b \times 3600}{\text{kg/h} \times \text{CV}} \text{ or } \frac{3600}{\text{kg/(kW h)} \times \text{CV}}$$

$$= \frac{77.7 \times 3600}{28.44 \times 44.5 \times 10^3} \text{ or } \frac{3600}{0.366 \times 44.5 \times 10^3}$$

$$= 0.22 \text{ or } 22\% \qquad\qquad \blacklozenge\blacklozenge\blacklozenge$$

Determine the bmep and brake thermal efficiency when a four cylinder four-stroke engine of 88 mm bore and 120 mm stroke consumes 7.755 l of fuel per hour developing 17.6 kW brake power at 1280 rev/min. (relative density of the fuel 0.72 and CV 45 MJ/kg)

$$\text{brake power} = \frac{\text{bmep} \times LAnN}{60 \times 2}$$

therefore

$$\text{bmep} = \frac{P_b \times 60 \times 2}{LAnN}$$

thus

$$\text{bmep kN/m}^2 = \frac{17.6 \times 60 \times 2 \times 4}{0.120 \times \pi \times 0.088^2 \times 4 \times 1280}$$

$$= 565 \text{ kN/m}^2$$

$$\text{brake thermal efficiency} = \frac{P_b \times 3600}{\text{kg/h} \times \text{CV}}$$

$$= \frac{17.6 \times 3600}{7.755 \times 1 \times 0.72 \times 45 \times 10^3}$$

$$= 0.252 \text{ or } 25.2\%$$ ◆◆◆

An engine having four cylinders and operating on the four-stroke cycle has a total swept volume of 2010 cm^3. At 4140 rev/min a bmep of 745 kN/m^2 is developed while consuming 16.4 kg of fuel per hour (CV of fuel 45 MJ/kg). Determine the brake thermal efficiency and the power available in the fuel consumed.

$$\text{brake power} = \frac{\text{bmep} \times LAnN}{60 \times 2} = \frac{745 \times 2010 \times 4140}{60 \times 10^6 \times 2} = 51.66 \text{ kW}$$

$$\text{brake thermal efficiency} = \frac{\text{brake power}}{\text{fuel power}} \text{ and fuel power} = \text{kg/s} \times \text{CV}$$

$$\text{thus fuel power kW} = \frac{16.4}{3600} \times 45 \times 10^3 = 205 \text{ kW}$$

$$\text{and brake thermal efficiency} \% = \frac{51.66}{205} \times 100$$

$$= 25.2\%$$ ◆◆◆

EXERCISES 2.7

Engine thermal efficiency (B6)

1. During a test on a CI oil engine, power of 22.38 kW was developed for a

fuel consumption of 6.36 kg of fuel oil per hour. If the mechanical efficiency was 80% and the fuel CV was 46 MJ/kg, determine the brake and indicated thermal efficiencies.

2. The engine of a car developed an output of 30 kW whilst travelling at 96 km/h. If the thermal efficiency is 25%, CV of fuel 45 MJ/kg and relative density 0.75, calculate the fuel consumption in kilometres per litre.

3. A CI engine consumes 8.6 litres of fuel oil per hour. The relative density is 0.84, brake thermal efficiency is 29.8%, the fuel has a calorific value of 45 MJ/kg and mechanical efficiency is 73%. What is the indicated power?

4. A CI engine consumes 7.9 kg of fuel per hour giving a brake thermal efficiency of 30.6%. If the CV of the fuel oil is 44 600 kJ/kg, calculate the indicated power if the mechanical efficiency is 78%.

5. Calculate the mechanical energy that one litre of petrol contains when its calorific value is 45 000 kJ/kg and relative density 0.718.

6. A fuel has a CV of 44 800 kJ/kg and is used at the rate of 4.35 kg/h. If the engine has a brake thermal efficiency of 20.9%, calculate the engine brake power.

7. A fuel of CV 43 600 kJ/kg is consumed at the rate of 0.0023 kg/s while developing 28 kW of power. Calculate the brake thermal efficiency.

8. Determine the brake thermal efficiency and bmep of a four-stroke cycle engine having a swept volume of 2624 cm^3 when it is developing a torque of 162.7 N m with a specific fuel consumption of 0.36 kg/(kW h). The fuel having a calorific value of 45 MJ/kg.

9. A four-stroke engine uses 20.6 kg of fuel per hour when developing a bmep of 896 kN/m^2 giving an engine torque of 57 N m. If the specific fuel consumption is 0.4 kg/(kW h) and calorific value of the fuel 44 MJ/kg, calculate the brake thermal efficiency and the engine capacity in cm^3.

10. The brake thermal efficiency of an engine is 26.7% when using fuel having a calorific value of 44.5 MJ/kg. The fuel consumed was 0.0022 kg/s. Find the brake power in kW.

11. A CI oil engine developed an indicated power of 51 kW when using 0.18 kg of fuel per minute having a calorific value of 45 MJ/kg. Pumping and friction losses reduce the indicated power by 11 kW. Calculate: (a) the brake power, (b) the mechanical efficiency, (c) the specific fuel consumption, and (d) the brake thermal efficiency.

12. An engine on test at 3000 rev/min overcomes a resistance of 142.35 N

acting at a radius of 0.355 m while consuming fuel at the rate of 7.784 litres per hour. If one litre per hour is equivalent to 10 kW, determine the engine brake thermal efficiency.

2.12 ENGINE TESTING AND CHARACTERISTIC CURVES

About engine testing

Indicated power (P_i) is not easily measured with accuracy. The finest engine indicators have a difficult task in trying to establish exactly what is happening within the engine cylinder and the exact time it happens, and transferring this knowledge to form an indicator diagram on paper or on the face of a cathode tube. The interpretation, phasing and calibration of such a diagram require trained staff if the final results are to be within 5% accuracy.

This type of testing and the information obtained is really in the nature of research and is carried out in expensively equipped laboratories organized and worked by engine and specialist component manufacturers often under the auspices of groups of companies or governments. Some very useful research is also carried out by certain universities, and elementary research-type engine tests are carried out in many technical colleges for the benefit of both full and part time students. Time and money are the more obvious limiting factors in such training, but the students do get some opportunity not only to study heat engine theory, but also to come to grips with an engine connected to a dynamometer, making a lot of noise while trying to fool the operatives as to its performance, if not most of the time at least some of the time.

Fortunately for industrial and most other purposes engine testing consists of checking performance against standard values, or comparing one type of power unit with another for power, torque and fuel consumption. Tuning and testing establishments where engines are stripped, modified and re-built for sports rally or racing have test benches for bmep, torque and power produced at the crankshaft, together with an accurate account of the amount of fuel it gorges in the process. This type of information and much more can be accurately obtained by a keen group of operatives working together as a team, using quite simple but accurate dynamometers and fuel measuring equipment.

Rolling road and chassis dynamometers produce very accurate results for such information as power at the roadwheels, acceleration and retardation figures, fuel consumption, air–fuel ratio, and ignition timing can be easily and accurately obtained by suitable trained technicians.

This type of equipment can be used for diagnostic work thereby reducing actual road testing to a minimum.

Engine characteristic curves

Power, torque and specific fuel consumption plotted on a revolution per minute base show the characteristics of an engine (Fig. 2.18)

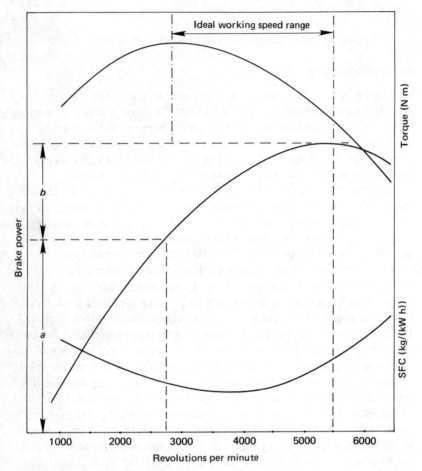

Fig. 2.18 Characteristic engine curves. *a* is the brake power produced in the first 2750 rev/min, and *b* the brake power produced in the second 2750 rev/min.

Brake power

A study of the power curve shows that it is steepest and straightest in the first part of the rev/min range. If the range is divided into two equal parts, up to maximum power, the power produced in the first half (a) can be compared with that of the second (b). The smaller increase in power during the latter half is mainly due to the fall in volumetric efficiency and the increasing frictional power (pumping and frictional losses). The rev/min at which maximum power takes place will influence the maximum road speed of the vehicle, and plays a role when determining the gear ratios for the vehicle.

The manufacturers' power curve is not a result of one or two tests through the rev/min range, taking fuel consumption and load readings at intervals and plotting the results. Their data and graphs are usually taken from a series of loops or hook curves (a description is given under *Consumption Loops* in Part 2) using a means of varying the air/fuel ratio and adjusting the ignition for optimum performance at each stage to give maximum bmep and power. Thus a curve produced in such a manner from a large series of loops may be considered as an 'ideal' power curve for that particular engine. No carburettor or ignition timing system, to date, is capable of giving optimum settings for all engine speeds and load conditions. The 'ideal' power curve, however, does give the engine tuner and tester a standard to aim for.

Torque

The shape of the torque and bmep curve decides the characteristic of the power unit. The horizontal distance between the point of maximum torque and maximum power, Fig. 2.18, is the efficient working engine speed range, and the ratio

$$\frac{\text{rev/min at maximum torque}}{\text{rev/min at maximum power}}$$

is called the engine speed ratio. It is employed when determining the number of gears for a vehicle and their ratios. (This is fully dealt with in Part 2.)

As torque is highly dependent on engine capacity, it is instructive to study the bmep figures if any comparison with other power units is to be made. Newtons or kilonewtons per square metre (N/m^2 or kN/m^2) reveal what force is available for a specific piston crown area, hence the higher the bmep, the higher the torque

Specific fuel consumption

This characteristic curve shows how much fuel is used (mass or volume) over a period of one hour in the production of one kW of power. The results and graph indicate how efficiently the engine uses the fuel supplied to it. A reflection of this curve in a mirror will show the shape of the thermal efficiency curve. Thus the lowest part of the specific consumption curve will become the highest part of the thermal efficiency curve. The figures can be used to compare different power units independent of their size and capacity.

Scale of graphs

It is of paramount importance to check the scale upon which graphs are produced when checking engine performance and/or comparing results from one engine with those from another. A comparative flat graph using one scale can be made to look entirely different if the scale was 'opened up'.

2.13 CONSERVATION OF ENERGY

Energy is defined as the capacity that a body possesses for doing work.

Principle of the conservation of energy

This principle states that types of energy are interchangeable. Although energy can neither be created nor destroyed, one form of energy may be converted to another form, but there will be losses due to incomplete conversion.

A good example is the mechanical loss in an engine due to the pumping and friction losses, and the heat loss in conversion of the liquid fuel into mechanical work is considerable.

Change of energy in a petrol engine

The energy changes taking place in a petrol engine are shown below.

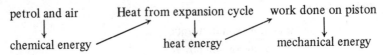

2.14 INDICATED POWER AND MECHANICAL EFFICIENCY

The Morse Method

An engine connected to a absorption-type dynamometer with load weighing gear and tachometer will enable the indicated power (P_i) and mechanical efficiency (η_m) to be calculated within reasonable limits of accuracy, providing care is taken to maintain the exact rev/min and particular attention is paid to the torque arm setting and the reading of the load figures.

The test consists of measuring the total brake power (P_b) with all the engine cylinders working normally under full throttle, and then cutting out each cylinder in turn. With spark ignition engines it is a simple matter to short out each cylinder in turn, and various gadgets are produced for this purpose. With oil engines, using in-line fuel injection pumps, the raising of the fuel pump cam follower with a screwdriver or similar tool will cut off the fuel supply to that cylinder without having fuel oil leaking around the test area which is the case if pipe unions are loosened to prevent injection. When a cylinder has been cut out, the remaining working cylinders have to overcome the frictional and pumping losses of the cut-out cylinder.

Consider a six cylinder four-stroke engine:

let A = brake power P_b of 6 cylinders which equals $6P_i - 6P_f$

(where P_i = indicated power and P_f = frictional power)

and $\qquad B = P_b$ of 5 cylinders which equals $5P_i - 6P_f$

thus case A − case B = $1P_i$, which is the indicated power of the cut-out cylinder.

When each cylinder's indicated power is known and added together, the result gives the total indicated power for the engine under those speed and load conditions. An example of a test carried out on a six cylinder four-stroke engine will help to understand this important test.

Worked examples

A six cylinder four-stroke engine was Morse tested at 2000 rev/min. The data is tabulated below:

Cylinder cut-out	Brake load w (N)	Brake power (kW)	Indicated power	Mechanical efficiency (%)
All firing	279.4	32.87	37.0	
1	227.2	26.73	6.14	
2	228.0	26.82	6.05	
3	227.6	26.77	6.10	
4	224.0	26.35	6.52	88.83%
5	226.2	26.61	6.26	
6	229.0	26.94	5.93	

Adding together the indicated powers of each cylinder gives a total of 37.0 kW, and 32.87 divided by 37 and multiplied by 100 equals 88.83%.

Note: To obtain the indicated power of a cylinder, subtract the brake power obtained when that cylinder was cut out from the total brake power. For example, consider no. 1 cylinder. The brake power when this was not working was 26.73, thus 32.87 − 26.73 = 6.14 the indicated power of no. 1 cylinder.

◆◆◆

A Morse test was completed on a four cylinder four-stroke petrol engine. The dynamometer torque arm had an effective length of 0.6 m. The following data was recorded at 2600 rev/min.

All cylinders firing	Load w = 141.6 N
no. 1 cut out	w = 100.0 N
no. 2 cut out	w = 104.0 N
no. 3 cut out	w = 101.2 N
no. 4 cut out	w = 103.2 N

Calculate the indicated power and mechanical efficiency at the quoted engine speed.

$$\text{brake power } P_b(\text{kW}) = \frac{w \times R \times 2\pi N}{60 \times 10^3}$$

and

$$\frac{R \times 2 \times \pi \times N}{60 \times 10^3} = \frac{0.6 \times 2 \times \pi \times 2600}{60 \times 10^3}$$

$$= 0.163 \text{ (a constant)}$$

thus $P_b = w \times 0.163$

P_b kW all cylinders firing $= 141.6 \times 0.163 = 23.08$ kW

P_b kW no. 1 cylinder cut out $= 100 \times 0.163$ $= 16.3$ kW

P_b kW no. 2 cylinder cut out $= 104 \times 0.163$ $= 16.95$ kW

P_b kW no. 3 cylinder cut out $= 101.2 \times 0.163 = 16.49$ kW

P_b kW no. 4 cylinder cut out $= 103.2 \times 0.163 = 16.82$ kW

P_i kW of no. 1 cylinder $= 23.08 - 16.3$ $= 6.78$ kW

P_i kW of no. 2 cylinder $= 23.08 - 16.95 = 6.13$ kW

P_i kW of no. 3 cylinder $= 23.08 - 16.49 = 6.59$ kW

P_i kW of no. 4 cylinder $= 23.08 - 16.82 = 6.25$ kW

$\overline{25.75 \text{ kW}}$ total indicated power

Mechanical efficiency $\eta_m = \dfrac{P_b}{P_i} = \dfrac{23.08}{25.75} = 0.896$ or 89.6%   ♦♦♦

An engine on a Morse test at 5000 rev/min recorded a brake power output, when all cylinders were operating, of 74.5 kW. The indicated power of each cylinder was: no. 1, 22.83; no. 2, 21.79; no. 3, 22.2; no. 4, 22.1 kW.

Determine the engine's mechanical efficiency at 5000 rev/min.

Total indicated power = 22.83 + 21.79 + 22.2 + 22.1 = 89.92 kW

$$\text{mechanical efficiency } \eta_m \% = \frac{P_b}{P_i} \times 100 = \frac{74.5}{89.92} \times 100$$

$$= 82.85\% \qquad \blacklozenge\blacklozenge\blacklozenge$$

EXERCISES 2.8

Morse test

1. The following results were recorded during a Morse test at 3000 rev/min on a four cylinder four-stroke cycle engine. The dynamometer torque arm had a 0.53 metre effective length. Determine the indicated power and mechanical efficiency of the engine.

All cylinders firing	load = 114 N
no 1 cylinder cut out	load = 78 N
no. 2 cylinder cut out	load = 82 N
no. 3 cylinder cut out	load = 80.4 N
no. 4 cylinder cut out	load = 82.8 N

2. A Morse test was completed on a four cylinder four-stroke engine. The dynamometer torque arm had an effective length of 0.6 m. The following data were recorded at an engine speed of 2600 rev/min:

All cylinders firing	brake load = 141.6 N
no. 1 cylinder cut out	brake load = 100 N
no. 2 cylinder cut out	brake load = 104 N
no. 3 cylinder cut out	brake load = 101.2 N
no. 4 cylinder cut out	brake load = 103.2 N

Calculate the engine mechanical efficiency.

3. The following torque figures were recorded on a Morse test of a four cylinder four-stroke engine operating at a constant 5000 rev/min.

All cylinders firing	142.4 N m
no. 1 cylinder cut out	98.8 N m
no. 2 cylinder cut out	100.8 N m
no. 3 cylinder cut out	100 N m
no. 4 cylinder cut out	100.2 N m

Determine the engine mechanical efficiency.

Mechanical efficiency by the motoring method

If an electrical swinging-field dynamometer is available the engine on test can be motored directly after the power curve readings have been recorded. The dynamometer motors the engine through the same rev/min range with ignition or fuel oil cut off (throttle wide open). Brake load readings are taken and frictional power (pumping + frictional losses) is obtained as follows:

$$\text{frictional power loss } P_f = w \times \frac{R \times 2\pi N}{60 \times 10^3} \text{ kW}$$

where R = length of torque arm (m), and

$$\text{brake power } P_b + \text{frictional power } P_f = \text{indicated power } P_i$$

$$\text{mechanical efficiency } (\%) = P_b/P_i \times 100$$

The temperature of the engine's pistons and cylinder walls, together with other working parts and also the engine oil, falls below that of normal working temperature during the motoring tests, and with the lack of exhaust gases, etc, the frictional and pumping losses are somewhat modified. If, however, the test is done quickly and smartly with good teamwork the results can be better than those produced by the Morse method. In the latter there is a torsional balance upset and the charge within the induction manifold has its flow modified together with a change in exhaust gas flow at the ports and manifold.

Calculation of indicated power and mechanical efficiency from indicator diagrams is not an easy matter and requires equipment more in keeping with research projects than routine engine test work. At least the motoring system is a speedy one and repeat tests can be quickly made. It is possible with such a dynamometer to evaluate the frictional and pumping losses of various engine parts by taking readings as parts have been dismantled.

The following worked example will show the principles of such a test.

Worked example

An engine under mechanical efficiency test is connected to a electrical swinging-field dynamometer. The brake load reading was 273 N at 1500 rev/min. The dynamometer torque arm had an effective length of 0.56 m. On motoring test at the same engine speed the load reading was 69 N. Calculate the brake power, frictional power, the indicated power and the mechanical efficiency.

$$\text{brake power } P_b \text{ (kW)} = \frac{w \times R \times 2\pi N}{60 \times 10^3} = \frac{273 \times 0.56 \times 2 \times \pi \times 1500}{60 \times 10^3}$$

$$= 24 \text{ kW}$$

power lost to pumping and friction P_f (kW) $= \dfrac{69 \times 0.56 \times 2 \times \pi \times 1500}{60 \times 10^3}$

$$= 6.07 \text{ kW}$$

indicated power $P_i = P_b + P_f$

where P_b = brake power and P_f = frictional power.

$$= 24 + 6.07$$

$$= 30.07 \text{ kW}$$

Mechanical efficiency $(\eta_m \%) = \dfrac{P_b}{P_i} \times 100 = \dfrac{24}{30.07} \times 100$

$$= 79.8\%$$

♦♦♦

EXERCISES 2.9

1. An engine tested for pumping and frictional losses lifted a brake load of 96.5 N at the end of a 0.53 m torque arm when motored at 2000 rev/min by the electrical dynamometer. At the same engine speed under full throttle the brake load lifted was 328 N. Determine the indicated power and mechanical efficiency.

2. An engine when motored at 3400 rev/min by an electrical swing field dynamometer gave a brake load reading of 108.6 N which represents 23.2 kW power. At the same speed the engine developed 27.6 kW. Determine the engine mechanical efficiency at this speed and the length of the dynamometer torque arm.

Mechanical efficiency

The mechanical efficiency can be calculated from the following equations:

$$\dfrac{\text{brake power}}{\text{indicated power}} \quad or \quad \dfrac{\text{bmep}}{\text{imep}} \quad or \quad \dfrac{\text{brake thermal efficiency}}{\text{indicated thermal efficiency}}$$

The pumping cycle of the engine pistons, and the friction between their rings and the cylinder walls, account for the greater part or percentage of the lost work and power, especially with the compression ignition oil engine.

The main factors which contribute to the lost power are:

1. the type of materials used and their surface finish;
2. the loading between materials in contact under boundary lubrication conditions;
3. the area of the contact surfaces and their rubbing speeds;

4. the engine compression ratio;
5. revolutions per minute (rubbing speeds);
6. the throttle position (petrol engine);
7. windage. Air resistance increases in proportion to the square of the speed. Thus twice the speed gives four times the resistance. The flywheel, clutch, generator and engine-operated cooling fan all introduce windage;
8. the churning of the lubricating oil (this is more apparent when gearbox and final drives are connected).

Results of transmission losses obtained from modern rolling road dynamometers can prove interesting, and the losses between the engine and road are sometimes quite alarming.

With the indicated power, brake power and mechanical efficiency plotted on a rev/min base (Fig. 2.19) it can be seen that the indicated power is somewhat higher than the brake power throughout the rev/min range, but not proportionally higher. If the vertical distance between the two curves is measured at each revolution point, this distance will represent the power lost

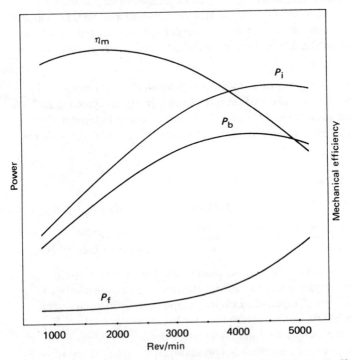

Fig. 2.19 Indicated power (P_i), brake power (P_b), mechanical efficiency (η_m) and frictional power (P_f) plotted on a rev/min base.

to pumping and friction at that engine speed. As engine speed rises so the losses increase, hence the increasing divergence between the brake power and indicated curve lines.

Worked examples

Two high performance four cylinder four-stroke engines have been bench tested, and their specification and performance figures are given below. Calculate the mean piston speed at maximum power, the bmep and torque figures for both engines.

Engine	A	B
Capacity (cm^3)	996	997
Bore diameter (mm)	64.6	80.96
Stroke (mm)	76.2	48.41
P_b (kW)	64.5	59.68
rev/min	6800	7200

$$\text{Mean piston speed } S \text{ (m/s)} = \frac{2LN}{60} = \frac{2 \times 0.0762 \times 6800}{60}$$

$$= 17.272 \text{ m/s for Engine A}$$

$$= \frac{2 \times 0.0484 \times 7200}{60}$$

$$= 11.62 \text{ m/s for Engine B}$$

$$\text{Engine torque: } P_b \text{ (kW)} = \frac{T2\pi N}{60 \times 10^3} \qquad \text{therefore } T\text{(Nm)} = \frac{P_b \times 60 \times 10^3}{2\pi N}$$

$$= \frac{64.5 \times 60 \times 10^3}{2 \times \pi \times 6800}$$

$$= 90.57 \text{ N m Engine A}$$

$$= \frac{59.68 \times 60 \times 10^3}{2 \times \pi \times 7200}$$

$$= 79.15 \text{ N m Engine B}$$

$$\text{Bmep:} \qquad \frac{T2\pi N}{60 \times 10^3} = \frac{P_b LAnN}{60 \times 2 \times 10^6}$$

$$\text{therefore} \quad \text{bmep (kN/m}^2) = \frac{T2\pi N \times 60 \times 2 \times 10^6}{60 \, LAnN \times 10^3}$$

(where LAn is in cm^3, and bmep kN/m^2)

therefore   bmep (kN/m^2) $= \dfrac{T \times 4 \times \pi \times 10^3}{LAn}$

$$= \frac{90.57 \times 4 \times \pi \times 10^3}{996} = 1142 \text{ kN/m}^2 \text{ for Engine A}$$

$$= \frac{79.15 \times 4 \times \pi \times 10^3}{997} = 997 \text{ kN/m}^2 \text{ for engine B}$$

Note: Although engine B makes 400 rev/min more than engine A, its mean piston speed is 5.652 m/s lower due to its shorter stroke.   ◆◆◆

A diesel engine and petrol engine both having four cylinders and operating on the four-stroke cycle were bench tested. From the data given below determine (a) the bmep at maximum torque and at maximum power; (b) the clearance volume of one cylinder of each engine; and (c) the bore and stroke dimensions for each engine in millimetres.

	CI	*Petrol*
Capacity (l)	3.47	3.26
Compression ratio	17:1	6.4:1
Stroke/bore ratio	1.16	1.21
Maximum power	48.5 kW	56 kW
Maximum torque	235 N m at 2300	247 N m at 2500
	rev/min	rev/min

(a)   *Diesel engine*

$$P_b = \frac{\text{bmep} \times LAn}{60 \times 2} \quad \text{therefore bmep kN/m}^2 = \frac{\text{kW} \times 60 \times 2}{LAn \times N} = \frac{48.5 \times 120}{0.003\,47 \times 2300}$$

$$= 729 \text{ kN/m}^2$$

$$\frac{T2\pi N}{60} = \frac{\text{bmep} \times LAn \times N}{60 \times 2}$$

therefore bmep at maximum torque $= \dfrac{T \times 2 \times \pi \times 60 \times 2}{60 \times LAn \times N \times 10^3}$

$$= \frac{235 \times 2 \times \pi \times 2}{0.003\,47 \times 10^3}$$

$$= 851 \text{ kN/m}^2$$

bmep at maximum torque = 851 kN/m^2

bmep at maximum power = 729 kN/m^2

Petrol engine

bmep at maximum power $= \dfrac{kW \times 120}{LAnN} = \dfrac{56 \times 120}{0.003\,26 \times 250}$

$$= 824 \text{ kN/m}^2.$$

bmep at maximum torque $= \dfrac{T2\pi2}{LAnN\,10^3} = \dfrac{247 \times 2 \times \pi \times 2}{0.003\,26 \times 10^3}$

$$= 952 \text{ kN/m}^2$$

bmep at maximum torque $= 952 \text{ kN/m}^2$

bmep at maximum power $= 824 \text{ kN/m}^2$

(b) *Diesel engine*

Compression ratio $r = \dfrac{V_s + V_c}{V_c} = \dfrac{V_s}{V_c} + 1$

therefore $V_c = \dfrac{V_s}{r-1} = \dfrac{3470}{17-1} = 216.875 \text{ cm}^3$

and for one cylinder $= \dfrac{216.875}{4} = 54.22 \text{ cm}^3$

Petrol engine

$V_c = \dfrac{V_s}{r-1} = \dfrac{3260}{6.4-1} = 603.7 \text{ cm}^3$

and for one cylinder $= \dfrac{603.7}{4} = 150.925 \text{ cm}^3$

(c) *Diesel engine*

$LAn = \text{cm}^3 = \dfrac{L\pi D^2 n}{4}$ and $L = 1.16\,D$

Therefore $\text{cm}^3 = \dfrac{1.16D^3\pi n}{4}$

therefore $D = \sqrt[3]{\left(\dfrac{\text{cm}^3 \times 4}{1.16 \times \pi n}\right)} = \sqrt[3]{\left(\dfrac{3470 \times 4}{1.16 \times 3.142 \times 4}\right)} = \sqrt[3]{(952)}$

$$= 9.835 \text{ cm}$$

$$= 98.35 \text{ mm diameter of piston}$$

and stroke $= 1.16D = 1.16 \times 98.35$

$$= 114 \text{ mm piston stroke}$$

Petrol engine

$L = 1.21D$

therefore $cm^3 = \dfrac{1.21D^2 \pi n}{4}$

Therefore $D = \sqrt[3]{\left(\dfrac{cm^3 \times 4}{1.21 \times \pi n}\right)}$

$= \sqrt[3]{\left(\dfrac{3260 \times 4}{121 \times 3.142 \times 4}\right)}$

$= \sqrt[3]{(875.5)}$

$= 9.449$ cm

$= 94.99$ mm piston diameter

and stroke $= 1.21D = 1.21 \times 94.99 = 114.94$ mm piston stroke

♦♦♦

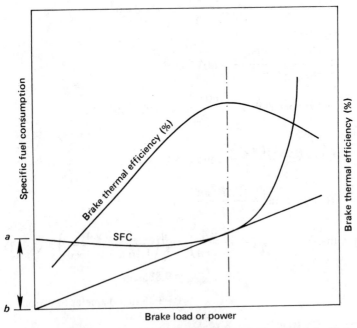

Fig. 2.20 Specific fuel consumption (SFC) and brake thermal efficiency plotted against a brake load or brake power base.

2.15 FUEL CONSUMPTION AND THERMAL EFFICIENCY

For an engine tested at constant speed with the load varied by throttle control and readings of brake load and fuel consumption noted, the specific fuel consumption (SFC) and brake thermal efficiency can be plotted against a brake load or brake power base. Fig. 2.20 shows these graphs. The steeper the slope of the consumption curve the lower the thermal efficiency, and where it cuts the vertical axis the distance between *a* and *b* represents the fuel consumed in overcoming the frictional, heat and pumping losses at this particular engine speed with no load. A Willan's line drawn from the origin tangential to the SFC curve will give the point of maximum thermal efficiency.

Another informative test is to plot fuel and brake power, brake thermal efficiency together with specific fuel consumption on a rev/min base (Fig. 2.21). It must be noted that this only gives results for one load or throttle position; therefore a series of part load or part throttle tests would provide more useful information. An automobile engine operates almost continuously at varying speeds and loads and one of the most informative series of tests are

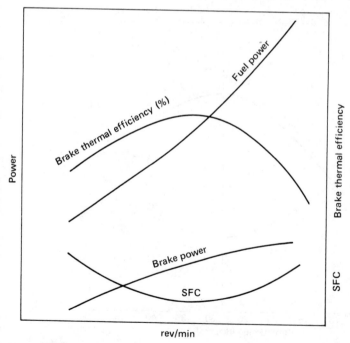

Fig. 2.21 Fuel and brake power, brake thermal efficiency and specific fuel consumption plotted on a rev/min base.

the 'hook' or consumption loops. The latter are described in some detail in Part 2.

2.16 IGNITION TESTS

The importance of correct ignition timing for all round performance and good fuel consumption with smooth running is well known to automobile engineers and technicians, and many motorists too. If the opportunity occurs and time permits, a series of ignition tests will prove interesting and informative.

Test 1

Bmep and specific fuel consumption are plotted on an ignition timing base (Fig. 2.22). Now that electronic ignition timing indicators are available for engine test—tuning work, accurate calibration can be made for the production of graphs and diagrams.

At a fixed engine speed, bmep and specific fuel consumption (SFC) are plotted on an ignition timing base starting at 0 degrees (TDC). From the curves it will be seen that at maximum power for that particular rev/min

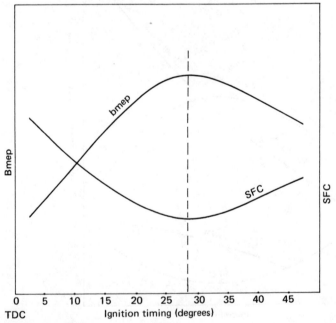

Fig. 2.22 Bmep and specific fuel consumption plotted on an ignition timing base.

(max bmep) the fuel consumption is at its lowest figure, and therefore highest thermal efficiency. During such a test the fuel consumption alters very slightly so the scale used for SFC should be fairly 'open'. Notice that as the ignition is retarded from the point of maximum bmep the power falls very rapidly, but for the same number of degrees on the advance side of maximum bmep the fall or decline is less severe; it is a point that should be remembered when vehicle ignition timing is being checked and corrected. From a series of these tests an 'ideal' ignition curve could be plotted, but results would have to be acquired for part load conditions also if the information is to be comprehensive.

Test 2

The modern ignition system, electronic or otherwise, with its automatic timing control, makes a large contribution to engine performance and reliability. To provide optimum ignition timing for all speeds and loads under all kinds of adverse conditions is a very difficult problem, and the manufacturers' design and research teams deserve high praise for their work in this field.

The following tests require time, patience and good teamwork. They could provide an interesting project for full-time college students or graduates. The object of the tests is to determine how the 'actual' ignition timing by centrifugal and vacuum control, compares with the optimum timing for a range of engine speeds and throttle positions. Similar types of tests could be introduced which are suitable for the latest electronic ignition systems, and indeed could compare the old systems with the new.

Part (a)

Consider that tests are to be made at full load, 3/4, 1/2 and 1/4 load. The engine is prepared for testing in the usual way with an electronic ignition timing tester connected. (The degree dial or quadrant should be as large as possible to ensure a reasonable interval between each degree marking). The ignition is set to zero (0) degrees advance (TDC) at a certain engine speed, then fuel and brake load readings are taken. (For added interest a heat balance test could be conducted at the same time). The ignition is then advanced by a fixed number of degrees, the brake load adjusted to maintain the same rev/min and the new set of readings taken. This procedure is repeated until the engine becomes rough or unstable. The whole sequence is then repeated at the same speed for 3/4, 1/2 and 1/4 load conditions. If time and interest permits, the series of tests may be repeated for a new engine speed.

Part (b)

With the correct distributor, set to maker's specification, load and fuel
consumption readings are taken at the same engine speed for the full, 3/4, 1/2
and 1/4 load conditions (four sets of readings for each engine rev/min).

Graphs

The bmep figures for all the results for a certain rev/min of part (a) are
plotted on an ignition timing base (Fig. 2.23) and the points of maximum
power are marked on each graph. These points, joined by a line, will represent
the *optimum* or *ideal* ignition timing curve for that particular engine speed at
four different loads or throttle positions. The four bmep readings obtained in
the part (b) test are plotted to the same scale (these points are unlikely to

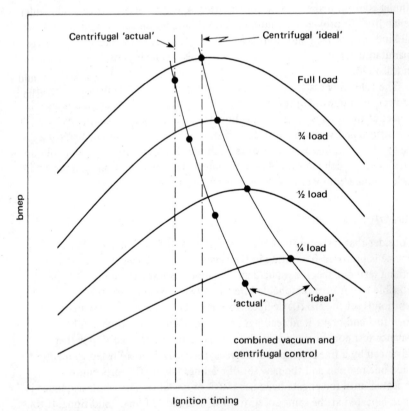

Fig. 2.23 Bmep figures for various loads with constant rev/min, plotted on an
ignition timing base.

appear exactly on the curves drawn from the part (a) test). A line drawn through these points will give a curve of *actual* ignition timing for that engine speed at four different loadings or throttle positions. The difference between the ideal or optimum and the actual ignition timing will be apparent. If a vertical is now dropped to the base from the maximum bmep point at full load in test (a), and the same done for test (b), they will represent the optimum and the actual centrifugal advance control, and the action of the vacuum control can be seen for each case.

Note: The difference between the actual and ideal timing results in Fig. 2.23 have been exaggerated slightly to show more clearly the difference between the curves and how they are produced.

2.17 HEAT BALANCE TESTS

An internal combustion engine is a mechanical device which is capable of converting a percentage of the heat energy supplied to it in the form of liquid fuel (petrol and oil engine) into useful work. Its overall efficiency is low, and it is not generally realized that more heat energy is lost to the cooling system and through radiation, and to the atmosphere via the exhaust system than is converted into useful work or power at the crankshaft. It is both interesting and informative to determine just where the heat which is supplied at so much expense really goes, and in what quantities. This account of heat energy is termed a *heat balance*.

Heat energy loss to the cooling system

The heat passing to the cooling system is easily determined on the test bed using a water flowmeter to measure the mass water flow, and suitable thermometers to record inlet and outlet water temperatures. The amount of heat carried away by the coolant per minute is recorded. Radiation losses are very difficult to evaluate accurately and for most practical purposes they are included with the exhaust losses. Subtracting the known energy losses from the energy supplied in the form of liquid fuel will provide the remaining losses.

energy supplied − (energy to power + energy lost to cooling, pumping and friction)

= energy lost to radiation and exhaust

When frictional losses are not known they would be included with the radiation and exhaust losses.

Heat energy loss via exhaust

Heat losses to the exhaust may be determined by using an exhaust gas calorimeter or by calculating the mass flow of exhaust gas. Where special equipment is unavailable the difference method may be adopted.

Heat energy loss to friction and pumping

A percentage of the total friction is lost as heat between pistons and cylinder walls, while the rest is lost at bearings, to lubricating oil, churning of the oil, windage and the pumping of the pistons. Thus part of the friction loss has already been accounted for with the cooling system losses. Therefore, if the heat energy lost to friction and pumping is included in the heat balance a small degree of inaccuracy has been introduced.

Some engineers, lecturers and the like consider that figures for the friction and pumping losses are sufficiently important in giving a better overall picture of the heat energy balance to be included in the heat balance whenever possible, as the inaccuracy introduced can be borne in mind and is quite small when the overall accuracy of a heat balance project is considered.

A heat balance may be made on the basis of heat or energy units, or on a power basis. The latter method may prove of greater interest to automobile technicians as the unit of power is a familiar term, and losses can be easily compared to the engine output.

Heat balance formulae

(a)   *Heat supplied* = mass of fuel consumed/min x calorific value (MJ/kg)

= kg/min x MJ/kg = MJ/min heat energy supplied.

(b)   *Heat energy converted to power* = $\dfrac{kW \times 60}{10^3}$ = MJ/min heat energy converted to power.

(c)   *Heat energy lost to cooling system* = mass of water flow x c x temperature rise MJ/min

$$= \frac{kg/min \times 4.2 \times (t_O - t_I)}{10^3} \, MJ/min$$

where c = specific heat capacity of water 4.2 kJ/kg $°$C

(d)   *Heat lost to exhaust gases*

(i)   *By exhaust calorimeter* Water flow through exhaust calorimeter (kg/min); inlet and outlet temperatures (t_I and t_O)

$$\text{Heat to exhaust gases} = \frac{kg/min \times c \times (t_O - t_I)}{10^3} \, MJ/min$$

(ii)   *By mass gas flow method*

mass of fuel consumed kg/min x air–fuel ratio by mass = mass of air consumed (kg/min)

mass of exhaust gases/min = kg/min of fuel + mass of air/min (kg/min)

heat energy lost to exhaust gases/min = $\dfrac{\text{kg/min} \times c \times (t_O - t_I)}{10^3}$ MJ/min

where c = specific heat capacity of the gases

(iii)   *Difference method*

Heat energy supplied − (heat energy lost to cooling, friction, radiation and heat converted to power) = heat energy lost to exhaust gases

(e)   *Heat energy loss to friction and pumping*

Indicated power (P_i) − brake power (P_b) = power lost to friction and pumping $(P_i - P_b = P_f)$

heat energy lost to friction and pumping = $\dfrac{P_f \text{ (kW)} \times 60}{10^3}$ MJ/min

Heat balance sheet

Total heat energy supplied MJ/min		Heat energy to brake power	%
		Heat lost to cooling	%
		Heat to friction, etc.	%
		Heat to exhaust and radiation	%
Total	100%	Total	100%

Note: t_O and t_I are outlet and inlet temperatures, respectively.

Worked examples

Heat balance

A CI oil engine developed 125 kW brake power and consumed fuel at the rate 32.2 kg/h (CV of the fuel 45 MJ/kg). The cooling water circulated at 12.6 kg/min and the inlet and outlet temperatures were 18°C and 87°C, respectively. An exhaust gas calorimeter was fitted and during the test registered a water flow of 46.5 kg/min with a temperature rise of 36°C. If the mechanical efficiency of the engine at the test speed was 72%, produce a full heat balance sheet on a MJ/min energy basis. (Specific heat capacity of water 4.2 kJ/kg °C).

heat energy to brake power/min = $\dfrac{\text{kW} \times 60}{10^3} = \dfrac{125 \times 60}{10^3} = 7.5$ MJ/min

$$\text{heat energy to cooling system/min} = \frac{\text{kg/min} \times c \times \text{temperature rise}}{10^3}$$

$$= \frac{12.6 \times 4.2\,(87 - 18)}{10^3} = 3.65 \text{ MJ/min}$$

$$\text{heat energy to exhaust gases/min} = \frac{\text{kg/min} \times c \times \text{temperature rise}}{10^3}$$

$$= \frac{46.5 \times 4.2 \times 36}{10^3} = 7 \text{ MJ/min}$$

Heat energy to friction and pumping:

$$\frac{P_b}{\eta_m} = P_i$$

thus $P_i = \dfrac{125}{0.72} = 173.6 \text{ kW}$

and $P_i - P_b = P_f$

therefore

power lost to friction and pumping $= 173.6 - 125 = 48.6 \text{ kW } P_f$

$$\text{heat energy to friction and pumping/min} = \frac{\text{kW} \times 60}{10^3} = \frac{48.6 \times 60}{10^3} = 2.92 \text{ MJ/min}$$

$$\text{heat energy supplied/min} = \frac{\text{fuel consumption kg/h} \times CV}{60}$$

$$= \frac{32.2 \times 45}{60} = 24.15 \text{ MJ/min}$$

heat energy to radiation/min = energy supplied − energy converted and lost

$$= 24.15 - (7.5 + 3.65 + 7 + 2.92)$$

$$= 3.08 \text{ MJ/min}$$

Heat energy balance sheet

Heat energy supplied/min 24.15 MJ/min		
	Heat energy to brake power	= 31.06%
	Heat energy to cooling system	= 15.11%
	Heat energy to exhaust gases	= 28.99%
	Heat energy to friction and pumping	= 12.09%
	Heat energy to radiation, etc.	= 12.75%
Total 100%		Total = 100.00%

Note: Exhaust gas heat loss not accounted for by the exhaust gas calorimeter is included with the radiation losses.

◆◆◆

A CI oil engine on test had a specific fuel consumption of 0.3 kg/(kW h), when developing 138 kW brake power. Water circulated the test-bed cooling system at the rate of 17.5 kg/min with inlet and outlet temperatures of 22°C and 91°C, respectively. Air enters the engine cylinders at an average temperature of 37°C and the exhaust gases leave at an average of 676°C. The specific heat capacities are: for water 4.19 kJ/(kg °C) and for gases 1.01 kJ/(kg °C). The air–fuel ratio by mass was 20.5:1 and the mechanical efficiency 78%. Produce a simple heat balance sheet on a MJ/min basis.

$$\text{heat energy converted to power (MJ/min)} = \frac{\text{kW} \times 60}{10^3} = \frac{138 \times 60}{10^3} = 8.28 \text{ MJ/min}$$

$$\text{heat energy to cooling system (MJ/min)} = \frac{\text{kg/min} \times c \times \text{temperature rise}}{10^3}$$

$$= \frac{17.5 \times 4.19 \, (91 - 22)}{10^3} = 5.06 \text{ MJ/min}$$

Heat energy to exhaust gases:

mass of air consumed (kg/min) = kg/min of fuel × air–fuel ratio

$$= \frac{0.3 \times 138}{60} \times 20.5 = 14.14 \text{ kJ/min}$$

mass of exhaust gases kg/min = kg/min of fuel + kg/min of air

$$= 0.69 + 14.14 = 14.83 \text{ kg/min}$$

$$\text{heat energy to exhaust gases (MJ/min)} = \frac{\text{kg/min gases} \times c \times \text{temperature rise}}{10^3}$$

$$= \frac{14.83 \times 1.01 \times (676 - 37)}{10^3}$$

$$= 9.57 \text{ MJ/min}$$

$$\text{heat energy to friction and pumping (MJ/min)} = \frac{\text{kW lost to friction} \times 60}{10^3}$$

$$= \frac{39 \times 60}{10^3} = 2.34 \text{ MJ/min}$$

$$(P_i = \frac{P_b}{\eta_m} = \frac{138}{0.78} = 177 \text{ kW}$$

$$P_i - P_b = P_f. \text{ thus } 177 - 138 = 39 \text{ kW})$$

heat energy supplied (MJ/min) = kg/min fuel x CV = 0.69 x 45

$$= 31.05 \text{ MJ/min}$$

heat energy lost to radiation, etc. (MJ/min)

$$= \text{energy supplied} - (\text{energy converted} + \text{energy lost})$$

$$= 31.05 - (8.28 + 5.06 + 9.57 + 2.34) = 5.8 \text{ MJ/min}$$

Heat balance sheet

Heat energy supplied = 31.05 MJ/min		
	Heat energy converted to P_b	26.66%
	Heat energy to cooling	16.29%
	Heat energy to exhaust gases	30.82%
	Heat energy to friction, etc.	7.53%
	Heat energy to radiation, etc.	18.70%
Total 100%	Total	100.00%

♦♦♦

A single cylinder four-stroke CI oil engine in a college heat engine laboratory has a cylinder bore of 254 mm and a stroke of 318 mm. From the following recorded data calculate the mechanical and brake thermal efficiencies and produce a simple heat balance sheet.

Recorded data:
- torque at 300 rev/min = 414 N m
- imep at 300 rev/min = 448 kN/m^2
- fuel consumption = 4.54 kg/h
- CV of fuel = 43 MJ/kg
- cooling water flow = 4 kg/min
- inlet water temperature = 14°C
- outlet water temperature = 66.6°C

$$P_i \text{ (kW)} = \frac{\text{imep } LAn(N/2)}{60} = \frac{448 \times 0.318 \times \pi \times 0.254^2 \times 300}{4 \times 60 \times 2} = 18 \text{ kW}$$

$$P_b \text{ (kW)} = \frac{T2\pi N}{60 \times 10^3} = \frac{414 \times 2 \times \pi \times 300}{60 \times 10^3} = 13 \text{ kW}$$

$$\text{mechanical efficiency} = \frac{P_b}{P_i} = \frac{13}{18} = 0.722 \text{ or } 72.2\%$$

$$\text{brake thermal efficiency} = \frac{\text{kW} \times 3600}{\text{kg/h} \times \text{CV}} = \frac{13 \times 3600}{4.54 \times 43 \times 10^3} = 0.239 \text{ or } 23.9\%$$

heat energy supplied/min $= \dfrac{\text{kg/h} \times \text{CV}}{60} = \dfrac{4.54 \times 43 \times 10^3}{60} = 3253$ kJ/min

heat energy converted to brake power/min = kW $\times$ 60 = 13 $\times$ 60 = 780 kJ/min

heat energy lost to cooling water/min = kg/min $\times c \times$ temperature rise

$$= 4 \times 1 (66.6 - 14) = 210.4 \text{ kJ/min}$$

heat energy lost to exhaust, radiation and friction =

heat energy supplied $- (P_b$ energy + cooling energy)

$3253 - (780 + 210.4) = 2262.6$ kJ/min

Heat balance sheet

Heat energy supplied/min 3253 kJ/min	= 100%	Heat energy to power	23.97%
		Heat energy to cooling	6.46%
		Heat energy to exhaust, radiation and friction	69.57%
Total 100%		Total 100.00%	

♦♦♦

EXERCISES 2.10

General engine questions

1. An engine on test at 2800 rev/min overcomes a resistance of 165.5 N acting at a radius of 0.355 m while consuming fuel at the rate of 6.9 l/h. If 1 l/h is equivalent to 12 kW, determine the brake thermal efficiency.

2. A CI engine consumes 0.12 kg of fuel per minute. The fuel has a CV of 45 MJ/kg. The brake thermal efficiency is 27.8%. Calculate the brake and indicated power if the mechanical efficiency is 77%.

3. A four cylinder four-stroke engine having a cylinder bore diameter of 88 mm and a 120 mm stroke gave the following results on test: fuel consumption 0.3 kg/(kW h) at 1280 rev/min; indicated power 17.5 kW at same engine speed; CV of fuel used 45 MJ/kg.
Calculate the imep and brake thermal efficiency when the mechanical efficiency was 82%.

4. An indicated power of 76 kW was developed by a CI engine when using 0.18 kg/min fuel oil of CV 44 MJ/kg. Pumping and frictional losses reduced power

output by 13 kW. Calculate: (a) the brake power, (b) the mechanical efficiency, (c) the specific fuel consumption, and (d) the brake thermal efficiency.

5. The brake thermal efficiency of an engine is 26.7% when using fuel having a CV of 44.5 MJ/kg. The fuel consumed was 0.0022 kg/s. Find the engine brake power.

6. A twelve cylinder four-stroke engine having a swept volume of 14 760 cm^3 on test at 3800 rev/min developed a bmep of 896 kN/m^2 and the mean piston speed was 914 m/min. What torque is being delivered at the crankshaft, and what force in tonnes is acting on a piston crown when the peak cylinder pressure is 4137 kN/m^2?

7. Determine the brake thermal efficiency and bmep for a four-stroke engine having a swept volume of 1600 cm^3 when it is producing a torque of 62.7 N m with a fuel consumption of 0.32 kg/(kW h). The CV of the fuel is 45 MJ/kg.

8. A four-stroke engine is connected to a dynamometer having a torque arm of 0.355 m effective radius. The fuel CV is 45 MJ/kg and has a relative density of 0.74. From the following data calculate the percentage of the fuel power converted into brake power, and the percentage lost to the cooling system, exhaust, radiation and friction. Produce a simple heat balance sheet. Rev/min, 4000; brake load, 181.56 N; water temperature, inlet 7°C, outlet 50°C; water flow, 7.71 kg/min; fuel consumption, 14.5 l/h.

9. An engine of 1640 cm^3 swept capacity has four cylinders and operates on the four-stroke cycle. A torque of 112 N m at 3000 rev/min is developed. The bore/stroke ratio is 1:1. Using the bmep, determine the average force on a piston in kN.

10. A four-stroke engine uses 18.6 kg of fuel per hour while developing a bmep of 796 kN/m^2 and torque of 59 N m. If the specific fuel consumption is 0.4 kg/(kW h) and the CV of the fuel 44 MJ/kg, calculate the brake thermal efficiency and the engine's cubic capacity.

11. Define bmep and mechanical efficiency. A six cylinder four-stroke engine has a total swept volume of 1624 cm^3 and develops 33.57 kW at 3000 rev/min. The mechanical efficiency is 80%. Determine the bmep and imep figures.

12. An oil engine developing 29.84 kW power consumes fuel oil at the rate of 0.150 kg/min; the CV of the fuel oil is 45 MJ/kg. Cooling water circulates at the rate of 8.4 kg/min having an inlet temperature of 20°C and an outlet temperature of 85°C. The specific heat capacity of water is 4.2 kJ/(kg °C). Draw up a simple heat balance sheet.

13. A petrol engine developing 33.57 kW consumes 12 kg of fuel per hour under full throttle. The CV of the fuel is 45 MJ/kg. Cooling water is supplied at the rate of 11.2 kg/min with inlet and outlet temperatures of 15.5°C and 83.3°C, respectively. If the mechanical efficiency is 90%, determine the indicated thermal efficiency, and draw up a simple heat balance sheet on a power basis.

2.18 FUELS USED IN IC ENGINES (B7)

Liquid fuels

The fuels normally used for the petrol or spark-ignition engine and those for the diesel or CI engine can be divided into two main groups: the volatile and non-volatile hydrocarbons.

Volatile fuels

Petrol is manufactured from crude petroleum and consists of fractions which boil at temperatures between approximately 40°C and 190°C. The three series of the fractions are: the paraffins, the naphthenes, and the aromatics.

Calorific value

The calorific or heat value of a fuel is the quantity of heat energy given out during the complete combustion of a unit mass of fuel (kJ/kg or MJ/kg). A calorimeter is used to measure the heat given out, but, with fuels containing hydrogen, water vapour is formed as one of the products of combustion. As water vapour or steam has a high latent heat value (2260 kJ/kg) and passes through the engine, the latent heat value must be deducted from the total heat energy generated, thus the net figure is termed the *lower calorific value* (LCV).

Volatility

Volatility is a measure of the rate of evaporation and the amount of pre-heating necessary to create the change. Engines using carburettors must use fuels which vaporize readily to maintain good cylinder distribution. The amount of pre-heating of the charge via hot-spots depends to a large extent on the volatility of the fuel. Very high volatility can produce pinking and detonation and the formation of vapour locks. The vaporization of the fuel before discharge through the carburettor needle valve unit and jets upsets the metering, and over-rich mixtures may disrupt idling and cause difficult starting with a hot engine.

Latent heat of vaporization

During evaporation a fuel will absorb heat from its surroundings thus cooling these surfaces. A fuel of high latent heat such as alcohol will make cold starting difficult. However, at working temperatures, a high latent value can improve an engine's breathing ability.

Detonation

Detonation occurs after the mixture has been ignited and the progressive flame spread compresses the unburnt gases (often termed the end gases) until they burn almost instantaneously in the form of an explosion. The shock waves produce a hammer-type blow to the piston crown and cylinder walls, causing a pronounced knock. Loss of power and engine flexibility is apparent and prolonged periods of detonation will lead to overheating and mechanical failure. Sir Harry Ricardo has shown that the paraffin series of fuels are more likely to detonate, and the aromatics less likely.

High octane fuels reduce the tendency to detonate the end gases. In 1921 Charles Kettering and his colleague Thomas Midgley discovered that the addition of some 0.04% of tetraethyl lead, $Pb(C_2H_5)_4$, allowed compression ratios to be increased without detonation or pinking taking place under normal running conditions.

Mixture ratio

The ratio of air to fuel for complete combustion varies for different fuels. This can be seen in Table 2.5.

Thermal efficiency of fuels

The thermal efficiency at a given compression ratio is almost identical for all hydrocarbon fuels irrespective of their chemical composition. Alcohol fuels give a higher thermal efficiency due to their improved latent heat value and lower burning temperatures, thus reducing the overall temperature of the working cycle. Fig. 2.24 shows thermal efficiency plotted on a compression ratio base. Note the large difference in the air standard cycle and a correct air–fuel ratio mixture. A 20% weak mixture is about the limit burnable under light load conditions for a modern engine.

Boiling point

A low boiling point is necessary for fuels used in spark-ignition engines to reduce the precipitation of fuel on the cylinder walls which, if pronounced, would lead to lubrication problems and oil dilution in the crankcase. Most

Table 2.5

Fuel	Symbol	Boiling point (°C)	Relative density	Latent heat of Vaporization (kJ/kg)	Air–fuel ratio, by mass	Calorific value (MJ/kg)
Paraffin series						
Hexane	C_6H_{14}	70	0.66	362	15.2	45–46
Heptane	C_7H_{16}	96	0.69	308	15.1	45–46
Octane	C_8H_{18}	125	0.7	297	15.05	45–46
Naphthene series						
Cyclohexane	C_6H_{12}	81	0.78	362	14.7	44
Hexahydrotoluene	C_7H_{14}	100	0.77	320	14.7	44
Hexahydroxylene	C_8H_{16}	120	0.756	308	14.7	44
Aromatic series						
Benzene	C_6H_6	80	0.884	399	13.2	41.5
Toluene	C_7H_8	110	0.87	350	13.4	41.5
Alcohols						
Ethyl alcohol	C_2H_6O	78	0.805	921	8.95	24.8
Methyl alcohol	CH_4O	65	0.8	1188	6.44	24.8

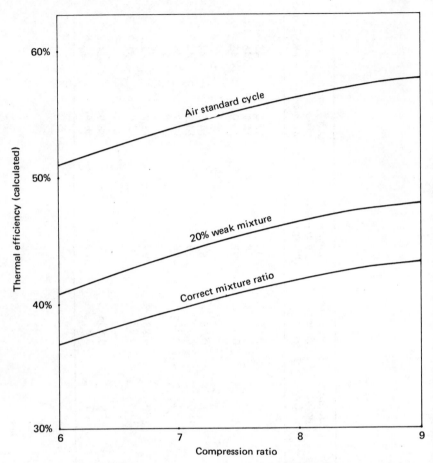

Fig. 2.24 Thermal efficiency plotted on a compression ratio base.

hydrocarbon fuels are mixtures of the paraffins, naphthenes and aromatics which have slightly different boiling points, thus some fractions will condense before others. For cold starting in winter a larger percentage of the lower boiling point fractions must be present.

Flash point

The flash point is the lowest temperature at which the vapours given off by the fuel when heated will 'flash up' or burn when a flame is initiated near the fuel surface.

The flash point of a fuel oil should not be less than 65°C.

Non-volatile fuels

Diesel fuel oil is a hydrocarbon fuel composed of approximately 85% carbon and some 15% hydrogen possibly with minute quantities of sulphur and ash. The fuel must be free from dirt, gum, water and other foreign substances. Fuel oil is inert, non-explosive and difficult to ignite in bulk. It is not subject to spontaneous ignition or combustion, but the vapour is explosive when mixed with the necessary oxygen. It is heavier than air and tends to settle or collect in low places.

Cetane number

The cetane number is a measure of the ignition-delay or delay period. A four-stroke cycle CI engine at 2000 rev/min, having an injection period of 15 degrees, has only some 0.001 25 seconds for the burning process to take place efficiently.

A mixture of cetane, $C_{16}H_{34}$, and alpha-methyl-napthalene, $C_{11}H_{10}$, which has the same ignition quality as a fuel under test would be given a cetane number according to the percentage by volume of cetane in the mixture. Thus, if the volume of cetane was 62% the fuel under test would be given a cetane number of 62.

Cetane numbers for fuel oils vary from 45 to 65 and over. A small addition of amyl nitrate or ethyl nitrate will reduce the ignition-delay period and thus raise the cetane number.

High relative density represents a higher calorific value per litre, but since the calorific value on a mass basis decreases as the relative density increases, the benefit in heat energy per litre is small, so the lighter fuels in a given boiling point range have the best ignition quality. Relative density varies between 0.815 to 0.850 and CV from some 44 MJ/kg to 45 MJ/kg.

Diesel engine compression temperatures can be as high as 820°C and should always be high enough to ignite the fuel without too much delay. Some vaporization of the fuel oil must take place as the fuel will not commence to burn while in a liquid state, thus the time lag or delay period is determined by the size of fuel spray droplets, fuel volatility, air swirl and turbulence, and the general composition of the fuel oil.

Combustion of hydrocarbon fuels

If a high bmep is to be attained, combustion of the charge within the cylinder must be rapid and complete. Both petrol and fuel oil consist of hydrocarbons with a composition of approximately 85% carbon (C) and 15% hydrogen (H). When combustion is complete, the carbon unites with the oxygen (O) which is supplied in the air (21% oxygen and 79% nitrogen, N, by mass) to form carbon dioxide (CO_2) and the oxygen also combines with the hydrogen to form water vapour or steam.

$$C + O_2 = CO_2$$

and $$2H + O_2 = 2H_2O$$

Nitrogen, which forms about four fifths of the air by volume, takes no active part in actual combustion, but does, however, play an important role in reducing the velocity of the flame rate. If a hydrocarbon fuel was mixed with oxygen only, a violent detonation would take place when ignited and the explosion would be similar to that of the propellant burnt behind a projectile in a gun. The inert nitrogen present in air slows the flame rate because the carbon molecules have to seek out the few oxygen molecules which are greatly outnumbered by nitrogen molecules. Detonation can provide flame rates in excess of 2000 m/s when something in the region of 2 to 5 m/s is required.

If there is sufficient oxygen present to unite with all the carbon and hydrogen molecules, there will be three gases present in the exhaust: carbon dioxide (CO_2), water vapour (H_2O) and nitrogen (N). In practice, perfect mixing of the oxygen and fuel is not always possible, and some excess air must be provided, particularly in the case of the CI oil engine where the fuel is only in close contact with the induced air for very short periods (10 to 5 ms). Thus only about 65 to 85% of the induced air can be used to keep the exhaust below the visible smoke point.

Lack of oxygen, as in the case of cold starts, results in burning carbon incompletely and the formation of carbon monoxide (CO) takes place. This represents a direct heat energy loss and pollution. Carbon burnt to form carbon dioxide provides a heat energy in the region of 34 MJ/kg, but carbon burnt to form carbon monoxide provides only about 10 MJ/kg heat energy, which represent some 70% energy loss. A weak mixture will result in the exhaust gases containing carbon dioxide, water vapour, nitrogen and some oxygen (see Fig. 2.25(a) and (b)). With the oil engine the mixing of the fuel with the induced and compressed air ensures that little or no carbon monoxide is present in the exhaust, providing the injectors, pump and fuel stops are correctly adjusted. This is one of the main reasons for the high thermal efficiency of the CI oil engine.

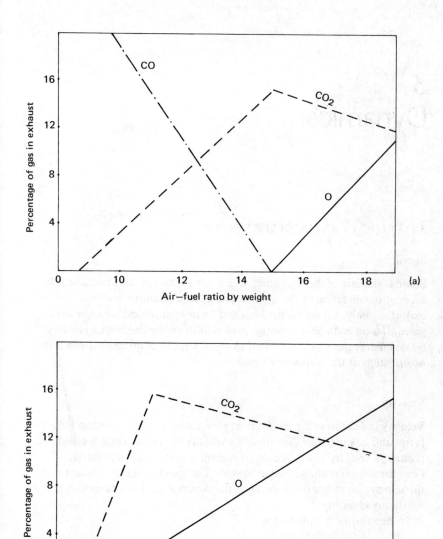

Fig. 2.25 Percentage of exhaust gases. (a) Petrol engine and (b) oil engine.

3
Dynamics

3.1 VELOCITY AND ACCELERATION (C8)

Speed

Speed is the rate of distance covered in a given time and does not take into account the direction of the motion. It is a scalar quantity involving magnitude only. Kilometre per hour and metres per second are both terms of speed. If a car is driven on average road conditions for one hour and covers 60 kilometres this would represent an average speed of 60 km/h. Note that no direction of travel was mentioned.

Velocity

Velocity is defined as the rate of change of distance within a certain time factor and in a specified direction. If a velocity in one direction is called positive, a velocity in the opposite direction would be called negative. Consider a car travelling in a curved path. The speed could be constant, but the velocity is constantly changing as the direction of the car's motion is constantly changing.

If the velocity is uniform then:

$$\text{velocity } (v) = \frac{\text{change of space}}{\text{change of time}} = \frac{S}{t} \text{ and } S = vt$$

where v = metres/second (m/s), S = space moved metres (m), t = change of time (s).

Fig. 3.1(a) shows uniform velocity.

Note: To change km/h to m/s: $\dfrac{\text{km/h} \times 1000}{60 \times 60} = \dfrac{\text{km/h}}{3.6} = \text{m/s}$

and km/h = m/s $\times$ 3.6

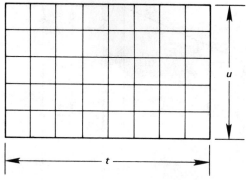

u = metres per second (m/s)
t = time in seconds
the area equals the distance travelled in metres
$S = u \times t$
  = 5 × 8
  = 40 m

Fig. 3.1(a) Uniform velocity

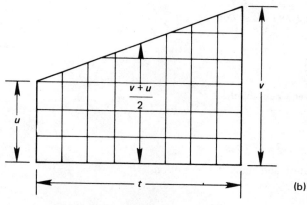

(b)

u = initial velocity, metres per secomd (m/s)
v = final velocity, metres per second (m/s)
t = change of time, seconds
the area equals the distance travelled, metres
(average height x base)

$$S = \frac{v + u}{2} \times t$$

$$S = \frac{6 + 3}{2} \times 8$$

  = 36 m

Fig. 3.1(b) average velocity and distance moved,

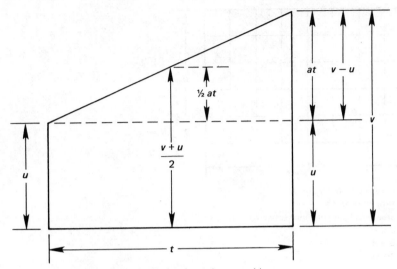

From the graph the following formulae are evident

$v - u = at$ and $v = u + at$

$S = \dfrac{v + u}{2} \times t$ and $u \times t + \tfrac{1}{2} at \times t = ut + \tfrac{1}{2} at^2$

now $v - u = at$

and $v + u = \dfrac{2S}{t}$

multiply these equations together

$v^2 - u^2 = \dfrac{2aSt}{t}$

$v^2 - u^2 = 2aS$ and $v^2 = u^2 + 2aS$

Fig. 3.1 (c) acceleration and equations of motion.

When the velocity is not uniform during the whole period of motion then the average velocity must be found.

$$\text{average velocity} = \frac{v + u}{2}$$

where u is the initial and v the final velocity. Thus

$$\text{space moved } S = \text{average velocity} \times \text{time}$$

$$= \frac{v + u}{2} \times t$$

Fig. 3.1(b) shows how the average velocity and the distance moved are obtained.

Acceleration (uniform)

Uniform acceleration is the rate of change of velocity. If the velocity of a vehicle has changed, acceleration or retardation has taken place. An acceleration cannot be expressed without stating both units of velocity. Fig. 3.1(c) shows how acceleration and the equations of motion are obtained.

$$v - u = at$$

This can be seen from the figure. Thus

$$v = u + at$$

The area of the diagram equals the distance moved, S metres

therefore area of rectangle $= u \times t$

area of triangle $= 1/2 at \times t = 1/2 at^2$

thus distance S $= ut + 1/2 at^2$

The slope of the graph indicates the magnitude of the acceleration. A steep slope indicates high acceleration and therefore a higher final velocity.

A study of Fig. 3.1(c) will help in understanding the equations of motion. Acceleration or retardation is metre per second per second (m/s^2). Only uniform accelerations are required for all technicians examinations. The equations of motion are as follows:

$$\text{acceleration } a(m/s^2) = \frac{v - u}{t}$$

thus $at = v - u$ and $v = u + at$

$$\text{distance moved } S(m) = \frac{v + u}{2} \times t \text{ and } \frac{2S}{t} - v = u$$

or $\dfrac{2S}{t} - u = v$ and $t = \dfrac{2S}{v + u}$

If the equation $v + u = 2S/t$ is multiplied by the equation $v - u = at$ then

$$(v - u)(v + u) = at \times \frac{2S}{t}$$

and $v^2 - u^2 = 2aS.$

The above equations are sufficient to solve most problems concerning velocity, distance moved and uniform acceleration and retardation. One other equation produced by substitution is obtained from Fig. 3.1(c):

$$\text{area of rectangle} = u \times t$$

and area of triangle = $1/2 \, at^2$ thus the total area = S metres = $ut + 1/2at^2$.

Equations of linear motion

1. $S = vt$ when velocity is uniform

2. $v = u + at$

3. $S = \dfrac{v + u}{2} \times t$

4. $v^2 = u^2 + 2aS$

5. $S = ut^2 + 1/2at^2$

Worked examples

A truck is uniformly accelerated at 5 m/s² when travelling at 36 km/h. Calculate: (a) the time taken to reach 60 km/h. (b) the distance travelled during the acceleration, (c) the uniform retardation if when the brakes are applied the truck comes to rest in 105 m.

$$\frac{36 \text{ km/h}}{3.6} = 10 \text{ m/s} \qquad \frac{60 \text{ km/h}}{3.6} = 16.66 \text{ m/s}.$$

(a) $\quad v = u + at \quad$ and $\quad t = \dfrac{v - u}{a} = \dfrac{16.66 - 10}{5}$

$$= 1.332 \text{ s}$$

(b) $\quad S = \dfrac{v + u}{2} \times t = \dfrac{16.66 + 10}{2} \times 1.332$

$$= 17.75 \text{ m}$$

(c) $\quad v^2 = u^2 + 2aS$

$$\text{therefore } a(\text{m/s}^2) = \frac{v^2 - u^2}{2S} = \frac{0^2 - 16.66^2}{2 \times 105}$$

$$= -1.32 \text{ m/s}^2 \text{ (deacceleration)} \qquad \blacklozenge\blacklozenge\blacklozenge$$

A car is moving at a steady velocity of 16 m/s, and is then accelerated at the rate of 5.6 m/s^2 until a speed of 72 km/h is reached. Calculate the distance travelled during the acceleration (72 km/h = 20 m/s).

$$v^2 = u^2 + 2aS \text{ and } S = \frac{v^2 - u^2}{2a} = \frac{20^2 - 16^2}{2 \times 5.6}$$

$$= 12.85 \text{ m} \qquad \blacklozenge\blacklozenge\blacklozenge$$

A vehicle travelling at a steady velocity of 8 m/s is accelerated at 3.2 m/s^2. Determine its velocity after 4 s, and the distance travelled during the fourth second.

$$v = u + at = 8 + 3.6 \times 4$$

$$= 22.4 \text{ m/s}$$

$$\text{distance travelled in 4 s} = \frac{v + u}{2} \times t = \frac{22.4 + 8}{2} \times 4$$

$$= 60.8 \text{ m}$$

$$\text{distance travelled in 3 s} = S = ut + 1/2at^2$$

$$= 8 \times 3 + 1/2 \times 3.2 \times 3^2$$

$$= 38.4 \text{ m}$$

distance travelled during 4th second = 60.8 − 38.4

$$= 22.4 \text{ m}$$

Therefore the velocity is 22.4 m/s and the distance travelled during 4th second is 22.4 m. $\qquad \blacklozenge\blacklozenge\blacklozenge$

A car having a mass of 1300 kg is decelerated at the rate of 8.2 m/s^2 from 112 km/h. What is the retarding force and the stopping distance?

$$\text{retarding force} = mg \times a = 1300 \times 9.81 \times 8.2$$

$$= 104\ 574 \text{ N}$$

$$\frac{112}{3.6} = 31.1 \text{ m/s}$$

Now $\qquad v = u + at \text{ and } t = \dfrac{v - u}{a}$

$$= \frac{0 - 31.1}{-8.2}$$

$$= 3.79 \text{ s}$$

and $\qquad S = \dfrac{v+u}{2} \times t = \dfrac{0+31.1}{2} \times 3.79$

$$= 58.93 \text{ m}$$

♦♦♦

If the above vehicle increases its speed from 48.3 km/h to 96.6 km/h in 2.2 seconds, what is the value of the accelerating force and the distance travelled during the acceleration?

$$\dfrac{48.3}{3.6} = 13.4 \text{ m/s}$$

and 96.6 km/h = 26.83 m/s

$$v = u + at$$

so $\qquad a = \dfrac{v-u}{t} = \dfrac{26.83 - 13.4}{2.2} = 6.10 \text{ m/s}^2$

retarding force $f_R = mg \times a$

$$= 1300 \times 9.81 \times 6.1$$

$$= 77\ 793 \text{ N}$$

$$t = \dfrac{v-u}{a} = \dfrac{26.83 - 13.4}{6.1}$$

$$= 2.2 \text{ s}$$

distance travelled $= S = \dfrac{v+u}{2} \times t = \dfrac{26.83 + 13.4}{2} \times 2.2$

$$= 44.253 \text{ m}$$

♦♦♦

EXERCISES 3.1

Dynamics, velocity and acceleration (C8)

1. A car is accelerated at 2.5 m/s² when travelling at 20 km/h, calculate the time taken to reach 78 km/h and the distance travelled during the acceleration. When the brakes are applied the car comes uniformly to rest in 200 m; what is the retardation?

2. A car starting from rest accelerates uniformly in first gear and reaches 28.8 km/h in 18 s. Second gear is engaged and a speed of 80 km/h is reached in a further 28 s. Determine the total distance travelled and the acceleration in first and second gears, respectively.

3. A car starting from rest accelerates uniformly until at the end of 20 s it is travelling at 50 km/h. Calculate the average acceleration and the distance travelled.

4. A vehicle moves at a uniform velocity of 7 m/s for a period of 164 s, and then accelerates uniformly at the rate of 2.5 m/s^2 for 15 s. Calculate the final velocity and distance travelled.

5. A truck is moving at a velocity of 4 m/s and then accelerates at the rate of 2.3 m/s^2 until a velocity of 14 m/s is reached. Find the distance travelled during the acceleration.

6. A car having an initial velocity of 11 m/s is accelerated at 2.6 m/s^2. Determine its velocity in 5 s, and the distance moved in the last second.

3.2 FREE FALLING AND PROJECTED BODIES

Free falling bodies

When a body is falling freely it moves with uniform acceleration produced by the gravitational attraction of the earth. In general this acceleration has an accepted value of 9.81 m/s^2, and g is the symbol used.

The gravitational pull of the earth is proportional to the size of the mass, and all bodies, whatever their size, will fall with the same uniform acceleration towards the earth's surface (neglecting air resistance). In a vacuum a feather will fall at the same rate as a stone or piece of lead. The equations of linear motion are modified by substituting g for a. Vertical velocities may be considered as plus ($+v$) and descending velocities as minus ($-v$). The negative sign may be omitted when a body is falling from rest as it can only fall downwards.

The linear equations of motion under the influence of gravity on a free falling body become:

$$v = u - gt \qquad \text{and from rest} \quad v = -gt$$

$$S = ut - 1/2gt^2 \quad \text{and from rest} \quad S = -1/2gt^2$$

$$v^2 = u^2 - 2gS \qquad \text{and from rest} \quad v^2 = -2gS$$

where $g = 9.81$ m/s^2 and S is the distance from the starting point.

The exact value of S must be understood as the distance of the body at that precise moment from the starting point. This may not be the same as the distance through which the body has moved. To make this quite clear consider a body which is projected vertically 200 m and at the end of t s has dropped 150 m. The total distance travelled by the body is 350 m, but the body now lies only 50 m from the starting point and it is this second distance which represents the value of S in the above equations. Again if this body had been projected 200 m vertically from the top of a 20 m high tower the value of S will be at a maximum at the top of its flight (200 m) and then decreases to zero as the body in falling passes its starting point, and until striking the ground S becomes increasingly negative. Thus S is the distance of the body from the starting point at any precise period of t seconds. A few simple worked examples will help to understand the principles.

Worked examples

A body is allowed to fall freely from rest. What is its velocity after falling:
(a) for 10 s, (b) for 20 s, and (c) how far did it fall during the first 10 s?

(a) velocity of body falling from rest (after 10 s) $= v = gt = 9.81 \times 10$

$$= 98.1 \text{ m/s}$$

(b) velocity after falling for 20 s $\qquad\qquad v = gt = 9.81 \times 20$

$$= 196.2 \text{ m/s}$$

(c) metres from starting point after 10 s $S = 1/2gt^2 = 1/2 \times 9.81 \times 10^2$

$$= 490 \text{ m}$$

Note: By using the formula $v^2 = 2gS$ the above results may be checked

$$v^2 = 2gS \text{ thus } v = \sqrt{(2gS)}$$

$$= \sqrt{(2 \times 9.81 \times 490)}$$

$$= 98 \text{ m/s} \qquad\qquad ◆◆◆$$

A body falling freely from rest reaches a velocity of 56 m/s. Determine the time taken to reach the velocity and the distance travelled from the point of release.

$$\text{velocity from rest} = v = gt \text{ thus } t = \frac{v}{g} = \frac{56}{9.81} = 5.708 \text{ s}$$

$$\text{distance travelled from rest} = S = 1/2gt^2 = 1/2 \times 9.81 \times 5.708^2$$

$$= 159.8 \text{ m}$$

Note: Check answers by using formula $v^2 = 2gS$

$$\text{thus } S = \frac{v^2}{2g}$$

$$\text{and } S = \frac{56^2}{2 \times 9.81}$$

$$= 159.8 \text{ m} \qquad\qquad ◆◆◆$$

A stone is projected vertically at a velocity of 23 m/s. Neglecting air resistance determine: (a) the height reached by the stone, (b) the time taken to reach the point of projection, and (c) its velocity at this point.

(a) The equation $v^2 = 2gS$ may be used as the stone started its flight from rest.

$$v^2 = 2gS$$

therefore $S = \dfrac{v^2}{2g} = \dfrac{23^2}{2 \times 9.81} = 26.96$ m

(b) The time taken to reach the point of projection or starting point will be twice the time taken to reach the height of 26.96 m. In other words, the time of ascent is equal to the time of descent to the projection point.

$$\text{from rest } v = gt \quad \text{and} \quad t = \frac{v}{g} = \frac{23}{9.81} = 2.344 \text{ s}$$

Thus time taken to reach projection point is 2.344 x 2 = 4.688 s. Incidently the velocity on return to the projection point will be the same as the projection velocity, thus the answer to (c) is 23 m/s.

♦♦♦

Relative acceleration

If two masses are dropped freely at the same time they would move vertically downwards together (neglecting air resistance) and the relative acceleration between them would be zero. If, however, one of the masses were projected downwards, its velocity after t(s) would be $v_p = u - gt$, but the mass allowed free fall would have a velocity after t seconds of $v_f = 0 - gt$, and $v_p - v_f = u$ (m/s) is the difference in their velocities. The separation would continue with this difference of velocity.

Free falling bodies having horizontal motion

Gravitational attraction is entirely vertical and does not influence any horizontal motion the body may possess. A body projected horizontally from a point above ground level will reach the ground in the same time that it would take to fall freely from the same elevated point at which the projection had been made.

A vehicle to be scrapped is propelled over a cliff 100 m in height at a uniform velocity of 20 m/s, on a level run. On passing the edge of the cliff, vertical acceleration of 9.81 m/s^2 due to the earth's pull takes place, but this has no influence on the horizontal uniform velocity of 20 m/s. In equal intervals of time (neglecting air resistance) the vehicle travels 20 m for every second, but the vertical distances are increasing every second due to the gravitational acceleration. Using the equation of distance travelled from rest by a free falling body $S = 1/2gt^2$, the following table was made.

Time t (s)	1	2	3	4	5
Horizontal distance (m)	20	40	60	80	100
Vertical distance (m)	4.9	19.6	44.1	78.4	122.6

The fall of the vehicle is shown below.

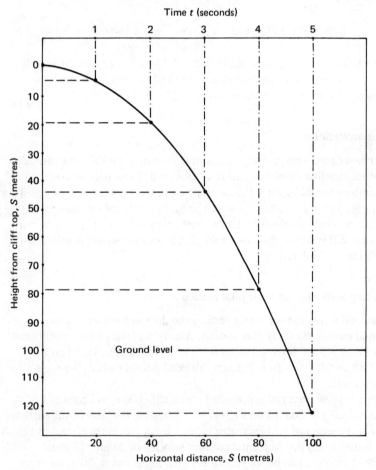

Fig. 3.2 Falling vehicle having horizontal motion.

It will be seen that the horizontal motion is one of uniform velocity, and the vertical motion one of uniform acceleration. Thus a body having uniform motion in one direction (horizontal in this case) when subjected to uniform acceleration acting at right angles to the other motion (vertical in this case) the resultant motion will form a parabolic curve.

The horizontal distance from the cliff to the point of impact of the vehicle may be calculated by finding the time taken to fall freely 100 m and multiplying this time factor by the uniform horizontal velocity.

$$S = 1/2gt^2$$

therefore $\quad t = \sqrt{\left(\dfrac{S}{1/2\,g}\right)} = \sqrt{\left(\dfrac{100}{0.5 \times 9.81}\right)} = 4.51 \text{ s}$

space moved with uniform velocity $= S = v \times t$

$$= 20 \times 4.51$$

$$= 90.3 \text{ m}$$

Worked examples

A casting is moving at a uniform velocity of 1.3 m/s along the floor of a truck and falls off the back striking the ground 1.6 m below truck floor level:
(a) With what velocity did it strike the ground? (b) How long did it take to reach the ground? (c) At what horizontal distance from the rear of the truck was the point of impact?

(a) $\quad v^2 = 2gS$

thus $v = \sqrt{(2gS)} = \sqrt{(2 \times 9.81 \times 1.6)}$

$$= 5.6 \text{ m/s}$$

(b) $\quad S = 1/2gt^2$

thus $t = \sqrt{\left(\dfrac{S}{1/2 \times g}\right)} = \sqrt{\left(\dfrac{1.6}{0.5 \times 9.81}\right)}$

$$= 0.571 \text{ s}$$

(c) $\quad$ horizontal distance from truck to point of impact = velocity x time

$$S = v \times t = 1.3 \times 0.571$$

$$= 0.074\ 23 \text{ m}$$

$$= 74.23 \text{ mm} \qquad\qquad \blacklozenge\blacklozenge\blacklozenge$$

A scrap vehicle is pushed off the edge of a cliff 122 m in height. What velocity

will it attain after 2 s, and how far will it have travelled at the end of 3 s?
When will it reach the base of the cliff and with what velocity?

as vehicle is at rest initially $v = -gt$

$$= -9.81 \times 2$$

$$= -19.62 \text{ m/s (velocity after 2 s)}$$

distance after 3 s $= S = ut - 1/2gt^2$

and from rest $\qquad S = -1/2gt^2$

$$= \frac{-9.81 \times 3^2}{2}$$

$$= -44.145 \text{ m after 3 s}$$

time taken to reach base of cliff

$$t = \sqrt{\left(\frac{S}{1/2g}\right)}$$

$$= \sqrt{\left(\frac{122 \times 2}{9.81}\right)}$$

$$= 4.98 \text{ s to reach base of cliff}$$

velocity at which vehicle strikes the ground

$$v = \sqrt{(2gS)}$$

$$= 48.9 \text{ m/s velocity on striking the ground} \qquad \blacklozenge\blacklozenge\blacklozenge$$

A body is projected vertically at 30.5 m/s. Neglecting air resistance
determine the height reached by the body and the time to return to the point
of projection. Note that at maximum height the velocity of the body will be
zero, and the time of ascent is equal to the time of descent. The velocity on
return to the point of projection will be equal to the original projection
velocity.

thus $\qquad S = \dfrac{v^2 - u^2}{2g} = \dfrac{0^2 - 30.5^2}{2 \times 9.81} = 47.41 \text{ m}$

$$\frac{v - u}{g} = t$$

therefore $\quad t = \dfrac{0 - 30.5}{9.81} = 3.106 \text{ s}$

If it takes 3.106 s to return, it must take the same period to reach the maximum height of 47.41 m.

hence total time = 3.106 x 2

$$= 6.204 \text{ s}$$ ◆◆◆

Body projected at an angle

As the horizontal velocity of a body is not influenced by gravitational acceleration it is possible to determine how far a body projected at some angle will travel until it crosses the same horizontal plane from which it was projected.

Let a body be projected with a velocity of V (m/s) at an angle ϕ degrees (Fig. 3.3). The horizontal component of this velocity will be $V \cos \phi$ and this velocity remains unchanged (neglecting air resistance). But the vertical component $V \sin \phi$ is changed uniformly by the pull of gravity, and the body starting upwards with an initial velocity of $u = +V \sin \phi$, will return to the same level with a velocity $v = -V \sin \phi$.

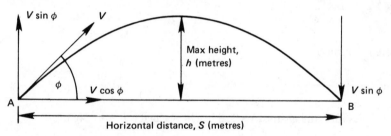

Fig. 3.3 Body projected at an angle.

Time taken to travel from point A to B:

$$v = u - gt \text{ and } t = \frac{u - v}{g} = \frac{+V \sin \phi - (-V \sin \phi)}{g}$$

$$t = \frac{2V \sin \phi}{g}$$

and during this period the body is still moving with a horizontal velocity $V \cos \phi$.

Distance moved from point A to point B = velocity x time = $v \times t$

thus
$$S = v \times t = V \cos \phi \times \frac{2V \sin \phi}{g}$$

$$= \frac{2V^2 \cos \phi \times \sin \phi}{g}$$

and since $\cos\phi \times \sin\phi = \dfrac{(\sin 2\phi)}{2}$

$$S = \frac{2V^2(\sin 2\phi)}{2g} = \frac{V^2 \sin 2\phi}{g}$$

The maximum range occurs at $45°$ when $2\sin\phi = 90° = 1$, thus the maximum range at $45° = V^2/g$.

It is of interest to note that there are two angles namely $30°$ and $60°$ where with the same projected velocity the body would move through the same horizontal distance.

$$\sin 30° = 0.5 \qquad \cos 30° = 0.866$$

$$\sin 60° = 0.866 \quad \cos 60° = 0.5$$

$$\sin 2 \times 30° = 0.866 \quad \sin 2 \times 60° = 0.866$$

The greatest height the body reaches is found from the equation $v^2 = 2gh$.

thus $h = \dfrac{v^2}{2g}$

where $v = V\sin\phi$

then $h = \dfrac{V^2 \sin^2\phi}{2g}$

At $45°$ elevation the greatest vertical height reached is $h = V^2/4g$ m.

Worked examples

Falling bodies having horizontal motion
A stunt car is driven at a steady 25 m/s velocity up a take-off ramp with the object of clearing a fence 4.5 m in height with a clearance of 5 cm. At what angle must the ramp be laid, and where must the fence be placed (neglect the height of the ramp)?

$$\text{height } h\text{(m)} = \frac{V^2 \sin^2\phi}{2g} \quad \text{and} \quad \sin^2\phi = \frac{h2g}{V^2}$$

therefore $\sin\phi = \sqrt{\left(\dfrac{h2g}{V^2}\right)} = \sqrt{\left(\dfrac{4.55 \times 2 \times 9.81}{25^2}\right)}$

$$= 0.3777$$

$$= 22.2° \text{ angle}$$

The ramp must be set at an angle of $22.2°$.

Total distance travelled $= S = \dfrac{V^2 \sin 2\phi}{g} = \dfrac{25^2 \times 2 \times 0.3777}{9.81}$

$$= 48.12 \text{ m}$$

The fence should be placed at half this distance where the height of the flight is at a maximum, 24.06 m from the point of projection.   ♦♦♦

A high speed grinding wheel without safety guard bursts and a large piece flies off at an angle of 48°, and another at 20°, both pieces moving with a velocity of 125 m/s. What respective maximum heights will the pieces reach, and what horizontal distance will be travelled when they reach the same level from which they were projected?

$$h = \dfrac{V^2 \sin^2 \phi}{2g} \text{ m}$$

$$h_1 = \dfrac{125^2 \times 0.743^2}{2 \times 9.81}$$

$$= 439.64 \text{ m height}$$

$$h_2 = \dfrac{125^2 \times 0.342^2}{19.62}$$

$$= 93.147 \text{ m height}$$

$$S = \dfrac{V^2 \sin 2\phi}{g} \text{ m}$$

$$S_1 = \dfrac{125^2 \times 0.9945}{9.81}$$

$$= 1\,584 \text{ m distance}$$

$$S_2 = \dfrac{125^2 \times 0.6427}{9.81}$$

$$= 1\,023 \text{ m distance} \qquad\qquad ♦♦♦$$

What horizontal distance would a piece of the above wheel reach if projected at 45 degrees, and what would be its highest point in flight?

$$S \text{ at } 45° = \dfrac{V^2}{g} = \dfrac{125^2}{9.81} = 1592 \text{ m distance}$$

$$h \text{ at } 45° = \dfrac{V^2}{4g} = \dfrac{125^2}{4 \times 9.81} = 398 \text{ m height}$$

Note: At a projected angle of 45° the distance travelled and height of flight are at the maximum.   ◆◆◆

A stone travelling at 10.75 m/s is thrown up at an angle of 42° by the rear tyre of a automobile. Two cars are following behind at intervals of 5.6 m and 11 m from the rear wheels of the leading car. The height of each car is 1.7 m. Will either of the cars be hit by the flying stone?

$$\text{maximum height of stone's flight} = h = \frac{V^2 \sin^2 \phi}{2g}$$

$$= \frac{10.75^2 \times 0.699^2}{2 \times 9.81}$$

$$= 2.878 \text{ m height}$$

$$\text{horizontal distance travelled by stone} = S = \frac{V^2 \sin 2\phi}{g}$$

$$= \frac{10.75^2 \times 0.994\ 5}{9.81}$$

$$= 11.715 \text{ m}$$

The stone will miss the first of the following cars, but hit the second.   ◆◆◆

A stunt motorcyclist moving at a steady 26 m/s velocity runs up a platform placed at an angle of 32° to the horizontal, with the object of landing on a similar platform placed some distance away. What would be the maximum height of the parabolic curve traced by rider and machine? When, and in what horizontal distance, would the landing take place?

$$\text{maximum height} = h = \frac{V^2 \sin^2 \phi}{2g} = \frac{26^2 \times 0.529\ 9^2}{2 \times 9.81}$$

$$= 9.67 \text{ m height}$$

$$\text{distance travelled horizontally} = S = \frac{V^2 \times \sin 2\phi}{g}$$

$$= \frac{26^2 \times 0.898\ 8}{9.81}$$

$$= 61.935 \text{ m distance}$$

$$\text{time taken to travel distance} = t = \frac{2V \sin \phi}{g}$$

$$= \frac{2 \times 26 \times 0.529\ 9}{9.81}$$

$$= 2.8 \text{ s}$$ ◆◆◆

EXERCISES 3.2

Free falling bodies, etc. (C8)

1. A stone of 0.2 kg flies off a vehicle's wheel at an angle of 37° and travels 17.4 m. At what velocity did it leave the wheel, and what was its maximum height during flight? What kinetic energy did the stone attain?

2. An object is dropped from a height of 3500 m. Neglecting air resistance, calculate the time of fall and the velocity on impact.

3. A mass is projected upwards with a velocity of 12 m/s. To what height will it rise, and how long will it take to reach the ground?

4. A 100 g balance mass flies off a vehicle's wheel at an angle of 47°, and travels a horizontal distance of 26 m. At what velocity did it leave the wheel?

5. A jet of water from a fire hose leaves the nozzle at 8.9 m/s. What would be the maximum horizontal distance travelled by the jet of water, and what maximum height would it reach?

6. A stunt car moving at 22 m/s rides up a short take-off ramp set at an angle of 25°. What is the highest point in its flight, and how far will it travel before touching down at ramp level?

7. An engine being raised by a crane falls from its sling at a height of 9 m. What velocity will the engine attain after falling 0.25 s, and how far will it have travelled in 1.2 s? When will it impact the shop floor and at what velocity?

8. A lead balance weight becomes detached from a road wheel and is projected at an angle of 35° at a velocity of 6.2 m/s. What height will the weight reach and what horizontal distance will it travel before reaching the height at which it was projected?

3.3 ANGULAR AND LINEAR MOTION(C9)

Angular and linear displacement

If two circular discs, A of 20 cm and B of 10 cm diameter, are connected to a shaft (Fig. 3.4) and the shaft rotated through 360° then point P on disc A and Q on disc B will have completed one revolution, thus both points have moved through the same angle or angular displacement, namely 360°, but the linear displacement around the circumference by point P will be twice that of Q.

$$P \text{ cm} = 2\pi R = 2 \times \pi \times 20 = 125.66 \text{ cm}$$

and $\qquad Q \text{ cm} = 2\pi r = 2 \times \pi \times 10 = 62.83 \text{ cm}$

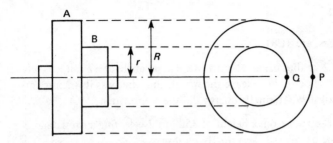

Fig. 3.4 Angular and linear displacement.

Hence the angular displacement of wheels, discs and shafts is independent of their diameters, but circumferential or linear displacement will vary according to their diameters for a given speed of rotation.

Angular displacement is denoted by the symbol θ and is usually in radians.

Radians

Radians are used to simplify calculations for angular displacement and angular velocity and acceleration. A radian is defined as the angle subtended at the centre of a circle by an arc equal in length to the radius (Fig. 3.5(a)).

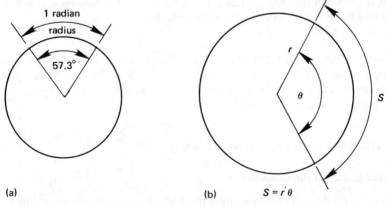

(a)   (b) $S = r'\theta$

Fig. 3.5 (a) Definition of a radian. (b) Linear displacement.

Since an arc r units in length subtends an angle of one radian, the number of radians in the circumference of a circle must be equal to the number of times the radius is contained in that circumference.

$$\text{circumference} = 2\pi r$$

hence radians for one revolution $= \dfrac{2\pi r}{r} = 2\pi$

therefore $360° = 2\pi$ radians and $\dfrac{360°}{2\pi} = 57.295°$ or one radian

thus 2π radians $= 360°$

and π radians $= 180°$

The angular displacement in radians is represented by the symbol θ.

the length of the arc for one radian $= r$

and   the length of the arc for θ radians $= r\theta$

thus if the arc is denoted by S (linear space moved) then (see Fig. 3.5(b))

$S = r\theta$

and if $S = 360°$ or $2\pi r = r\theta$ then $2\pi = \theta$ and 2π radians $= 360°$ or one revolution.

Angular velocity

This may be defined as the rate at which the angle θ (in radians) changes with respect to time t(s).

$$\text{angular velocity} = \frac{\text{angle moved through (radians)}}{\text{time taken}} = \frac{\theta}{t} \text{ rad/s}$$

and the Greek letter ω (omega) represents angular velocity in radians/second

thus $\omega = \dfrac{\theta}{t}$ rad/s

Angular and linear velocity

Consider the discs A and B which have rotated through θ radians in t(s) (Fig. 3.6) then the circumferential distance $= S = r\theta$. Divide each term by t then:

$$\frac{S}{t} = \frac{r\theta}{t} = v \text{ m/s and } \frac{\theta}{t} = \omega \text{ thus } r\theta/t = \omega r$$

and linear velocity $v = \omega r$ (angular velocity x radius).

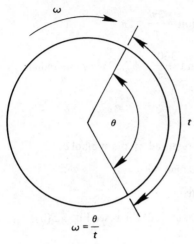

Fig. 3.6 Angular velocity.

Now consider points P and Q on discs A and B rotating at N = 6000 rev/min.

linear velocity of point $P = \dfrac{2\pi RN}{60} = \dfrac{\pi RN}{30} = \dfrac{\pi \times 0.01 \times 6000}{30}$

$$= 6.28 \text{ m/s}$$

linear velocity of point $Q = \dfrac{2\pi rN}{60} = \dfrac{\pi rN}{30} = \dfrac{\pi \times 0.005 \times 6000}{30}$

$$= 3.14 \text{ m/s}$$

The angular velocity of discs A and B:

$$\text{rad/s} = \dfrac{2\pi N}{60} = \dfrac{\pi N}{30} = \dfrac{\pi \times 6000}{30} = 628 \text{ rad/s}$$

Note that point Q has only half the linear velocity of point P, but the same angular velocity.

Worked examples

Express an angle of 321° in radians.

$$\text{radians} = \dfrac{321°}{57.295°} = 5.6$$

◆◆◆

A flywheel of 17.5 cm radius is rotating at 4900 rev/min. Find the velocity of a point on the rim.

$$\text{linear velocity } v(\text{m/s}) = \frac{2\pi rN}{60} = \frac{2 \times \pi \times 0.0175 \times 4900}{60}$$

$$= 8.97 \text{ m/s} \qquad \blacklozenge\blacklozenge\blacklozenge$$

The exhaust valve opening is marked on the rim of a diesel engine flywheel of 0.42 m diameter, and represents a circumferential distance of 9.6 cm before the bottom dead centre mark. What does this indicate in degrees?

$$S \text{ metres} = r\theta$$

$$\text{therefore} \quad \theta \text{ radians} = \frac{S}{r} = \frac{0.096}{0.21} = 0.457 \text{ radians}$$

$$1 \text{ radian} = 57.295°$$

thus $0.457 \times 57.295 = 26.18°$ $\qquad \blacklozenge\blacklozenge\blacklozenge$

A vehicle engine is producing a brake power of 56 kW with a torque of 132.2 N m. The final drive reduction ratio is 5.21:1 and the roadwheels have an effective radius of 0.4 m. Calculate the angular velocity of the crankshaft and the road speed of the vehicle in top gear.

$$\text{kW} = \frac{T2\pi N}{60 \times 10^3} \text{ thus } N = \frac{\text{kW} \times 60 \times 10^3}{T \times 2\pi} \text{ where } T \text{ is in N m.}$$

$$= \frac{56 \times 60 \times 10^3}{132.2 \times 2 \times \pi} = 4045 \text{ rev/min}$$

$$\omega = \frac{2\pi N}{60} = \frac{2 \times \pi \times 4045}{60} = 423.6 \text{ rad/s}$$

$$\text{roadwheel rev/min} = \frac{\text{engine rev/min}}{\text{final drive ratio}} = \frac{N}{f} = \frac{4045}{5.21}$$

$$= 776.4 \text{ rev/min}$$

$$\text{road speed (km/h)} = \frac{\text{roadwheel rev/min} \times \text{circumference of wheel} \times 60}{10^3}$$

$$= \frac{776.4 \times \pi \times 0.8 \times 60}{10^3}$$

$$= 117 \text{ km/h} \qquad \blacklozenge\blacklozenge\blacklozenge$$

A motor-cycle engine crankshaft has an angular velocity of 523.6 rad/s and is in third gear of ratio 1.62:1. The final chain reduction is 4.7:1 and the effective wheel diameter 0.73 m. Calculate the road speed of the machine in km/h.

$$\omega = \frac{2\pi N}{60}$$

and

$$N = \frac{\omega \times 60}{2 \times \pi} = \frac{523.6 \times 60}{2 \times \pi} = 5000 \text{ rev/min}$$

roadwheel rev/min $= N_r = \dfrac{\text{engine rev/min}}{\text{overall reduction ratio}}$

$$= \frac{5000}{1.62 \times 4.7} = 656.68 \text{ rev/min}$$

$$\text{km/h} = \frac{N_r \times \pi \times D \times 60}{10^3}$$

$$= \frac{656.68 \times \pi \times 0.73 \times 60}{10^3}$$

$$= 90.36 \text{ km/h} \qquad\qquad\qquad \blacklozenge\blacklozenge\blacklozenge$$

The phase angle of a diesel fuel injection pump was $90°$. Injection intervals were observed to occur every 0.008 s by electronic timing. At what speed was the four-stroke cycle engine running?

$$\omega \text{ of pump} = \frac{\theta}{t} = \frac{1.57}{0.008} = 196.25 \text{ rad/s} \ (90° = 1.57 \text{ radians})$$

$$N_p = \frac{\omega \times 60}{2 \times \pi} = \frac{196.25 \times 60}{2 \times \pi} = 1874 \text{ rev/min}$$

thus engine speed $= 1874 \times 2 = 3748$ rev/min $\qquad\qquad \blacklozenge\blacklozenge\blacklozenge$

EXERCISES 3.3

Angular and linear motion (C9)

1. A vehicle having roadwheels with an effective diameter of 0.72 m is travelling in top gear at 63 km/h. The final reduction ratio is 4.83:1. Find (a) the angular velocity of the roadwheels, (b) the engine speed rev/min.

2. A vehicle's wheels and tyres give an effective rolling radius of 0.46 m. The vehicle speed is 72 km/h. Calculate the rev/min of the roadwheels and their angular velocity.

3. The linear velocity of a point on a wheel is 1.74 m/s and angular velocity with respect to another point X is 3.48 rad/s. What is the difference between the radii of the two points?

4. A roadwheel is making 20 rev/min. What angle in radians does the tyre valve move in one second, and what is the linear distance if it lies 0.38 m from the wheel axis?

5. A car engine is making 2600 rev/min in second gear of ratio 2.76:1. If the final drive ratio is 4.63:1 and the effective roadwheel diameter 0.76 m, what is the angular and linear velocity of a flaw in the centre of the tyre tread, and the speed of the vehicle in km/h?

6. An engine crankshaft is making 4200 rev/min. If the engine stroke is 78 mm, find the mean piston speed in m/s and the angular velocity of the crankshaft in rad/s.

7. The mean or average piston speed of an engine is 12.6 m/s. The engine stroke is 108 mm. Calculate the engine speed and angular velocity.

8. The test dwell angle of the distributor points for a four cylinder four-stroke engine was $62°$. This period was observed to take 0.005 s. At what engine speed was the test made?

9. The rim of a flywheel with a diameter of 38 cm has the valve timing marks etched upon it. Measurement on the rim surface was recorded as follows: (a) inlet valve opens 3.5 cm before TDC; (b) inlet valve closes 9.8 cm after BDC; (c) exhaust valve opens 10.4 cm before BDC; (d) exhaust valve closes 7.2 cm after TDC. Convert the readings to degrees and draw the valve timing diagram.

10. The dwell angle of the ignition contact points was $58°$ when the four cylinder four-stroke engine was making 5350 rev/min. For what period of time were the contacts closed?

11. An engine crankshaft has an angular velocity of 381.5 rad/s. The engine stroke is 90 mm. Calculate the mean piston speed in m/s.

12. The phase angle of a diesel fuel injection pump is $60°$. If injection commences at intervals of 0.02 s, at what speed was the four-stroke engine running, and how many cylinders does it have?

13. The firing order of a six cylinder four-stroke engine was 153624. With the engine running, spark production between plugs 1 and 4 was 0.03 s. Determine the engine speed and its angular velocity.

14. A vehicle travelling at 72 km/h has an angular velocity at its roadwheels of 58.8 rad/s. Determine their diameter in metres.

3.4 FRICTION AND BEARINGS (C10)

Even a surface which is considered smooth will provide a frictional resistance
to motion when one surface slides over the other. A block of material resting
on a level surface is the well-tried experiment to verify the laws of friction
for dry surfaces, and this apparatus serves a very useful function. Consider
such a block resting on a level surface (Fig. 3.7). The four forces acting on
the block are:

1. The weight W or mg acting normal to the surfaces.
2. The applied force P which moves the block without acceleration, and is
equal to the frictional force F, but opposite in sense or direction.
3. The reaction of the surface R acting vertically.
4. The frictional resistance force F acting horizontally or tangential to the
surfaces, which is equal but opposite to the applied or frictional force P.

$$\text{coefficient of friction } \mu = P/W = F/W$$

$$\text{and } F \text{ or } P = \mu W \text{ or } \mu mg$$

If the frictional resistance F increases, force P will increase, but when force
P becomes greater than the resistance force F the block will commence to
move in the direction of force P. It is found that once the surfaces are sliding
relative to each other, the value of P will fall slightly as static friction is
greater than kinetic friction.

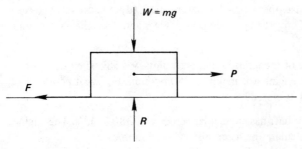

Fig. 3.7 Block resting on a level surface.

Laws of friction

1. Friction always opposes motion.
2. The frictional force under certain circumstances is independent of the
areas in contact. (There must be no penetration or change of conditions at
the surfaces.)

3. The frictional force is independent of sliding velocity.

4. The frictional force depends upon the type of materials in contact, and the quality of the surfaces in contact.

If the resultant of the forces R and F is considered as in Fig. 3.8, the reaction R will no longer be at right angles or normal to the surfaces, but inclined away from the direction of motion at an angle ϕ. The greater the friction the larger the angle which is known as the angle of friction.

$$\tan \phi = \frac{ca}{ab} = \frac{F}{R} = \frac{F}{W} = \mu$$

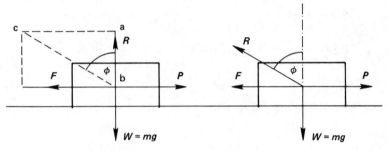

Fig. 3.8 Angle of friction.

Some values of the coefficient of friction

cast iron on cast iron	0.15
mild steel on brass	0.15
mild steel on cast iron	0.2
mild steel on white metal (oiled)	0.003–0.04
ball and roller bearings (thin oil)	0.0015–0.004
brake linings (moulded)	0.25 –0.38
brake linings (woven)	0.3–0.45
cork inserts in oil	0.17

Journal bearings and friction

When there is no motion the shaft rests at the bottom of the bearing. The load on the shaft and the bearing reaction are then in the same plane (point 1, Fig. 3.9). When the shaft starts rotating it climbs around the bearing in the *opposite* direction to the shaft rotation until 100% slip takes place between shaft and bearing surface. The shaft will remain in this position (point 2) unless there is a change in the coefficient of friction. The reaction R_N is normal to position 2, but the bearing reaction R_B will be inclined at an angle

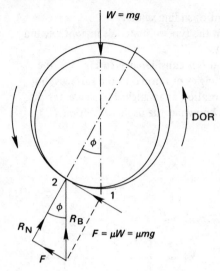

Fig. 3.9 Journal bearings and friction.

ϕ in relation to R_N, and the frictional force F is the tangential component of reaction R_B.

$$\sin \phi = \frac{F}{R_B}$$

therefore $R_B = W$ or mg and $\sin \phi = \dfrac{F}{W}$

therefore $F = W \sin \phi = mg \sin \phi$

angle of friction = $\tan \phi = \mu$

therefore $F = W \tan \phi = \mu W$ or μmg

For very small angles $\sin \phi$ is almost the same value as $\tan \phi$. Owing to the small working clearance in modern bearing design, the angle of climb by the shaft is infinitesimal; therefore, $\tan \phi$ may be used for $\sin \phi$. This relationship is very convenient as it shows that an increase in friction would produce a larger angle of climb ϕ, or a smaller angle would denote a lower coefficient of friction.

frictional force at shaft = $F = \mu W$ or μmg

frictional or resisting torque = $T = \mu mg \times r$ N m

where *mg* is in N, and *r* in m.

angular velocity of shaft $= \omega = \dfrac{2\pi N}{60}$ rad/s

linear velocity $v = \dfrac{2\pi r N}{60} = \omega r$ m/s

work lost to friction per minute $= F \times 2\pi r N$ J/min

$= \mu mg \times 2\pi r N$ J/min

$= T \times 2\pi N$ J/min

power lost to friction $\quad$ kW $= \dfrac{T 2\pi N}{60 \times 10^3}$

Heat generated by friction

The unit of heat energy is also the N m or J (Joule). The heat generated by friction may be required per second, per minute, or per hour, and in joules J, kJ or MJ.

1 watt = W = 1 N m/s = J/s, and 1 kW = 1000 W = 1000 J/s or 1 kJ/s. Thus kW = kN/s = kJ/s and kJ/s $\times 10^3$ = J/s. kJ/10^3 = MJ, and kW $\times$ 60 = kJ/min, and kW $\times$ 60 $\times$ 60 = kJ/h. Also (kJ/h)/10^3 = MJ/h.

Worked examples

The power lost to friction at a series of bearings was found to be 2.6 kW. Find the heat lost to friction in J/s, kJ/min, and MJ/h.

2.6 kW $= 2.6$ kJ/s $= 2.6 \times 10^3 = 2600$ J/s

J/min $= 2600 \times 60 = 156\,000$ J/min

kJ/min $= \dfrac{156\,000}{10^3} = 156$ kJ/min

MJ/h $= \dfrac{156 \times 60}{10^3} = 9.36$ MJ/h $\quad$ ♦♦♦

The combined gas and inertia load on a 6 cm diameter journal bearing averages 28 kN. The coefficient of friction at the bearing is 0.009 and the shaft speed 3500 rev/min. Find the power lost to friction and the heat generated in MJ/h.

power lost to friction kW $= \dfrac{\mu W r 2\pi N}{60 \times 100}$

$= \dfrac{0.009 \times 28 \times 3 \times 2 \times \pi \times 3500}{60 \times 100}$

$= 2.77$ kW

$$\text{heat generated MJ/h} = \frac{2.77 \times 60 \times 60}{10^3}$$

$$= 9.972 \text{ MJ/h} \qquad \blacklozenge\blacklozenge\blacklozenge$$

A shaft 65 mm in diameter rotating at 4000 rev/min carries a load of 2500 kg. The coefficient of friction between journal and bearing surfaces is 0.019. Calculate: (a) the frictional torque, (b) the lost power due to friction and (c) the heat generated at the bearing surface per minute.

(a) frictional torque T (N m) = μmgr

$$= \frac{0.019 \times 2500 \times 9.81 \times 65}{2 \times 10^3}$$

$$= 15.144 \text{ N m}$$

(b) lost power (kW) $= \dfrac{T2\pi N}{10^3 \times 60} = \dfrac{15.144 \times 2 \times \pi \times 4000}{10^3 \times 60}$

$$= 6.34 \text{ kW}$$

(c) Since 1 kW = 1 kJ/s

$$\text{heat generated per minute} = 6.34 \times 60$$

$$= 380.4 \text{ kJ/min} \qquad \blacklozenge\blacklozenge\blacklozenge$$

The coefficient of friction is 0.03 for a shaft of 0.052 m diameter operating at 2600 rev/min. Calculate the frictional torque if the load on the shaft is 11 000 N, and also the power lost to friction and the heat generated per second at the bearing. What work is done against friction per minute?

$$\text{frictional torque } T \text{ (N m)} = \mu Wr = 0.03 \times 11\,000 \times \frac{0.052}{2}$$

$$= 8.58 \text{ N m}$$

$$\text{power lost to friction (kW)} = \frac{T2\pi N}{10^3 \times 60} = \frac{8.58 \times 2 \times \pi \times 2600}{10^3 \times 60}$$

$$= 2.336 \text{ kW}$$

As 1 kW = 1 kJ/s heat energy,

$$\text{heat generated} = 2.336 \text{ kJ/s}$$

work done against friction per minute (kJ/min) = 2.336 × 60

$$\doteq 140.16 \text{ kJ/min} \qquad \blacklozenge\blacklozenge\blacklozenge$$

EXERCISES 3.4

Friction and bearings (C10)

1. The average gas and inertia load on a 68 mm diameter journal bearing is 25 kN and the coefficient of friction is 0.012. Determine the power lost to friction and the heat generated per hour when the shaft is making 4800 rev/min.

2. A test shaft (A) is fitted with two plain bearings, 60 mm in diameter, lined with white metal. The coefficient of friction with lubrication is 0.028. A similar shaft (B) is fitted with two ball race bearings having a mean diameter between the ball paths of 60 mm, and their coefficient of friction is 0.0008. A load of 8 kN is applied to each shaft acting at right angles to the shafts. Each shaft is rotating at 2500 rev/min. Determine the power lost to friction at each shaft and the heat generated per hour in each case.

3. The average of the gas and inertia loads on each of the five main crankshaft bearings is 7.6 kN. The bearings are 0.07 m in diameter and the heat generated per minute at an engine speed of 3700 rev/min is 865.8 kJ. Calculate the coefficient of friction at the bearings.

4. The four main bearings fitted to a crankshaft are 58 mm in diameter, and the coefficient of friction is 0.009. The average vertical load at each bearing is 1.35 kN. Calculate the power lost to friction and the total heat generated per minute when the shaft is making 4000 rev/min.

5. A shaft carrying an average load of 220 N is fitted with two needle roller bearings having an effective diameter of 5 cm. The coefficient of friction is 0.0002. Calculate the power lost to friction at 6000 rev/min and the heat generated per minute.

3.5 CLUTCHES

The plate clutch

The torque that a clutch can transmit depends upon the following:
1. The axial force acting normal to the pressure plate, driven plate and flywheel face. This force may be supplied by springs or centrifugal force, or a combination of the two (W) in newtons.
2. The coefficient of friction between clutch lining and operating faces (μ).
3. The mean or average leverage or mean radius (R) in metres.
4. The number of pairs of frictional surfaces in contact (n).

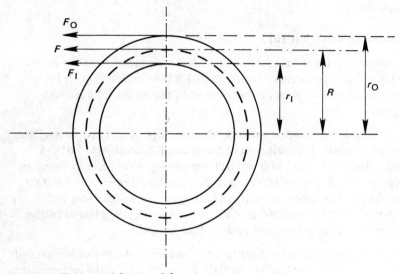

Fig. 3.10 Tangential frictional force.

$$\text{tangential frictional force} = \frac{F_I + F_O}{2} = F = \mu W \quad \text{(Fig. 3.10)}$$

$$\text{mean radius} = \frac{r_I + r_O}{2} = R \text{ m}$$

$$\text{torque transmitted (N m)} = T = \mu WRn$$

$$\text{power transmitted (kW)} = \frac{T \times 2\pi \times N}{60 \times 10^3} \text{ (where } N \text{ is in rev/min)}$$

Note: A single plate clutch has 2 pairs of frictional surfaces in contact, i.e. $n = 2$.

The cone clutch

The cone clutch (Fig. 3.11) will transmit a large torque for a given spring force due to the wedging action of the cone. The cone principle is to be found in overdrives, automatic transmissions and synchromesh units. The disadvantages are the possible fierce take-up of the drive due to the inclination to wedge.

$$\sin \theta = \frac{W}{Q} \quad \text{and} \quad Q = \frac{W}{\sin \theta}$$

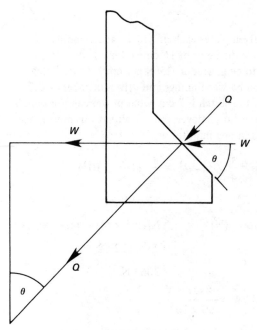

Fig. 3.11 The cone clutch.

$$\text{torque transmitted (N m)} = T = \mu QRn = \frac{\mu WRn}{\sin \theta}$$

$$\text{power transmitted (kW)} = \frac{t \times 2 \times \pi \times N}{60 \times 10^3}$$

where θ = angle of cone.

Note: For a single cone only one pair of frictional surfaces is in contact, thus $n = 1$.

Axial spring force

In certain cases the axial spring load or force in N or kN acting at right angles or normal to the pressure plate, clutch lining and flywheel face is not given directly, and in lieu of this the spring pressure per unit of clutch face area is stated. It may be in N/cm^2 or more likely in kN/m^2. In such cases the clutch lining face area must be calculated if it is not given directly and this figure multiplied by the spring pressure (pressure x area = force). Thus

$$\text{N/cm}^2 \times \text{lining face area cm}^2 = \text{axial spring force N}$$

and $\qquad \text{kN/m}^2 \times \text{lining face area } \text{m}^2 = \text{axial spring force kN}$

Worked examples

A multi-plate clutch has six driven plates each of which carries annular friction linings having an outside diameter of 16 cm and inside diameter of 10 cm. The spring pressure is to be limited to 25 N per cm^2 of face lining area. The coefficient of friction between linings and driven members is 0.3. If the effective mean radius of the clutch is 7 cm, what power can this clutch transmit at 4200 rev/min? If the clutch develops a 2% slip at this power, how much heat would be generated in one minute?

$$\text{face area of linings} = \frac{\pi}{4}(D^2 - d^2) = \frac{\pi}{4}(16^2 - 10^2)$$

$$= 122.52 \text{ cm}^2$$

$$\text{total axial spring force (N)} = \text{N/cm}^2 \times \text{lining face area cm}^2$$

$$= 25 \times 122.52$$

$$= 3063 \text{ N}$$

$$\text{power transmitted kW} = \frac{\mu W R n 2\pi N}{60 \times 10^3}$$

$$= \frac{0.3 \times 3063 \times 0.07 \times 6 \times 2 \times \pi \times 4200}{60 \times 10^3}$$

$$= 169.74 \text{ kW}$$

$$\text{heat developed with 2\% slip (kJ/min)} = \text{kW} \times 60 \times 0.02$$

$$= 169.74 \times 60 \times 0.02$$

$$= 203.68 \text{ kJ/min} \qquad \blacklozenge\blacklozenge\blacklozenge$$

Single plate clutch

A single plate clutch has a driven plate with an annular friction lining of 30 cm outside diameter and 25 cm inside diameter. The pressure between the flywheel face and pressure plate is to be limited to 198 kN/m^2, and the coefficient of friction is 0.35. The engine to which the clutch is to be fitted produces a maximum torque of 720 N m at 1890 rev/min, and a maximum power of 426 kW at 5650 rev/min. A safety factor of 10% at maximum power is essential. Will this proposed clutch prove satisfactory?

$$\text{area of clutch friction linings} = \frac{\pi}{4}(D^2 - d^2) \times 2$$

$$= \frac{\pi}{4}(0.3^2 - 0.25^2) \times 2$$

$$= 0.043 \text{ m}^2$$

axial spring force (total) = W = kN/m^2 × m^2 (kN)

$$= 198 \times 0.043$$

$$= 8.514 \text{ kN}$$

mean radius $R = \dfrac{(D + d)}{4} = \dfrac{0.3 + 0.25}{4} = 0.1375$ m

maximum torque transmitted (N m) = $\mu W R n$

$$= 0.35 \times 8.514 \times 10^3 \times 0.1375 \times 2$$

$$= 819.4 \text{ N m}$$

maximum power transmitted at 5650 rev/min $\dfrac{T 2\pi N}{60} = \dfrac{T \pi N}{30}$

$$= \frac{819.4 \times \pi \times 5650}{30}$$

$$= 484\ 811 \text{ W}$$

$$= 484.8 \text{ kW}$$

10% above maximum engine power of 426 kW

$$= 426 \times \frac{110}{100} = 468.6 \text{ kW}$$

The clutch can transmit a power of 484 kW which is well above the safety factor, and is therefore very suitable for the engine in question. ◆◆◆

Multi-plate clutch

An engine on test, giving maximum torque, produces 38 kW power at 1870 rev/min. The clutch designed for this engine has four asbestos-based annular friction linings having 30 cm outside diameter and 25 cm inside diameter, and their coefficient of friction with the five steel clutch plates is 0.34. What total axial spring force is necessary for the clutch if a 20% safety factor is to be provided?

$$P_b = \frac{T 2\pi N}{60} W$$

therefore $\quad T \text{ (N m)} = \dfrac{\text{kW} \times 10^3 \times 60}{2\pi \times N}$

$$= \frac{38 \times 10^3 \times 60}{2 \times \pi \times 1870}$$

$$= 194 \text{ N m maximum torque}$$

$$194 + 20\% \text{ safety factor} = 194 \times \frac{120}{100} = 232.8 \text{ N m}$$

mean radius of clutch $R = \dfrac{D+d}{4} = \dfrac{0.3 + 0.25}{4} = 0.137\ 5$ m mean radius

torque transmitted by clutch $(\text{max}) = \mu W R n$

and $\qquad W = \dfrac{T}{\mu \times R \times n} = \dfrac{232.8}{0.34 \times 0.137\ 5 \times 8}$

$$= 622.45 \text{ N axial spring force} \qquad \blacklozenge\blacklozenge\blacklozenge$$

A cone clutch used on a small garage crane has a coefficient of friction of 0.42 between the 26° angle steel cone and the driven member upon which an axial spring load of 198 N is applied. The mean diameter of the cone is 18.6 cm. What torque can be transmitted by the clutch?

torque transmitted T (N m) (max) $= \dfrac{\mu W R n}{\sin \theta} = \dfrac{0.42 \times 198 \times 0.093 \times 1}{0.438\ 3}$

$$= 17.64 \text{ N m} \qquad \blacklozenge\blacklozenge\blacklozenge$$

EXERCISES 3.5

Friction clutches (C10)

1. The coefficient of friction between the single driven plate of mean effective radius 11.43 cm and the pressure plate and flywheel face should be 0.35. Due to a faulty rear main bearing, oil has penetrated to the clutch lining, and the coefficient of friction is now only 0.16. The axial spring force is 3.2 kN. What percentage of the maximum transmitted torque has been lost?

2. A single cone clutch, having a mean diameter of 230 mm, has an axial spring force of 1.2 kN applied. The maximum torque transmitted by this clutch is 69.375 N m. The coefficient of friction is 0.28. Find the angle of the cone.

3. A single plate clutch of 400 mm mean diameter has a total spring load of 2.8 kN supplemented by a centrifugal assisted force of 1.2 kN produced by bell-cranked levers, suitably weighted at 3000 rev/min. The power transmitted is 187 kW. Determine the coefficient of friction between the friction lining and drive faces.

4. A multi-plate clutch has three annular friction linings of 275 mm outside diameter and 220 mm inside diameter, and their coefficient of friction is 0.35

with the driven surfaces. The axial spring load is 756 N. Find the torque transmitted by the clutch, and the power if the maximum safe rev/min is 5650.

5. An engine develops 40% of its maximum power of 78 kW at 2300 rev/min, which is the speed of maximum engine torque. A single plate clutch is fitted which has an axial spring load of 850 N. The coefficient of friction is 0.32. Find the mean effective diameter of the clutch.

6. A multi-plate clutch has six pairs of frictional surfaces of 280 mm outside and 206 mm inside diameters. The axial spring force is 520 N. If the coefficient of friction is 0.32, find the power which can be transmitted at 4750 rev/min.

3.6 BRAKES

Friction torque and brakes

When a brake is applied to the wheel of a car, a force is immediately introduced between the tyre and the road surface which tends to keep the wheel turning, and is the force opposing the motion of the vehicle. Stopping distance and braking efficiency depend upon:
1. The adhesive force, which in turn depends upon the coefficient of friction between tyre and road surface and upon the loading on the wheels normal or at right angles to the road surface.
2. Effort at the brake pedal, force at expander units and the load or force normal to brake shoes or disc pads.
3. Method of actuating the brakes, and their mechanical efficiency.
4. Coefficient of friction of linings and pads, diameter of drums or discs.
5. Thinking and action time.

Simple drum brake

If a simple drum brake is considered, as shown in Fig. 3.12, an important equation can be introduced. No servo action between shoe lining and drum is to be considered at this stage. In other words, there is no distinction between leading and trailing shoes.

The frictional force between tyre and road surface (F_R) multiplied by the leverage, which is the rolling radius of the wheel and tyre (r), will give the value of the braking torque, and this value must also equal the torque produced between brake shoe lining and drum.

braking torque between tyre and road = retarding torque between lining and drum or pad and disc

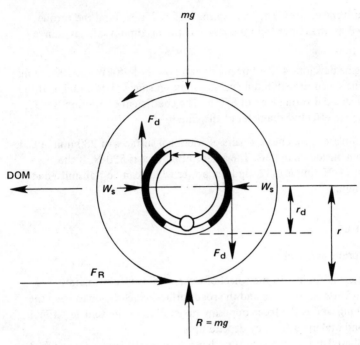

Fig. 3.12 The simple drum brake.

thus $\qquad F_R \times r = F_d \times r_d$

and $\qquad \mu \times mg \times r = \mu_s \times W_s \times r_d$

where $\quad F_R$ = frictional force between tyre and road surface (newtons)

$\qquad r$ = effective or rolling radius of roadwheels (metres)

$\qquad F_d$ = frictional force between shoe lining and drum or pad and disc (newtons)

$\qquad r_d$ = radius of brake drum or mean radius of disc pad lining (metres)

$\qquad \mu$ = coefficient of friction or adhesion between tyre and road

$\qquad \mu_s$ = coefficient of friction between lining and drum or pad lining and disc

$\qquad mg$ = vertical load on braked wheels (normal to the road) (newtons)

$\qquad W_s$ = load or force between shoe lining and drum or pad lining and disc (newtons)

$\qquad R$ = reaction to the load or force (mg)

Brake pedal travel

The force that is produced at the brake pedal by an average driver due to the toggle action of the leg is between 660 and 1550 N. Where high brake shoe or disc pad loads are necessary, a large leverage would be required between brake pedal and the brake shoes or disc pads. Large lever ratios entail large operating distances, and brake pedal travel should be kept to a minimum. Retardation will not commence until after the intervals of 'thinking' and 'action' time. A few figures will illustrate the problem of brake pedal travel.

If a braking system had an overall movement ratio of 100:1 and the brake pedal travels 38 mm, then the shoes travel 0.38 mm (this does not include clearance or free pedal travel). With this system the pedal will travel an additional 25 mm for every 0.25 mm of brake lining wear. To reduce the movement ratio and limit pedal travel, brake servos are fitted, thus high movement ratios and pedal travel are kept to a minimum, and the light pedal forces applied by the driver are supplemented by the brake servo unit.

Servo action of brake shoes

If the value of the coefficient of friction changes between brake lining and drum surface, the angle of the resultant force to F_d and W_s will also change. The small piece of the lining in Fig. 3.13(a) will create a resultant force that will tend to press it more firmly against the drum surface because this force passes to the right of the shoe pivot causing a clockwise moment on the shoe. In diagram (b) the resultant force on a piece of the brake lining close to the shoe pivot is causing a counter-clockwise moment on the shoe, tending to force this part of the lining away from the drum's surface.

The following observations may be noted:
(a) Extending the top or leading end of the shoe lining will aggrevate the tendency to jam.
(b) Raising the shoe pivot point will increase the servo action, but may lead to jamming.
(c) A change in the value of the coefficient of friction to a lower figure will alter the angle of the resultant force and reduce the servo and jamming effect.

Brake shoe factor

Sometimes the brake shoe factor is used to compare the efficiency of the leading and trailing shoes. The ratio of the brake drum drag force F_D to the shoe tip or actuating force P is called the *shoe factor*, and in the case of the leading shoe varies considerably with the coefficient of friction of the brake lining material, the distance between the pivot point and the drum centre, and the length of the lining arc. The trailing shoe is relatively insensitive to

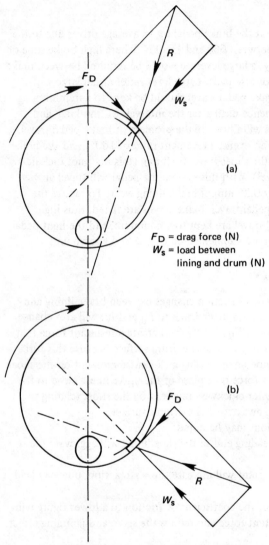

F_D = drag force (N)
W_s = load between
        lining and drum (N)

Fig. 3.13 Servo action of brake shoes.

changes of leverage or coefficient of friction. Fig. 3.14 shows shoe factor plotted against coefficient of friction for both leading and trailing shoes.

Braking efficiency and stopping distance

On a level road surface the coefficient of friction or the adhesion between

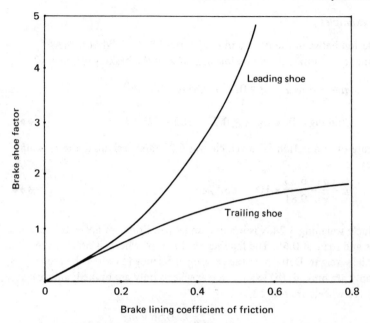

Fig. 3.14 Brake shoe factor for leading and trailing shoes.

tyres and road surface is considered as the maximum braking efficiency. Thus if μ = 0.65 the maximum braking efficiency possible under these conditions = 0.65 × 100 = 65%. Stopping distance for a given set of conditions is dependent on the braking force F_b (kN) which is available and thus relies upon the value of adhesion always assuming the braking system is serviceable.

$$\text{braking force } F_b = \mu W_t \text{ or } \mu mg$$

where W_t is the total vehicle weight and all wheels are braked.

$$\text{braking force } F_b = \text{mass} \times \text{retardation} = m \times a = \mu mg$$

thus $\qquad \mu = \dfrac{ma}{mg} = \dfrac{a}{g} \quad$ and $\quad \dfrac{a}{g} \times 100 = \text{braking efficiency \%}.$

where a = retardation (m/s^2) and g = acceleration due to gravity (9.81 m/s^2)
When certain wheels only are braked:

$$\text{retardation } a \text{ m/s}^2 = \mu g \times \frac{w}{mg}$$

where w = weight carried by the braked wheels. Further details including braking on gradients are given in Part 2.

Worked examples

The adhesion between the tyres and road surface is 0.72. What is the maximum rate of retardation possible and what is the braking efficiency?

$$\mu = \frac{a}{g} \text{ thus } a = \mu g = 0.72 \times 9.81 = 7.06 \text{ m/s}^2$$

braking efficiency % = 0.72 × 100 = 72%.   ◆◆◆

The rate of retardation for a vehicle was 6.23 m/s², calculate the braking efficiency.

$$\mu = \frac{a}{g} = \frac{6.23}{9.81} \times 100 = 63.5\%$$ ◆◆◆

A vehicle weighing 3.2 kN is braking under conditions of adhesion between the tyres and road of 0.66. The loading on the front wheels is 56% of the total vehicle weight. Determine the braking efficiency (a) when the front wheels only are braked; (b) when the rear wheels only are braked; and (c) when all the wheels are braked.

(a)   retardation $a = \mu g \times \dfrac{w}{mg} = 0.66 \times 9.81 \times \dfrac{0.56 \times mg}{mg} = 3.625$ m/s²

braking efficiency % $= \dfrac{a}{g} \times 100 = \dfrac{3.625}{9.81} \times 100 = 36.96\%$

(b)   retardation $a = \mu g \times \dfrac{w}{mg} = 0.66 \times 9.81 \times \dfrac{0.44 \times mg}{mg} = 2.848$ m/s²

braking efficiency % $= \dfrac{a}{g} \times 100 = \dfrac{2.848}{9.81} \times 100 = 29\%$

(c)   braking efficiency when all wheels are braked = μ% = 0.66 × 100

= 66%   ◆◆◆

The braking torque between a tyre and the road surface is 982 N m and the load between brake linings and drum is 17 166 N. If the drum diameter is 26 cm, what is the coefficient of friction between the brake linings and brake drum?

braking torque = $T_b = \mu_s \times W_s \times r$

where μ_s = coefficient between linings and drum,

W_s = load or force between linings and drum (N) and

r = radius of drum (m)

therefore

$$\mu_s = \frac{T_b}{W_s \times r} = \frac{982}{17\ 166 \times 0.13}$$

$$= 0.44$$

◆◆◆

The coefficient of adhesion between a tyre and road surface is 0.68 when carrying a load of 470 kg. The rolling radius of the wheel and tyre is 0.63 m, and the frictional force between pad and disc is 19.592 kN. At what distance is the pad from the disc axis?

retarding torque at wheel = retarding torque at drum

$$F_b \times R = F_d \times r$$

$$\mu \times mg \times R = F_d \times r$$

therefore $\quad \dfrac{\mu \times mg \times R}{F_d} = r$

$$\frac{0.68 \times 470 \times 9.81 \times 0.63}{19\ 592} = r \text{ m}$$

$$= 0.1 \text{ m mean radius}$$

◆◆◆

Leading and trailing shoe brakes

A shoe is a leading shoe when the movement of the drum over the lining is towards the pivot, and a trailing shoe when the movement is away from the pivot. From Fig. 3.15:

Trailing shoe
Taking moments about pivot

$$P \times A = W_T \times B + \mu W_T \times r$$

$$P \times A = W_T(B + \mu r)$$

and $\quad W_T = \dfrac{P \times A}{B + \mu r}$

now $\quad$ torque (N m) $= \mu W_T r$

$$= \frac{PA}{B + \mu r} \times \mu r$$

therefore $\dfrac{P \times A \times \mu r}{B + \mu r} =$

trailing shoe torque (N m)

Leading shoe
Taking moments about pivot,

$$W_L \times B = P \times A + \mu W_L \times r$$

$$W_L \times B - \mu \times W_L \times r = P \times A$$

$$W_L(B - \mu r) = P \times A$$

therefore $W_L = \dfrac{PA}{B - \mu r}$

torque $= \mu W_L r = \dfrac{P \times A \times \mu r}{B - \mu r} =$

leading shoe torque (N m)

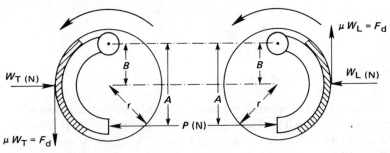

Fig. 3.15 (a) Trailing shoe and (b) leading shoe.

Worked examples

If $\mu = 0.45$ and $P = 445$ N, $A = 20$ cm and $B = 10$ cm, and if the radius of the drum is 12.7 cm, what is the retarding torque at the leading and trailing shoes? (See Fig. 3.15).

$$\text{torque at trailing shoe } T_T = \frac{PA\mu r}{B + \mu r} = \frac{445 \times 0.20 \times 0.45 \times 0.127}{0.10 + 0.45 \times 0.127}$$

$$= \frac{5.086}{0.157} = 32.39 \text{ N m}$$

$$\text{torque at leading shoe } T_L = \frac{PA\mu r}{B - \mu r} = \frac{445 \times 0.20 \times 0.45 \times 0.127}{0.10 - 0.45 \times 0.127}$$

$$= \frac{5.086}{0.043} = 118.3 \text{ N m} \qquad \blacklozenge\blacklozenge\blacklozenge$$

Brakes and braking

An actuating force is applied 18 cm from the pivot point of a leading and trailing shoe fitted to a 24 cm diameter brake drum, and operated by a hydraulic wheel cylinder (wc) having pistons each of 8 cm^2 area. The master cylinder (mc) piston is 4 cm in diameter, and the brake pedal has a lever ratio of 5:1. The coefficient of friction between linings and drum is 0.4. Determine the braking torque produced by each shoe if the efficiency of the system is 80% when the driver exerts a force of 700 N at the brake pedal.

$$\text{brake fluid pressure (N/m}^2) = \frac{\text{force at pedal} \times \text{leverage}}{\text{area of mc piston}}$$

$$= \frac{700 \times 5 \times 4 \times 10^4}{\pi \times 4^2}$$

$$= 2785\ 211 \text{ N/m}^2$$

actuating force by wc pistons = P = N/m^2 x area of wc piston

$$= 2785\ 211 \times 0.0008$$

$$= 2228\ N$$

actuating force P at 80% efficiency = 2228 x 0.8

$$= 1782\ N$$

torque by the trailing shoe = T_T (N m) = $\dfrac{PA\mu r}{B + \mu r} = \dfrac{1782 \times 0.18 \times 0.4 \times 0.12}{0.09 + 0.4 \times 0.12}$

$$= \frac{15.396}{0.138}$$

$$= 111.56\ N\,m$$

torque by the leading shoe = T_L (N m) = $\dfrac{PA\mu r}{B - \mu r} = \dfrac{15.396}{0.09 - 0.4 \times 0.12}$

$$= \frac{15.396}{0.042}$$

$$= 366.57\ N\,m$$

(*Note*: Hydraulic systems are reserved for TEC 415 MV Science 111 (Part 2) but a reference to hydraulic brakes was necessary to cover the subject matter of friction and brakes.)   ◆◆◆

Leading and trailing shoes

A leading and trailing shoe are operated in a 23 cm diameter drum by a force applied by a 3 cm wheel cylinder piston at 17.8 cm from the shoe pivot. The master cylinder piston of 2.4 cm diameter is operated by a brake pedal having a movement ratio of 4:1, with a brake lining coefficient of friction of 0.4. Determine the braking torque for each shoe, when the driver exerts a force of 890 N at the pedal, and the braking system efficiency is 80%.

brake fluid pressure (kN/m^2) = $\dfrac{\text{force at pedal x lever ratio}}{\text{Area of mc piston (m}^2)} = \dfrac{N \times MR}{m^2 \times 10^3}$

$$= \frac{890 \times 4 \times 4}{\pi \times 0.024^2 \times 10^3} = 7869\ kN/m^2$$

force by wheel cylinder piston (kN) = fluid pressure x area of wc piston

$$= kN/m^2 \times m^2$$

$$= \frac{7869 \times \pi \times 0.03^2}{4}$$

$$= 5.562\ kN$$

as efficiency is 80%, effective piston force = 5.562 x 0.8

$$= 4.45 \text{ kN}$$

$$= 4450 \text{ N}$$

torque at trailing shoe (N m) $= \dfrac{PA\mu r}{B + \mu r} = \dfrac{4450 \times 0.178 \times 0.4 \times 0.115}{0.089 + 0.4 \times 0.115}$

$$= \dfrac{36.43}{0.135} = 269.8 \text{ N m}$$

torque at leading shoe (N m) $= \dfrac{PA\mu r}{B - \mu r} = \dfrac{36.43}{0.089 - 0.4 \times 0.115}$

$$= \dfrac{36.43}{0.043} = 847 \text{ N m}$$

♦♦♦

Disc brakes

The main advantages of disc brakes are:

1. Less likely to fade due to better cooling.
2. Comparatively unaffected by grit and water as these are thrown off by centrifugal force.
3. Disc brakes operate equally well in forward or reverse mode as they are generally of the non-servo friction design, but are progressive in action.
4. There may be a reduction in unsprung weight.
5. Less maintenance.
6. Pedal travel does not vary (simple self-adjusting system) due to heat and expansion as in the case of highly stressed drum brakes.

Although the axial forces on a disc are balanced, there remains an unbalanced radial force acting on the disc when only one caliper unit per disc is employed, and this force is taken by the wheel bearings. This can be averted by using another caliper unit fitted diametrically opposite if adequate space is available to house the cylinders and pistons, especially on the wheel side of the disc. A floating system of calipers employing a single piston overcomes most of the space problem and reduces unsprung weight.

Hydraulic disc system (non-servo) (Fig. 3.16)

retarding torque at disc = $2Pa\mu rn$ N m

where P = line pressure (N/m^2), a = area of one piston per caliper (m^2), μ = coefficient of friction of pad material, r = mean radius of caliper unit to

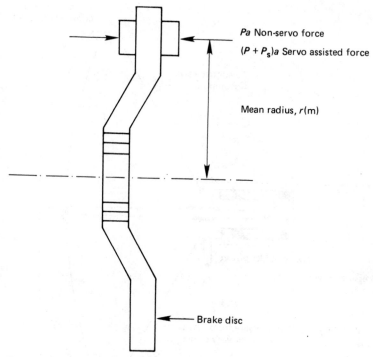

Fig. 3.16 Hydraulic disc system (non-servo).

disc axis (m), n = number of caliper units in system, and 2 = number of frictional surfaces per disc,

retarding torque at disc = $2Pa\mu rn$ N m, and,

$$\text{power absorbed} = \frac{2Pa\mu rn \times 2\pi N}{60} \text{ watts}$$

where N = rev/min of disc.

Disc brakes with servo assistance

retarding torque = $2(P_s + P)a\mu rn$ N m

where the servo system assists the normal brake fluid pressure created by the driver's effort via the master cylinder (Fig. 3.17) and P_s is the additional pressure produced by the servo unit.

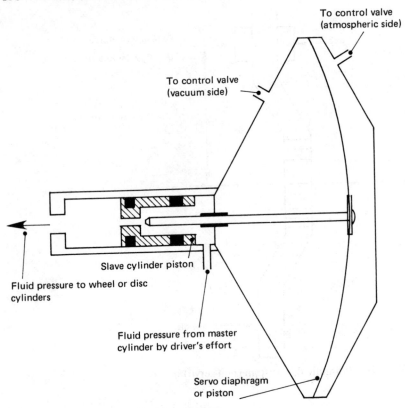

Fig. 3.17 Disc brakes with servo assistance.

$$P_s = \frac{\text{force produced by servo piston}}{\text{area of slave cylinder piston}} \text{ N/m}^2$$

$$= \frac{\text{pressure difference across servo piston (N/m}^2) \times \text{area of piston (m}^2)}{\text{area of slave cylinder piston (m}^2)} \text{ N}$$

P = brake fluid pressure due to driver's effort (N/m^2)

$$= \frac{\text{force produced by master cylinder piston (N)}}{\text{area of master cylinder piston (m}^2)} \text{ N/m}^2$$

$$= \frac{\text{pedal effort} \times \text{leverage} \times \text{efficiency (N)}}{\text{area of master cylinder piston (m}^2)} \text{ N/m}^2$$

$2a\mu r$ and n as for non-servo disc unit.

On the first stage of braking, the master cylinder pressure passes to the wheel or disc cylinders. In the second stage, the servo piston or diaphragm and rod forces the slave piston to the left thus boosting the original brake fluid pressure. In the third stage, the servo control valve closes, thus preserving the total pressure of P and P_s.

Worked examples

A vehicle having a mass of 1272 kg is brought to rest in a distance of 46 m from a speed of 96 km/h by its disc brakes fitted to all four wheels. The effective diameter of the wheels is 0.7 m. The disc units have two calipers fitted to each front wheel, and one to each rear wheel. The caliper pistons each have an area of 25.8 cm² (2 pistons per caliper) and the brake pads are situated at a radius of 102 mm from the disc axis (their coefficient of friction is 0.4). Determine the brake fluid pressure in the system during the braking period.

$$96 \text{ km/h} = \frac{96}{3.6} = 26.66 \text{ m/s}$$

$$V^2 = 2aS \quad (\text{where } a = \text{acceleration})$$

thus
$$a \text{ m/s}^2 = \frac{V^2}{2S} = \frac{26.66^2}{2 \times 46} = 7.725 \text{ m/s}^2$$

braking force $F_b = ma = 1272 \times 7.725 = 9826 \text{ N}$

braking torque T_b (N m) = braking force × wheel radius

$$= 9826 \times 0.35 = 3439 \text{ N m}$$

braking torque (N m) = $2Pa\mu rn$ = 3439 N m (where a = area)

therefore P (kN/m²) $= \dfrac{3439}{2a\mu rn \times 10^3}$

$$= \frac{3439}{2 \times 0.002\ 58 \times 0.4 \times 0.102 \times 6 \times 10^3}$$

$$= 2722.5 \text{ kN/m}^2 \text{ line pressure} \qquad \blacklozenge\blacklozenge\blacklozenge$$

The front wheels of a vehicle are fitted with two calipers per wheel. The disc pads operate at a radius of 150 mm from the disc axis and they have a coefficient of friction of 0.45. The opposed pistons in each unit are 36 mm in diameter. The driver's pedal effort via the master cylinder raises the line pressure to 3560 kN/m² and this is raised to 5980 kN/m² by the action of the brake servo unit. The rear drum brakes account for 36% of the front brake retarding torque figure. Determine the total braking torque during the retardation.

retarding torque by front brakes

$$= T_b \text{ (kN m)} = 2(P + P_s)a\mu rn$$

$$= \frac{2 \times 5980 \times \pi \times 0.036^2 \times 0.45 \times 0.150 \times 2}{4}$$

$$= 1.643 \text{ kN m or } 1643 \text{ N m}$$

retarding torque for rear brakes (N m) = 36% of 1643 = 591 N m

total braking or retarding torque = 1643 + 591

$$= 2234 \text{ N m} \qquad \blacklozenge\blacklozenge\blacklozenge$$

The friction pads of a single caliper unit pressing on each side of the brake discs fitted to all four wheels of a car are placed at a mean radius of 11.4 cm. The coefficient of friction between pad and disc is 0.38 and the force applied to a disc pad is 3560 N. The rolling radius of the wheels is 0.32 m. Find the retarding torque per disc unit, the total braking force between tyres and road surface, and the heat generated at the discs when the wheels are rotating at 600 rev/min.

retarding torque per disc = $2Pa\mu rn$ N m

$$= 2 \times 3560 \times 0.38 \times 0.114 \times 1$$

$$= 308 \text{ N m}$$

braking force $F_b = \dfrac{\text{torque at disc} \times 4}{\text{wheel rolling radius}} = \dfrac{308 \times 4}{0.32}$

$$= 3850 \text{ N}$$

heat generated (kJ/min) = $\dfrac{T2\pi N}{10^3}$

$$= \frac{308 \times 4 \times 2\pi \times 600}{10^3}$$

$$= 4645 \text{ kJ/min} \qquad \blacklozenge\blacklozenge\blacklozenge$$

A car fitted with disc brakes on the front wheels which have servo assistance. This increases the line pressure of 6000 kN/m^2 by 2400 kN/m^2. The diameter of the caliper pistons is 40 mm, and they operate at a mean radius of 16 cm from the disc axis. One caliper is fitted per disc. The coefficient of friction between pad and disc is 0.45. What retarding torque is produced at the front wheels which remain turning?

retarding torque by the front wheels (N m) = $2(P_s + P) a\mu rn \times 2$

$$= 2(2400 + 6000) \times 10^3 \times \frac{\pi \times 0.04^2}{4} \times 0.45 \times 0.16 \times 2 \times 2$$

$$= 6080 \text{ N m}$$

◆◆◆

EXERCISES 3.6

Friction and brakes (C10)

1. The coefficient of friction between the brake linings and brake drum is 0.43. The brake drum diameter is 28 cm and the total load between brake linings and drum is 3850 N. Neglecting any servo action determine: (a) the braking torque in N m, (b) the power absorbed in bringing the drum to rest from 650 rev/min, and (c) the heat generated per minute.

2. A vehicle wheel of 0.74 m diameter carries a vertical loading of 1.6 kN when the brakes are applied. The coefficient of friction between the tyres and road is 0.62. The brake drums have a radius of 146 mm and the total loading between brake linings and drum is 7.17 kN. Find the coefficient of friction between brake linings and drum, neglecting any servo action.

3. The force between the brake linings and the 29 cm diameter brake drum is 2.8 kN and the coefficient of friction is 0.43. After a period of service, the oil seal fails and oil contacts the brake linings. The coefficient of friction is reduced to 0.125. Determine the percentage reduction in the braking torque.

4. A vehicle having a mass of 7.6 Mg has roadwheels of 1.2 m rolling diameter. The brake drums are 38 cm in diameter and the coefficient of adhesion between the tyres and road surface is 0.62. What would be the maximum retarding force at the brake drums?

5. A caliper unit of a disc brake is placed at a mean radius of 8.9 cm from the wheel axis. The caliper pistons are 56 mm diameter operating pads with a coefficient of friction of 0.44 between pad and disc. The brake fluid pressure is 5516 kN/m². The vehicle weighs 11 570 N and is fitted with disc brakes to the front wheels which have an effective diameter of 0.43 m. The rear brakes account for 20% of the retardation. What braking force is applied by the front wheels?

6. A high-performance car has disc brakes fitted to the front wheels having two calipers per disc operating at a mean radius of 16 cm. The pads are operated by opposed pistons of 3.8 cm diameter. The coefficient of friction

between pad and disc is 0.42. The driver through the brake pedal and master cylinder raises the line pressure to 1430 kN/m^2 during moderate retardation and this pressure is increased to 3260 kN/m^2 by brake servo assistance. The rear brakes account for 32% of the front brakes' retarding torque. Determine the total braking torque during the retardation.

4
Lubrication (D 11)

4.1 PRINCIPLES OF BEARINGS AND THEIR USES

Plain engine bearings

As engine crankshaft speeds increase, the gas and inertia loads become greater per minute, thus the heat generated increases.

The running temperature of a bearing depends to a large extent upon the rate at which heat is generated and the rate of heat removal by conduction, air cooling and the heat removal by the oil flowing through the bearing. The cooler the bearing, the higher is the working load factor. The pressure on a bearing and its rubbing speed are two important factors which influence bearing temperature.

The width of bearings is limited by the space between the cylinders and the overall engine length. The larger the bearing area, the greater are the loads it can carry. Unfortunately narrow large diameter bearings, although the answer to the engine dimension, increase the rubbing velocities and a compromise has to be made.

Bearing materials

A bearing should possess a combination of hardness to resist abrasion at the higher rubbing speeds and compressive strength to support the journal under heavy and shock loads. A certain degree of plasticity is needed to allow good mating of journal to bearing, but it must not allow creep at the higher temperatures.

Good oil retention and low coefficient of friction are necessary together with high thermal conductivity to enable heat to flow rapidly from the bearing surfaces. Altogether this is a very complex set of problems which is ably met by the modern bearing.

White-metal shell bearings

Thin steel shell bearings about 1 mm thick with a layer of white-metal about 0.35 mm thick are used in most production-type automobile engines (see

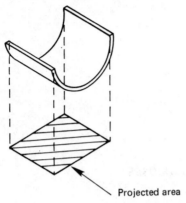

Projected area

Fig. 4.1 Thin steel wall shell bearings.

Fig. 4.1). Steel strips are prepared with the white-metal layer *in situ* . They are then fed into a machine and the shells are stamped into shape with oil holes and an indentation made in one corner as a location point to fit a slot in the bearing housing.

A composition of the bearing metal could consist of 85% tin, 11% antimony, and 4% copper. In certain cases the percentage of tin is reduced and instead a larger percentage of copper is used with the addition of a small amount of lead.

Lead–bronze bearings

For high performance petrol engines and compression-ignition oil engines, lead–bronze bearing metal consisting of about 67% copper and 33% lead is used. The metal is harder, so crank journals must be hardened and larger clearances given which calls for higher oil pressures with greater flow rate. The oil must also possess a high degree of oiliness and be capable of upholding its viscosity at working temperatures.

The thermal conductivity of the metal is good, but it has poor anti-corrosion properties and is attacked by the acidic products which build up in the engine sump oil. A very thin layer of tin or indium is used for protection, but frequent oil changes are necessary.

Pre-lubricated bearings and bushes

Bushes and bearings can be made by the powder metallurgy process. This method enables alloys to be manufactured into bushes and small bearings which it would not be possible to make by a normal metal melting process as the ingredients would not 'mix' and remain in separation.

A large degree of porosity is possible and the processed metal can be impregnated with oil or graphite. The metallic powder is produced by an electrolytic process and has the consistency of fine sand.

A cold pressing is made into steel dies under very high pressures, and then the pressing is heated (sintered) in an electrically heated furnace for some 40 to 60 minutes. Sintered bronze is used for bearings and bushes for such units as dynamos and electric motor bearings, distributor bushes, and clutch spigot bearings where oil in a fluid state would be undesirable.

Pressure and loads on bearings

When calculating the vertical loading or pressure on a bearing, the area to be considered for such calculations is the projected area of the bearing surface (Fig. 4.1). The diameter of the bearing multiplied by its width is the projected surface area.

Worked example

The peak gas pressure on a piston crown of 85 mm diameter is 1256 kN/m^2. The crankshaft big-end journal has a diameter of 50 mm and is 26 mm in width. Calculate the pressure on the big-end bearing.

force in connecting rod = pressure x piston crown area

$$= p \times \frac{\pi D^2}{4}$$

$$= \frac{1256 \times \pi \times 0.085^2}{4} \text{ kN (kN/m}^2 \times \text{m}^2 = \text{kN)}$$

$$= 7.127 \text{ kN}$$

$$\text{pressure on bearing kN/m}^2 = \frac{\text{force in con-rod}}{\text{projected bearing area}}$$

$$= \frac{7.127}{0.026 \times 0.05}$$

$$= 5482 \text{ kN/m}^2$$

◆◆◆

4.2 BALL AND ROLLER BEARINGS

The contrast between the resistance to movement when sliding a loaded crate along the shop floor to that when rollers are placed between crate and floor is very noticeable. The drag or frictional forces are very much smaller when there is a rolling contact instead of a sliding one. The friction between the finished surfaces of a crankshaft journal and white-metalled bearing suitably lubricated is a sliding one with a possible coefficient of friction of 0.013. A suitable ball race bearing under the same load could be 0.0013 and thus only introduces oı tenth the friction.

Brief construction details

A ball bearing consists of one or more rows of balls interposed between an inner and outer race or track. The balls are held spaced in relation to each other by cages. The balls are of hardened steel, ground and polished to very high standards and close limits. The races are also of hardened steel ground and polished. The inner race is fitted to the shaft and the outer to the housing.

A basic type of roller race bearing consists of a series of cylindrical rollers interposed between two plain ground and polished races (Fig. 4.6). Cages are used to separate the rollers.

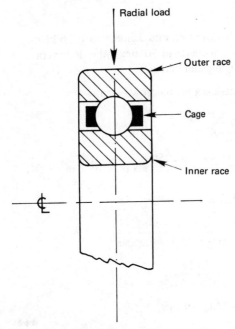

Fig. 4.2 Single row journal bearing.

Main types of ball type bearings used in automotive work

1. Single row journal bearing (Fig. 4.2)
2. Double row journal bearing
3. Double row self-aligning bearing (Fig. 4.3)

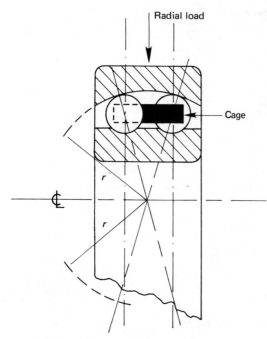

Fig. 4.3 Double row self-aligning bearing.

4. Combined journal and thrust bearing (Fig. 4.4)
5. Flat seated single or double thrust bearing (Fig. 4.5)

1. Suitable for radial loads acting at right angles or normal to the shaft axis, such as gearbox shafts with double helical gears, generator shafts and certain rear axles.

2. Can be fitted where there is no misalignment of the shaft and greater radial loads are applied. The balls are staggered by the ball cage to reduce the overall width of the bearing.

3. The outer race or path is a segment of a sphere with its centre on the bearing or shaft axis. It allows for a normal load when shaft is running with a slight misalignment.

4. Designed to take radial and certain thrust loads. Note that the thrust is taken in one direction only. Certain deep groove races are designed to take moderate lateral thrust in each direction and may be of single or double row.

5. Designed to take side thrusts only, such as those associated with clutches, king pins, worm and wheel final drives and steering boxes.

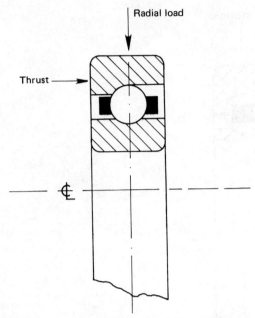

Fig. 4.4 Combined journal and thrust bearing.

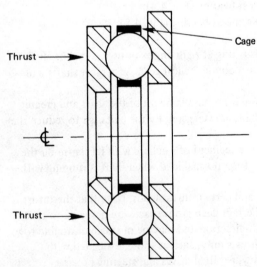

Fig. 4.5 Single thrust bearing.

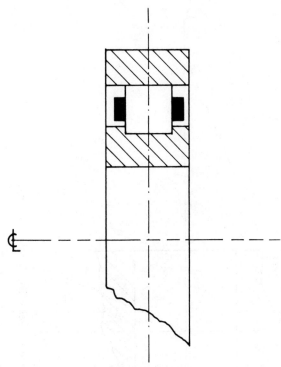

Fig. 4.6 Single row roller bearing.

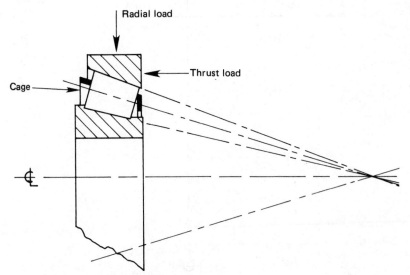

Fig. 4.7 Tapered roller bearing.

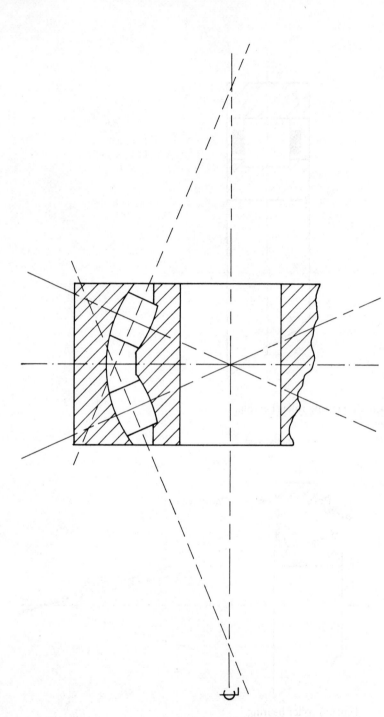

Fig. 4.8 Double row spherical self-aligning roller bearing.

Roller bearings

1. Single row roller bearing (Fig. 4.6)
2. Tapered roller bearing (Fig. 4.7)
3. Double row self-aligning spherical roller bearing (Fig. 4.8)
4. Needle roller bearing (Fig. 4.9)

1. This bearing uses cylindrical rollers having a similar width as their diameter. This ensures high radial loading is possible with safety.

2. Tapered roller bearings have conical inner and outer races and together with the tapered rollers have a common intersection or apex to ensure true rolling of the rollers. When mounted in pairs such as for wheel hub bearings, they are fitted so that the smaller diameters face each other. Such a bearing is capable of sustaining considerable radial and thrust loads.

3. Spherical roller self-aligning bearings can take higher radial loads than the double row self-aligning ball bearing with a similar degree of misalignment.

4. Needle roller bearings consist of small diameter rollers in the order of four times the diameter in length. No cages are fitted and these bearings can take very high radial loads for their construction size, and are usefully employed where space is limited; such as for layshafts, camshafts and universal joints.

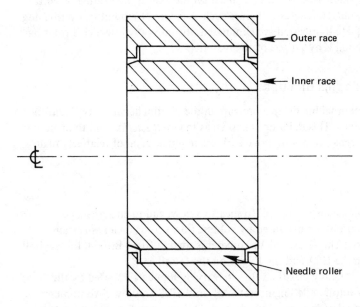

Fig. 4.9 Needle roller bearing.

Lubrication of ball and roller bearings

In theory there is either point or line contact between ball or roller and race. Under load, very slight deformation of the materials in contact takes place and provides a definite, if small, area of contact, which in size will depend upon the degree of loading, and the hardness and elasticity of those materials used. This minute deformation prevents true rolling of the balls and rollers, thus introducing a small sliding action with its higher friction. Therefore some form of lubrication is necessary to cope with this and also to protect the highly finished surfaces from corrosion and rust formation. Ball and roller bearings operate over wide speed ranges and load-carrying capacities are reduced with an increase in speed. Temperatures at which the bearings are running are important, and although the self-induced heat is low with this type of bearing, heat from the surrounding air or by conduction from other parts of the machine could create problems unless some suitable form of lubrication is present.

Geometrical conditions for pure rolling

The balls or rollers should roll accurately around their races with the minimum of slip or spin about the point or line of contact. The generating lines for the rolling line are shown in Figs. 4.3, 4.7 and 4.8 and indicate that the generators are either parallel to each other or meet on the axis of the bearing or sahft.

If all extraneous causes of failure such as incorrect mounting, overloading and inadequate lubrication are eliminated, the only way in which a rotating bearing can fail is by fatigue of the material.

4.3 PROPERTIES OF LUBRICATING OILS

A rotating journal builds up a pressure in the oil film between itself and the bearing surface. This build-up is known as the *wedge action* and to maintain a complete separation of the two surfaces requires an oil of relatively high viscosity.

Viscosity

This is the resistance of the oil to shear, to flow, and to change shape. Viscosities of oils are measured by volume flow through a jet at certain temperatures. The Redwood Viscometer is used in Great Britain, the Saybolt Universal in the USA and the Engler on the Continent.

Oils are generally classified for viscosity by numbers imposed by the Society of Automobile Engineers (SAE) in the USA. A low SAE number indicates an oil of low viscosity, thus an SAE rating of 5 would indicate a 'thin' engine oil suitable for very cold conditions, a 50 rating would be an engine oil suitable for warm or hot climatic conditions, and a rating of 140 is a 'thick' oil suitable for final drives, etc.

This SAE rating only classifies the oil for viscosity within a limited range of temperatures, and does not indicate how the oil would behave at the more extreme temperatures. It gives no indication of the other properties of the oil.

Oiliness

This property is very important, especially where high rubbing speeds and loads are applied. It is the molecular attraction that the oil possesses for metal. An oil with a high degree of oiliness will form an intimate molecular bond of oil, termed a boundary layer, which is very difficult to remove, and even solvents such as petrol cannot always erase the film. Castor and rape oil have high oiliness values.

Boundary lubrication

Boundary lubrication is a molecular film of oil which clings to the surfaces of both journal and bearing. It is only a few microns thick and unless the surface finishes are very smooth the 'peaks' will protrude and will contact one another under load.

An engine starting from cold after a period of inactivity may have boundary conditions for a few revolutions. Unfortunately the gas loading is high at such times, due to the rich mixtures and delay periods, and hence a high degree of oiliness will provide good boundary oil films.

Fluid lubrication

This is lubrication at its highest efficiency. A fluid film of oil under pressure is imposed between journal and bearing, taking up the entire clearance between these surfaces thus keeping them separated under all working conditions. This fluid oil film is on the move the whole time and is capable of absorbing and removing some heat from the bearing.

Viscosity index

This is a method of estimating the degree of viscosity change at varying temperatures. A high index figure such as 110 would indicate that the oil maintains a very high viscosity level when hot. A 0 index indicates high viscosity when cold, but becoming very low (thin) when the oil is hot. Thus multi-grade oils have a high viscosity index.

Oxidation

The oxygen contained in air is 'kneaded' into the hot oil when in the form of spray or mist. The rate is doubled for every 7°C rise in temperature. The oil turns a dark colour and becomes thick and gummy, and is known as *hot sludge*. There are a large variety of oxidation inhibitors or anti-oxidants in use, most are soluble organic compounds of various types.

Detergent and dispersant additives

Mineral oils and water tend to separate when mixed slowly, but in the crankcase, due to the heat and degree of churning, they are forced into an emulsion. Cold running engines produce a high percentage of acidic water, sooty combustion products, dirt and rust which turns the emulsion black and is termed *cold sludge*. By the use of dispersants, the soot, water and oxidation products are prevented from accumulating together by being kept in suspension as very small particles, thereby preventing them from depositing on the metal surfaces. Although the oil may look black due to the soot content, the 'dirt' particles are so finely divided that they are unlikely to cause wear.

There are three types of anti-wear additives as follows:

(a) *Anti-scuffing*

These are compounds containing phosphorus or sulphur or both. They decompose at high temperature at the points of rubbing contact where the high temperatures are generated, and form a layer to prevent metal-to-metal contact under high load conditions. Cams and tappets are items which benefit from such additives.

(b) *Extreme pressure*

On highly loaded gear teeth and/or where sliding action between teeth is severe, a safety film is necessary to withstand this high loading and sliding action. Phosphorus, sulphur, chlorine and certain metal soaps such as lead naphthenate are some of the chemicals used to reduce the tendency for metal-to-metal contact taking place.

(c) *Anti-corrosive*

Corrosion begins by oxidation of the metal surfaces when the oil film breaks down. Condensed moisture from the products of combustion forms an acidic solution. Running engines below their working temperature is a main cause of

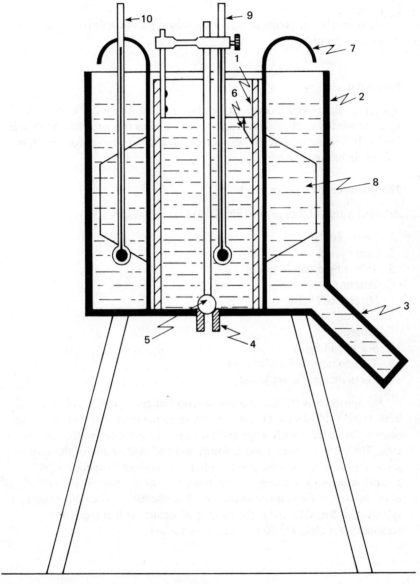

Fig. 4.10 The Redwood viscometer no. 1.

corrosion, and oil dilution increases as engine temperature falls, thus special chemical inhibitors are introduced to prevent the formation of these acidic solutions.

There are also anti-foam and anti-rust inhibitors and additives to increase the oiliness property.

Pour point

The pour point of an oil is the temperature approximately 2.8°C above the figure at which the oil will just cease to flow when a test jar is laid on its side for 5 s. It is influenced by the wax formation and the viscosity of the oil in this region of temperature.

The Redwood viscometer, no. 1

An explanation of this device (Fig. 4.10) is as follows:

1. Inner vessel
2. Outer vessel
3. Tube where heat is applied
4. Metering jet
5. Silvered ball valve
6. Oil level pointer
7. Stirrer
8. Stirrer paddles
9. Thermometer (oil under test)
10. Thermometer (water jacket)

The apparatus is levelled and the metering jet closed by the ball valve. The inner vessel is filled with the oil to be tested to the level of the pointer. The outer jacket is filled with water and the heat source applied to the heating tube. The stirrer is rotated continuously and the temperature of the water jacket regulated to maintain the test oil at the required temperature. A 50 cm^3 vessel is placed under the metering jet, the ball valve lifted and 50 cm^3 of oil allowed to flow, timed in seconds. The viscosity of the oil is expressed as Redwood Seconds, and is the number of seconds at that particular temperature it takes for 50 cm^3 of the oil to flow.

5
Statics

5.1 TRIANGLE AND POLYGON OF FORCES (E13)

Triangle of forces

If three forces acting in the same plane are acting upon a body which is at rest and in equilibrium, the forces must be applied to the same point and can be represented by force vectors drawn to scale in both direction and magnitude, which will form a closed triangle.

Space and force diagram

The space diagram indicates the forces and their position. Fig. 5.1(a) is a space diagram, and (b) represents the force diagram.

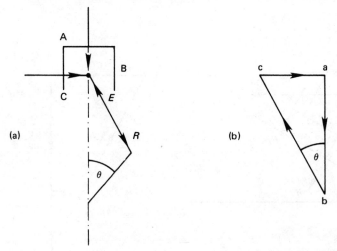

Fig. 5.1 Triangle of forces. (a) Space diagram and (b) force diagram.

Bow's notation

This is a useful method to indicate the forces and their sense of direction. The spaces separating the two forces can be lettered in capitals in a clock or anti-clock direction in the space diagram. In the space diagram in question, it is lettered A, B and C clockwise. Thus the force acting on the piston crown is drawn as ab in the force diagram. The reaction force in the connecting rod becomes force bc, and force ca represents the reaction at the cylinder wall. If one of these forces were taken away, the piston would not remain in equilibrium. If either force did not act at the same point as the others, the piston would not be in equilibrium, as a turning moment would have been introduced.

The minimum data necessary for the solution of a triangle of forces is:

1. One side and two angles, or
2. two sides and the included angle, or
3. three sides.

A series of worked examples are given later with their space and force diagrams.

Resultant and equilibrant forces

The triangle of forces can be used to find the resultant of the two other forces, but the sense or direction of the resultant will be opposite to the equilibrant. Fig. 5.2 shows a vehicle travelling on a curved banked road. The centrifugal force (CF) and the gravitational force (*mg*) act through the

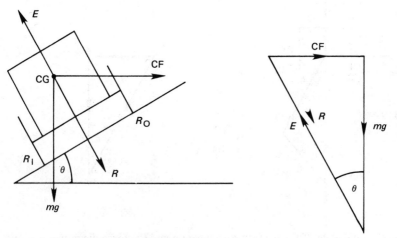

Fig. 5.2 Resultant and equilibrant forces.

vehicle's centre of gravity (CG). In this case the vehicle has no tendency to slide up or down the banking as the equilibrant force E is acting upon the centre-line of the vehicle, and the resultant force equal to E but acting in the opposite sense is at right angles or normal to the road surface. As it could replace the two forces CF and mg these forces are not creating any moment or couple, thus no weight is being transferred from one set of wheels to the other.

Looking again at the piston/crank/connecting rod, Fig. 5.1, the force acting along the connecting rod towards the gudgeon pin is the equilibrant E of the other two forces. Acting in the opposite sense is the resultant force R which, through the effective crankshaft leverage or radius, develops the torque at the crankshaft.

Resultant of two inclined forces

If a body is under the action of two forces acting in different directions they can, when drawn as force vectors, be replaced by a single force vector which is their resultant and is the diagonal of the parallelogram ABCD (Fig. 5.3) drawn from that point.

$$\text{Consider the triangle CBE:} \quad \sin \phi = \frac{CE}{CB}$$

therefore $\quad CE = CB \sin \phi$

$\qquad\qquad = Y \sin \phi$

$\qquad \cos \phi = \dfrac{BE}{CB}$

therefore $\quad BE = CB \cos \phi$

$\qquad\qquad = Y \cos \phi$

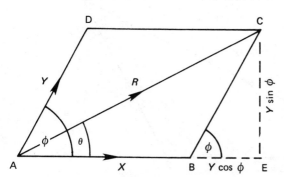

Fig. 5.3 Parallelogram of forces (the parallelogram is ABCD).

Taking the triangle CAE:

$$\tan \theta = \frac{Y \sin \phi}{X \cos \phi} + Y \cos \phi = \frac{Y \sin \phi}{X + Y \cos \phi}$$

then

$$R^2 = (AB + BE)^2 + (CE)^2$$

$$= (X + Y \cos \phi)^2 + (Y \sin \phi)^2$$

and

$$R = \sqrt{[(X + Y \cos \phi)^2 + (Y \sin \phi)^2]}$$

or

$$R = \sqrt{(X^2 + Y^2 + 2X \times Y \cos \phi)}$$

The above formulae apply when the angle between the two forces X and Y is below 90°. For an angle between 90° and 180° (obtuse) cos ϕ becomes negative, and the term $2X \times Y \cos \phi$ becomes negative.

Thus

$$R = \sqrt{(X^2 + Y^2 - 2XY \cos \phi)}$$

and

$$\tan \theta = \frac{Y \sin \phi}{X - Y \cos \phi}$$

Worked example

Consider two forces of 8 kN and 6 kN acting from a point with an angle of 60° between them (see Fig. 5.4). Draw the parallelogram and scale off the resultant force. Calculate the force and find the angle between it and force X.

$$R = \sqrt{[(X + Y \cos \phi)^2 + (Y \sin \phi)^2]}$$

$$= \sqrt{[(8 + 6 \times 0.5)^2 + (6 \times 0.866)^2]}$$

$$= \sqrt{(11^2 + 5.196^2)}$$

$$= 12.165 \text{ kN}$$

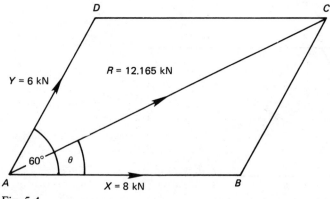

Fig. 5.4

$$\tan \theta = \frac{Y \sin \phi}{X + Y \cos \phi} = \frac{6 \times 0.866}{8 + 6 \times 0.5}$$

$$= 0.4723$$

$$\theta = 25.28°$$

◆◆◆

Polygon of forces

If there are more than three forces acting at a point, but in the same plane, and the body is in equilibrium, then these forces may be represented as force vectors in magnitude and direction when drawn to scale, and the sides will produce a closed polygon (see Fig. 5.5). If the body was not in equilibrium such as with the forces shown in Fig. 5.6 then the closing line will represent the resultant or equilibrant force, depending on the direction shown by the arrowheads.

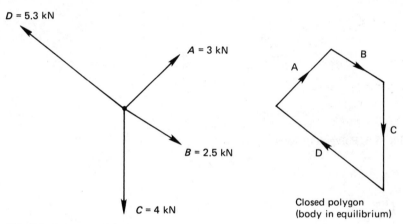

Fig. 5.5 Polygon of forces.

Resolution of forces

If a resultant of two unknown forces was given in both magnitude and direction, and it was required to replace the resultant by the two forces or components (often necessary with problems in statics) this process is termed the resolution of a force into its components.

The resolution can be made by graphical construction of the force vectors drawn to scale in magnitude and direction, or by trigonometry. Consider a force of 60 kN is applied to a body at an angle of 30° to the horizontal. The vertical and horizontal components can be drawn graphically as shown in Fig. 5.7 and the values scaled off, or the solution found by trigonometry.

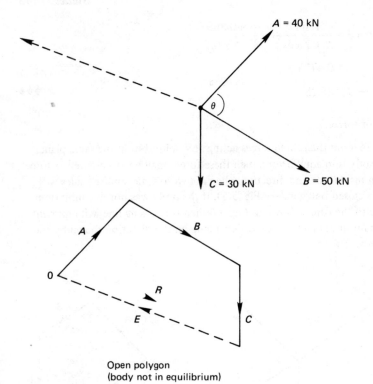

Open polygon
(body not in equilibrium)

Fig. 5.6 Polygon of forces.

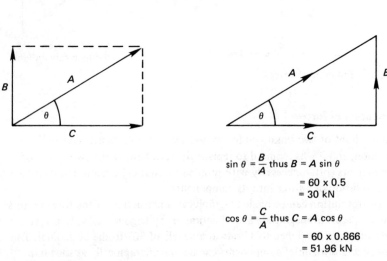

$\sin \theta = \dfrac{B}{A}$ thus $B = A \sin \theta$

$= 60 \times 0.5$

$= 30$ kN

$\cos \theta = \dfrac{C}{A}$ thus $C = A \cos \theta$

$= 60 \times 0.866$

$= 51.96$ kN

Fig. 5.7 Resolution of forces.

5.2 PISTON, CONNECTING ROD AND CYLINDER WALL FORCES

The forces acting upon the piston, connecting rod and the reaction of the cylinder wall were used to illustrate the triangle of forces. Owing to the importance of these forces it is repeated in more detail. The expansion of the burning gases produces a load or force upon the piston crown (F_p). Two resisting forces are introduced, one in the connecting rod (F_c) and the other by the reaction of the cylinder wall (F_w). When the effective crank radius is known, the torque delivered to the crankshaft can be determined.

From the angle between the connecting rod, the cylinder bore axis and the value of one of the forces, the value of the other two forces may be calculated. A simple space diagram, Fig. 5.8(a), and force diagram (b) shows the three forces acting towards the gudgeon pin axis.

$$\sin \theta = \frac{ca}{bc}, \quad \cos \theta = \frac{ab}{bc}, \quad \text{and} \quad \tan \theta = \frac{ca}{ab}.$$

Consider the angle θ and the force on the piston crown F_p are known:

$$\text{thrust in the connecting rod } F_c = bc = \frac{ab}{\cos \theta}$$

$$\text{reaction of cylinder wall } F_w = ca = ab \times \tan \theta$$

If the thrust in the connecting rod is known:

$$\text{reaction of cylinder wall } F_w = ca = bc \sin \theta$$

$$\text{force on piston crown } F_p = ab = bc \cos \theta$$

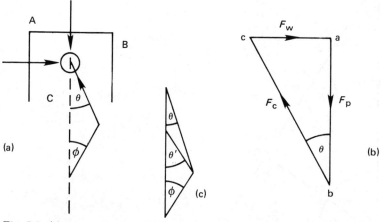

Fig. 5.8 (a) Space diagram, (b) force diagram, (c) effect of shorter connecting rod.

If the reaction of cylinder wall is known:

$$\text{force on piston crown } F_p = ab = \frac{ca}{\tan \theta}$$

$$\text{Thrust in connecting rod } F_c = bc = \frac{ca}{\sin \theta}$$

It will be seen from the diagram, Fig. 5.8(c), that for the same crankshaft angle ϕ a shorter connecting rod would increase the angularity of the connecting rod from θ to θ' in relation to the cylinder bore axis. From the force diagram the vector ca would be greater, thus the thrust between piston and skirt would be higher. An increase in the crank throw or engine stroke for a given connecting rod length would have a similar effect. Either of the changes would modify the piston movement and acceleration.

5.3 TORQUE AT THE CRANKSHAFT

The torque at the crankshaft is the product of the force or thrust produced by the connecting rod force (F_c) acting on the effective crank radius r. Thus

$$\text{torque} = T \text{ (N m)} = F_c \times r$$

Let angle ABC in Fig. 5.9 = X, and angle CBD = Y, therefore

$$\theta + \phi + X = 180°$$

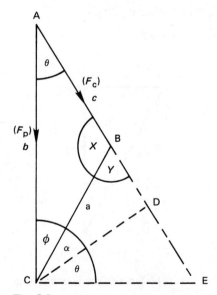

Fig. 5.9

and $\qquad\qquad X + Y = 180°$

thus $\qquad\quad \theta + \phi + X = X + Y$

and $\qquad \theta + \phi + X - X = Y$

therefore $\qquad\qquad X = 180° - (\theta + \phi)$

$\qquad\qquad$ angle CBD $= Y = \theta + \phi$

and $\qquad\quad \sin(\theta + \phi) = \dfrac{CD}{BC}$

thus $\qquad\quad$ BC $\sin(\theta + \phi)$ = CD

hence torque at the crankshaft T (N m) $= F_c \times r = F_c \times$ CD

angle ACD $= 90° - \theta$, and angle BCD $= (90° - \theta) - \phi = \alpha$

and length CD (effective crank leverage) $= \dfrac{BC}{\cos \alpha}$

Note: The sine rule may be used to determine some unknown angle, force or measurement:

$$\frac{a}{\sin A} = \frac{b}{\sin B} = \frac{c}{\sin C}$$

Crankshaft torque may also be found by calculating the length of a perpendicular to AC at C namely CE which cuts the produced line ABD.

$\qquad\qquad$ angle DAC = angle DCE = angle θ

$$\cos \theta = \frac{CD}{CE} \text{ and CE} = \frac{CD}{\cos \theta}$$

hence crankshaft torque T (N m) $= F_c \times$ CD $= F_p \times$ CE

$$= \frac{F_p \times CD}{\cos \theta}$$

Worked examples

Reactions to force on engine piston

A six cylinder two-stroke oil engine develops 89.52 kW power at a mean piston speed of 365.78 m/min giving an engine speed of 2000 rev/min. A bmep of 689.5 kN/m² is available. If the pressure in the engine cylinder is 58.6 kN/m² when the connecting rod is displaced 20° from the cylinder bore axis, what is the force along the connecting rod and the reaction to the piston thrust at the cylinder walls?

$$\text{brake power } P_b = \frac{\text{bmep} \times LAn \times N}{60}$$

and
$$LAn \text{ (m}^3) = \frac{P_b \times 60}{\text{bmep} \times N}$$

$$= \frac{89.5 \times 10^3 \times 60}{689.5 \times 10^3 \times 2000}$$

$$= 0.003\ 894 \text{ m}^3$$

mean piston speed (m/min) $= S = 2LN$

and
$$L = \frac{S}{2N} = \frac{365.78}{2 \times 2000}$$

$$= 0.0914 \text{ m}$$

area of a piston (m^2) $= A = \dfrac{\text{m}^3}{Ln} = \dfrac{0.003\ 894}{0.0914 \times 6} = 0.007 \text{ m}^2$

force on piston crown F_p = pressure (kN/m^2) $\times$ piston crown area (m^2)

$$= 58.6 \times 10^3 \times 0.007 \text{ N}$$

$$= 410.2 \text{ N}$$

Reaction at con-rod (see Fig. 5.8):

$$\cos \theta = \frac{ab}{bc} \text{ thus bc} = \frac{ab}{\cos \theta} = \frac{410.2}{0.939\ 7} = 436.5 \text{ N}$$

Reaction at cylinder wall:

$$\tan \theta = \frac{ca}{ab}$$

thus
$$ca = \tan \theta \times ab = 0.364 \times 410.2 = 149.3 \text{ N}$$

force on piston crown = 410.2 N

force along con-rod   = 436.5 N

reaction at cylinder wall = 149.3 N   ◆◆◆

Torque at the crankshaft

If the force acting along the connecting rod was 2.6 kN and the crankshaft is at the angle of 25° from TDC, determine the torque at the crankshaft in N m if the engine stroke was 88 mm and the connecting rod lies 6° from the cylinder bore axis (Refer to Fig. 5.9).

$$\text{crank throw or radius} = \frac{L}{2} = \frac{88}{2 \times 10^3} = 0.044 \text{ m} = \text{BC}$$

$$\text{effective crank leverage} = \text{CD} = \text{BC} \times \sin(\theta + \phi)$$

$$= 0.044 \times \sin(6° + 25°)$$

$$= 0.044 \times 0.515$$

$$= 0.0226 \text{ m}$$

$$\text{torque at crankshaft} = \text{force con-rod} \times \text{CD}$$

$$= 2.6 \times 0.0226$$

$$= 0.058 \ 76 \text{ kN m or } 58.76 \text{ N m torque}$$

◆◆◆

5.4 PISTON DISPLACEMENT

It is established in Part 2 that piston movement is not uniform. The shorter the connecting rod for a given stroke or the longer the stroke for a given connecting rod length, the greater the variation in piston movement and acceleration. It is sometimes necessary to know the position of the piston relative to the crankshaft angle. The method and formulae may be determined with the aid of a simple diagram (see Fig. 5.10).

$$X = r \sin \phi, \text{ and } X = L \sin \theta$$

thus $r \sin \phi = L \sin \theta$

piston displacement $= S$

$$= (L + r) - (a + b)$$

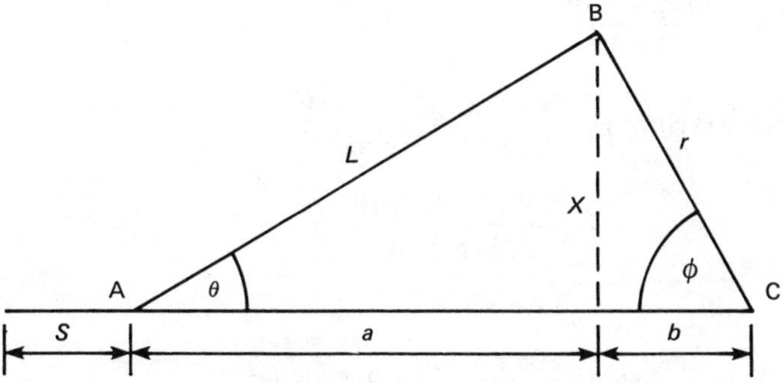

Fig. 5.10 Piston displacement.

and $a = L \cos \theta$, $b = r \cos \phi$

thus $a + b = (L \cos \theta + r \cos \phi)$

therefore $S = (L + r) - (L \cos \theta + r \cos \phi)$

Worked examples

An engine having a stroke of 60 mm with the crankshaft $40°$ from top dead centre has a connecting rod angularity of $12°$ in relation to the cylinder bore axis. How far has the piston moved from TDC? From Fig. 5.10:

$$a = L \cos \theta \text{ and } b = r \cos \phi$$

thus $$L = \frac{r \cos \phi}{\cos \theta}$$

$$= \frac{30 \times 0.766}{0.9781}$$

$$= 23.49 \text{ mm}$$

$$S = L + r - (L \cos \theta + r \cos \phi)$$

$$= 23.49 + 30 - (23.49 \times 0.9781 + 30 \times 0.766)$$

$$= 7.53 \text{ mm} \qquad\qquad \blacklozenge\blacklozenge\blacklozenge$$

The capacity of a four cylinder four-stroke engine is 2025 cm^3. It produces a maximum power of 70.8 kW at 5200 rev/min, and the maximum bmep figure is 20% greater than the bmep at maximum power. The engine cylinder bore is 98 mm and stroke 66 mm. Calculate the average thrust between piston skirt and cylinder wall at maximum bmep, and the thrust in the connecting rod when displaced $12°$ from the cylinder bore axis.

$$kW = \frac{bmep \times LAnN}{2 \times 60}$$

therefore $$bmep \ (kN/m^2) = \frac{kW \times 2 \times 60}{LAn \times N}$$

$$= \frac{70.8 \times 2 \times 60 \times 10^6}{2025 \times 5200}$$

$$= 806.8 \text{ kN/m}^2$$

$$\text{maximum bmep} = \frac{806.8 \times 120}{100} = 968 \text{ kN/m}^2$$

force on piston crown (average) = bmep x area

$$= \frac{968 \times \pi \times 0.098^2}{4}$$

$$= 7.3 \text{ kN}$$

From Fig. 5.8:

thrust at cylinder wall = ca = ab tan θ

$$= 7.3 \times 0.2126$$

$$= 1.55 \text{ kN}$$

force in connecting rod = bc = $\dfrac{ab}{\cos \theta} = \dfrac{7.3}{0.9781} = 7.46 \text{ kN}$

◆◆◆

5.5 WHEEL BALANCE

Unbalance is divided into two forms: static and dynamic.

Static unbalance

Consider a wheel which has been jacked up and is free-running. The wheel will come to rest with the heavier part of the wheel and tyre at the bottom due to the gravitational force. This force is expressed as mass x distance from the wheel axis or the mass-moment. When the wheel is rotating an out-of-balance force exists and its value will equal mV^2/r or $mr\omega^2$. This force, unless balanced, will cause wheel hop or patter.

Dynamic unbalance

Dynamic unbalance is made up of a rotating couple, sometimes termed *couple unbalance*. If an excess mass exists on one side of the wheel and tyre centre, then, on rotation, a centrifugal or unbalance force is set up which will attempt to move the wheel inwards when at the top, and outwards when at the bottom. It is corrected by adding a mass opposite to the unbalanced mass, but on the other side of the wheel. Fig. 5.11(a) to (f) shows the unbalanced couples and their correction.

(a) This wheel without any balance weight would not be in static balance, and on the road this would cause wheel hop due to the unbalanced force CF (centrifugal force). The balance weight so fitted would give static balance, but on rotation the wheel would flap or wobble about its axis owing to the reversing couple CF x X N m. The dotted arrows show the effect when the wheel has moved through 180°.

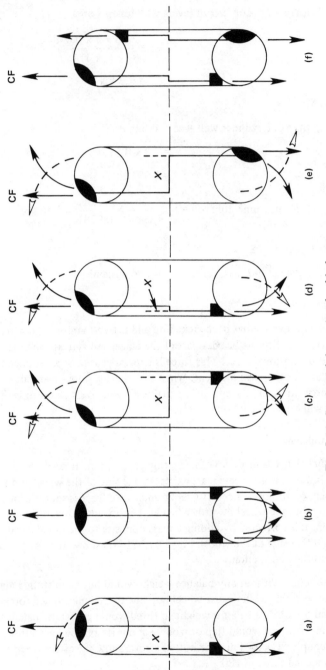

Fig. 5.11 Static and dynamic wheel balance.

(b) The wheel of (a) has now been balanced by two weights, each half the value of the previous single weight. The couples created by the weights cancel each other and the wheel will be in both static and dynamic balance.

(c) This wheel has been balanced statically, but there remains a large reversing unbalanced couple CF x X N m, and this would create bad wheel wobble or shimmy.

(d) The wheel of (c) has now been balanced by the addition of a single weight which may still leave a small reversing couple due to the slight displacement of the centre of gravity of the unbalanced tyre mass and that of the balance weight.

(e) This wheel may be in static balance but would tend to shimmy on rotation due to the reversing unbalanced couple CF x X N m.

(f) The wheel of (e) is now balanced by the addition of two weights fitted opposite each other, but at either side of the wheel rim.

Worked examples

Wheel balancing

The centre of gravity of a tyre and wheel is 3 mm from the axis of rotation. The mass of the complete wheel is 17 kg, and its overall diameter 0.625 m. Determine the value of the out-of-balance force and the amount of balance mass to be applied at the wheel rim, which is 355 mm in diameter. The vehicle's speed is 72 km/h.

$$m/s = \frac{km/h}{3.6} = \frac{72}{3.6} = 20 \text{ m/s}$$

$$\text{angular velocity of wheel} = \frac{v}{r} = \frac{20}{0.3125} = 64 \text{ rad/s}$$

$$\text{out-of-balance force} = CF = mr\omega^2$$

$$= 17 \times 0.003 \times 64^2$$

$$= 208.9 \text{ N}$$

CF of balance mass must equal CF of unbalanced mass

$$mr\omega^2 = 208.9$$

therefore
$$m = \frac{208.9}{0.1775 \times 64^2}$$

$$= 0.2873 \text{ kg balance mass required (287 g)} \qquad \blacklozenge\blacklozenge\blacklozenge$$

A tyre having a section height of 13.5 cm is fitted to a wheel rim 0.5512 m in diameter. An unbalanced mass of rubber of 0.22 kg is situated at the centre of the tyre tread. If the tyre is running at 83 km/h, what is the value of the out-of-balance force and what values of balance weights are to be applied to each side of the wheel rim to balance the wheel statically and dynamically?

$$83 \text{ km/h} = \frac{83}{3.6} = 23 \text{ m/s}$$

$$\text{radius of complete wheel} = \frac{\text{tyre section height} \times 2 + \text{rim diameter}}{2}$$

$$= \frac{0.135 \times 2 + 0.5512}{2} = 0.4106 \text{ m}$$

$$\text{angular velocity of wheel (rad/s)} = \frac{v}{r} = \frac{23}{0.4106} = 56 \text{ rad/s}$$

$$\text{out-of-balance force CF} = mr\omega^2 = 0.22 \times 0.4106 \times 56^2$$

$$= 283.28 \text{ N}$$

CF of balance mass equals CF of unbalanced mass

$$mr\omega^2 = 283.28$$

therefore

$$m = \frac{283.28}{0.2756 \times 56^2}$$

$$= 0.3278 \text{ kg (328 g)}$$

Thus 328 g is divided equally and so a balance mass of 164 g is placed on each side of the wheel rim opposite the unbalanced mass of rubber.   ♦♦♦

Triangle of forces, etc.
A diagram of a wall crane is shown Fig. 5.12. ab represents the tie and ca the jib. If the angle between the jib and tie is 35° and the mass lifted at the end of the jib is 2.6 tonne, what forces are there in the jib and tie and state which is in tension and which in compression.

From triangle of forces, Fig. 5.12:

$$\sin \theta = \frac{bc}{ab}$$

thus

$$ab = \frac{bc}{\sin \theta} = \frac{2.6 \times 10^3 \times 9.81}{0.5735}$$

$$= 44\,474 \text{ N or } 44.474 \text{ kN}$$

$$\tan \theta = \frac{bc}{ca}$$

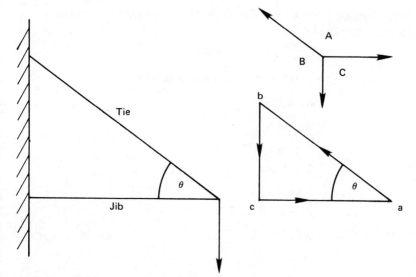

Fig. 5.12 Wall crane.

thus $\qquad ca = \dfrac{bc}{\tan \theta} = \dfrac{25\ 506}{0.7002} = 36.426$ kN

The jib is in compression and the tie in tension. ◆◆◆

Two forces acting from the same point are 130° apart as shown in Fig. 5.13.

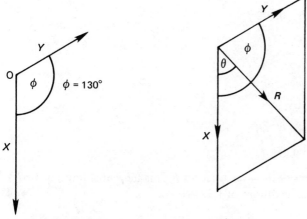

Fig. 5.13 Two inclined forces.

Their values are $Y = 6$ kN and $X = 10$ kN. Determine their resultant and direction from the force X.

$$R = \sqrt{(X^2 + Y^2 - 2XY \cos \phi)}$$
$$= \sqrt{(10^2 + 6^2 - 2 \times 10 \times 6 \times 0.6427)}$$
$$= \sqrt{(58.876)}$$
$$= 7.673 \text{ kN}$$

$$\tan \theta = \frac{Y \sin \phi}{X - Y \cos \phi}$$
$$= \frac{6 \times 0.766}{10 - 6 \times 0.6427}$$
$$= 0.748$$
$$= 36.8°$$

The resultant force is 7.673 kN acting at 36.8° from position of force X. ◆◆◆

A 2.6 kN force is acting on the crankpin at an angle of 40° between it and the crank throw. Determine the tangential force acting on the crankpin and the force in the crankshaft webs by resolving the given force into its components. From Fig. 5.14:

$$\sin \theta = \frac{bc}{ac}$$

thus $bc = ac \sin \theta$
$$= 2.6 \times 0.642 \, 7$$
$$= 1.67 \text{ kN}$$

$$\cos \theta = \frac{ab}{ac}$$

thus $ab = ac \cos \theta$
$$= 2.6 \times 0.766$$
$$= 1.99 \text{ kN}$$

The two components of the given force are F_t, the tangential force, of 1.67 kN and force F_r in crank throw of 1.99 kN. ◆◆◆

Two balance weights acting in the same plane are attached to a roadwheel

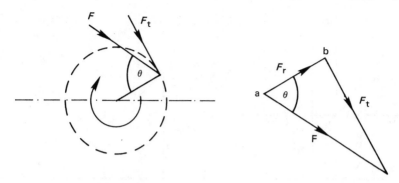

Fig. 5.14 Forces acting on a crankpin.

for static balance and are 130° apart (Fig. 5.16). Weight Y is 0.4 N and X 0.56 N. Determine the value of a single weight which will replace weights X and Y and its relative position to weight X.

From parallelogram Fig. 5.3:

$$R = \sqrt{(X^2 + Y^2 - 2\,XY \cos \phi)}$$
$$= \sqrt{(0.56^2 + 0.4^2 - 2 \times 0.56 \times 0.4 \times 0.6427}$$
$$= \sqrt{(0.1856)}$$
$$= 0.43 \text{ N and } \frac{0.43 \times 10^3}{9.81} = 43.84 \text{ g.}$$

$$\tan \theta = \frac{Y \sin \phi}{X - Y \cos \theta}$$

$$= \frac{0.4 \times 0.766}{0.56 - 0.4 \times 0.6427}$$

$$= \frac{0.3064}{0.3029}$$

$$= 45.33°$$

The value of the single replacement weight is 0.43 N (43.83 g) placed 45.33° from weight X. ◆◆◆

A roadwheel has a loading normal to the road surface of 2.8 kN. The centrifugal force due to cornering is 1.76 kN. Determine the equilibrant force on the wheel bearing and its direction in relation to the wheel axis.

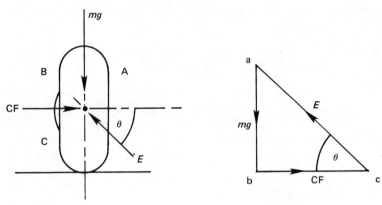

Fig. 5.15

From the diagrams in Fig. 5.15

$$\tan \theta = \frac{ab}{bc} = \frac{mg}{CF} = \frac{2.8}{1.76}, \theta = 57.84°$$

$$\sin \theta = \frac{ab}{ca} = \frac{mg}{E}$$

thus

$$E = \frac{mg}{\sin \theta} = \frac{2.8}{0.8465}$$

$$= 3.3 \text{ kN}$$

◆◆◆

EXERCISES 5.1

Triangle of forces, etc. (E13)

1. A vehicle of 6 tonnes mass is held on a gradient of 30° by a steel rope and tractor. Calculate the tension in the tow rope and the reaction to the vehicle normal to the road surface. Neglect rolling resistance.

2. A vehicle having a mass of 2.2 Mg is negotiating a 12° banked road bend. If there is no tendency to slide, what is the value of the resultant force, and the centrifugal force?

3. A crate weighing 10.6 kN is held at rest on a ramp having an angle of 15°. What force is required to hold the crate, neglecting any friction, and what value has the resultant force?

4. Four forces of 5 kN, 7 kN, 3 kN and 6 kN are displaced at angles of 100°,

60° and 55°, respectively. Find the resultant force and its direction relative to the 3 kN force.

5. The tangential force acting upon a crankpin is 3.2 kN and the force in the crank throw 1.86 kN. Find the value of the resultant of these two forces.

6. Three wire cables are attached to the same point on a vehicle which has to be recovered from a ditch. The cable directions and tensions are 2.5 kN due west, 2.25 kN due north, and 2 kN south-west. By drawing find the magnitude and direction of a fourth cable attached to the same point which will hold the vehicle in a state of equilibrium.

7. The force pressing a roadwheel to the road surface is 1.2 kN and the lateral force due to cornering is 0.7 kN. Determine the resultant force and its direction in relation to the road surface.

8. The angle between the frictional force of 650 N acting at a brake pad and the force 1720 N pressing the pad to the disc is 86°. Determine the resultant of these two forces and the angle it makes with each force.

9. Two balance masses X and Y as shown in Fig. 5.16 are acting in the same plane but 137° apart. The masses are X 25 g and Y 46 g. Determine the value of a single mass to replace X and Y, and its relative angle to X. What force does this mass produce at a roadwheel speed of 200 rev/min if it lies 0.6 m from the wheel axis?

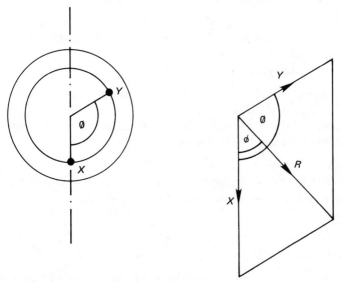

Fig. 5.16 Static wheel balance. Question 9.

10. The frictional force between a brake pad and disc is 0.8 kN. The force acting normally between pad and disc is 2.6 kN. Calculate the resultant of these forces and its direction relative to the frictional force.

11. The resultant force between a brake lining and brake drum and the tangential frictional force, is 1.6 kN. The angle between the resultant force and frictional force is 26°. Determine the value of the two components.

12. Two balance masses in the same plane, balance a wheel statically. Mass A of 30 g is 15° from the tube valve and mass B of 55 g 76° from A. Find the value of a mass, and its position, which can replace masses A and B.

13. A recovery vehicle is winching a vehicle out of mud. The winch rope is applying a force of 5 kN applied at an angle of 17° to the centre line of the stuck vehicle. Calculate the force causing the vehicle to move in the direction of its axis, and the force tending to slide the vehicle at right angles to its towed path.

14. A single throw crankshaft of a motorcycle engine has a stroke of 86 mm. The big-end journal of 0.3 kg mass is to be balanced at a radius of 30 mm in the form of two equal masses applied opposite the journal. Find the value of these masses and the value of the unbalanced force at 5800 rev/min.

15. Two forces 38° apart are acting at the same point on a chassis member. The horizontal force is 3 kN and the other 2.5 kN. Determine the value of the resultant force and its direction in relation to the horizontal force.

16. The force on a piston is 2 kN and the connecting rod is making an angle of 10° to the cylinder axis. Friction between piston and cylinder wall accounts for 35 N of the effective force. Calculate the force along the connecting rod and the reaction of the cylinder wall on the piston.

17. When an engine crankshaft has moved through an angle of 19° from TDC, the connecting rod is displaced 4° 30′ from the cylinder axis and the force on the piston crown is 792 kN. The engine stroke is 92 mm. Calculate the torque being delivered to the crankshaft at this precise moment.

18. The force acting upon the engine piston is 860 kN when the crankshaft has moved 17° from TDC, which displaces the connecting rod 3° from the cylinder bore axis. The engine stroke is 115 mm. Calculate the torque delivered to the crankshaft.

5.6 PRINCIPLE OF MOMENTS (E14)

The principle of moments is so important that it is given as a reminder and is as follows:

If any number of forces, acting in one plane, on a body free to rotate about some fixed point produce equilibrium, then the sum of the moments of the clockwise effect forces is equal to the sum of the moments of the anti-clockwise effect forces, when the moments are taken about a single fixed point or fulcrum.

Worked examples

Some worked examples covering straight and bell-cranked levers and the reaction of beam supports.

Straight levers
Consider the lever in Fig. 5.17. From the diagram determine the effort required to produce equilibrium.

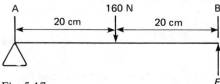

Fig. 5.17

Taking moments about the fulcrum:

clockwise (CW) moments = anti-clockwise (ACW) moments

$$160 \times 20 = E \times 40$$

therefore $\dfrac{160 \times 20}{40} = 80 \text{ N} = E$ ◆◆◆

Determine the effort E N to produce a state of equilibrium, and the upward thrust at the fulcrum R of the loaded beam in Fig. 5.18.

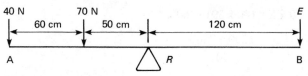

Fig. 5.18

Taking moments about R:

CW moments = ACW moments

$$E \times 120 = (70 \times 50) + (40 \times 110)$$

therefore E (N) $= \dfrac{3500 + 4400}{120}$

$= 65.83$ N

force at fulcrum = algebraic sum of all forces operating on lever

$= 40 + 70 + 65.83$

$= 175.83$ N

or by taking moments about some point:

taking moments about point A:

CW moments = ACW moments

$(65.83 \times 230) + (70 \times 60) = R \times 110$

$\dfrac{15\ 140.9 + 4200}{110} = 175.83$ N   ◆◆◆

A lever has two forces applied to it (Fig. 5.19). At what distance must the 30 N force be applied to create equilibrium?

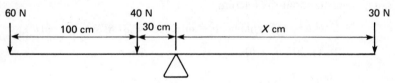

Fig. 5.19

Taking moments about the fulcrum:

CW moments = ACW moments

$30 \times X = (40 \times 30) + (60 \times 130)$

and $X = \dfrac{1200 + 7800}{30}$

$= 300$ cm   ◆◆◆

A single cylinder crankshaft has a mass of 4.4 kg. The centre of gravity of the shaft lies 4.4 cm from the shaft axis. What mass must be placed opposite the crank throw at 7.4 cm from the shaft axis to balance the whole shaft (Fig. 5.20)?

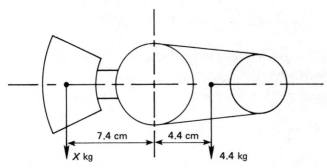

Fig. 5.20

Mass moments may be used.

$$4.4 \times 4.4 = X \text{ kg} \times 7.4$$

therefore $\dfrac{4.4 \times 4.4}{7.4} = 2.616 \text{ kg}$

Note: If this balance mass was equally divided and placed each side of the main journal, the crankshaft would be in balance both statically and dynamically. ◆◆◆

Bell-cranked levers

The principle of moments is used with bell-cranked and curved levers providing the pivot point is established, and all the distances are measured or calculated at right angles to the line of action of the forces.

Worked examples

Consider the lever in Fig. 5.21. If the effort was acting in the direction E_1

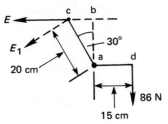

Fig. 5.21

then:

$$\text{CW moments} = \text{ACW moments}$$

$$86 \times 15 = E_1 \times 20$$

and $\dfrac{86 \times 15}{20} = 64.5 \text{ N} = E$

but the actual effort E is acting through the perpendicular distance ab, and this distance must be calculated.

angle bac = 30°

$\cos 30° = \dfrac{ab}{ac}$

and   ab = ac cos 30°

= 20 x 0.866

= 17.32 cm

therefore   86 x 15 = E x 17.32

and $\dfrac{86 \times 15}{17.32} = 74.48 \text{ N}$

♦♦♦

A two bell-crank lever system is shown in Fig. 5.22. The length of the levers are as follows:

lever ab = 14 cm; bc = 37 cm; de = 27 cm; ef = 18 cm. Determine the effort E N required to balance the force of 190 N operating on bell-crank lever A.

length of leverage ge:

$\cos 30° = \dfrac{ge}{ef}$

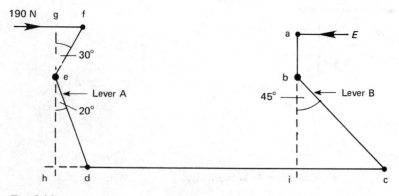

Fig. 5.22

and   ge = ef cos 30°

            = 18 x 0.866

            = 15.58 cm

length of leverage bi:

$$\cos 45° = \frac{hi}{bc}$$

and   bi = bc cos 45°

            = 37 x 0.707

            = 26.12 cm

length of leverage eh:

$$\cos 20° = \frac{eh}{de}$$

and   eh = de cos 20°

            = 27 x 0.9396

            = 25.37 cm

Taking moments about pivot e:

            190 x ge   = F x eh

            190 x 15.58 = F x 25.37

thus $\dfrac{190 \times 15.58}{25.37}$ = 116.74 N

Taking moments about pivot b:

            E x ab   = F x bi

            E x 14   = 116.74 x 26.12

thus E $= \dfrac{116.74 \times 26.12}{14}$

            = 217.8 N

Note: Connecting link cd is in tension.

♦♦♦

5.7 CENTRE OF GRAVITY

All pieces of matter consist of large numbers of molecules, each of which is a mass and subjected to the pull of gravity. All these forces are considered as being parallel to each other, and their resultant is the weight of the body. This acts through some point of the body. Thus the centre of gravity of a body is the point at which all forces or the weight of body is taken to act.

Equilibrium

Consider a block of steel (Fig. 5.23) on a bench. In position (a) the block is in equilibrium and is considered to be in a stable condition. Its weight acting downwards is supported by the reaction of the bench. If the block is tilted as in (b) the block is acted upon by two forces, the reaction at the point of contact x and the weight W acting through the centre of gravity CG which will return the block to its stable position. If the block was tilted to a position (c) where W and the reaction R are equal and opposite, this would be considered as unstable equilibrium, and any further tilt would result in the force W acting to the left of the pivot point x (Fig. 5.23(d)). The block would then topple over. It may be noted that as the block is tilted from position (a) to position (c) the point of CG is rising and stable conditions exist, but beyond position (c) the CG begins to lower and unstable conditions exist.

To determine the position of a vehicle's centre of gravity Method 1

Position of CG on wheelbase (Fig. 5.24)

The weight of the vehicle must be known, and also the load carried by the front or rear wheels on a level surface. A vehicle weighbridge can be used. Moments can then be taken about the front or rear wheels.

Taking moments about R_R:

$$R_F \times b = W_t \times y \text{ and } \frac{R_F \times b}{W_t} = y$$

therefore $x = b - y$

Position of CG on track (Fig. 5.25)

The loadings on the nearside (R_N) or offside wheels (R_O) must be known, then moments are taken about R_N or R_O.

Taking moments about the offside wheels R_O (Fig. 5.25):

$$R_N \times t = W_t \times y$$

then $\dfrac{R_N \times t}{W_t} = y$

and $t - y = x$

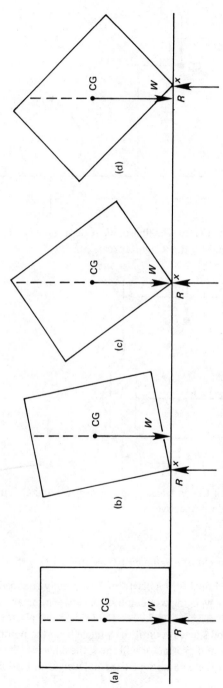

Fig. 5.23 Equilibrium considerations for a block of steel on a bench.

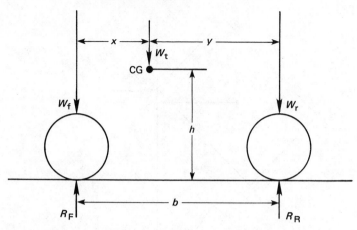

Fig. 5.24 Position of CG on wheelbase. W_t is the total weight, W_f the weight at front and W_r the weight at rear.

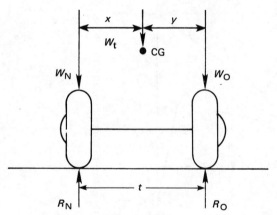

Fig. 5.25 Position of CG on track. The subscripts N and O denote nearside and offside, respectively.

To determine the height of a vehicle's CG: Method 1 (Fig. 5.26)

The vehicle is placed on a tilting platform, and usually the road springs are made inoperative by wedging wooden blocks between the axles and the chassis. Ropes or chains are attached to the vehicle and platform for safety. The platform is tilted sideways until the vehicle is on the point of overturning sideways. A pointer and protractor will show the angle of tilt, or a clinometer may be used. Under these conditions the total weight or load line (W_t) will

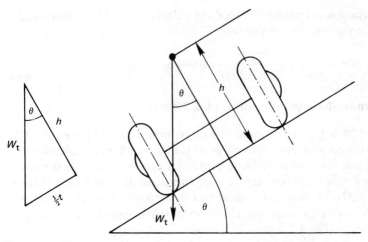

Fig. 5.26 Determination of the height of a vehicle's CG. Method 1.

be passing through the centre of the loaded wheels contact area. If the CG is considered to be in the centre of the vehicle's track, therefore:

$$\tan \theta = \frac{1/2t}{h}$$

therefore $\quad h = \dfrac{1/2t}{\tan \theta}$ or $\dfrac{t}{2 \tan \theta}$

If CG is not in the centre of the track then the line of the CG and the outer or inner wheels distance will be substituted for $1/2t$.

Worked example

To determine the position of a vehicle's CG
A vehicle having a total weight of 10 600 N carries 60% on its front wheels when on a level surface. The wheelbase is 3 m and track 1.5 m. Calculate the position of the CG relative to the rear wheels.

$$0.6 \text{ of } 10\ 600 = 6360 \text{ N}$$

$$R_F \times b = W_t \times y$$

therefore $\quad y = \dfrac{R_F \times b}{W_t} = \dfrac{6360 \times 3}{10\ 600}$

$$= 1.8 \text{ m}$$

then $\quad b - y = x, \quad 3 - 1.8 = 1.2 \text{ m}$

If this vehicle is at a point of balance when tilted through 42°, at what height lies the centre from the road surface?

$$h = \frac{t}{2 \tan \theta} = \frac{1.8}{2 \times 0.9004} = 0.999 \text{ m}$$

◆◆◆

To determine the height of a vehicle's CG. Method 2

This method may be a little more difficult to understand, but if the rule of moments (force x perpendicular distance) is always applied, the calculations are quite easy. In practice no tilting platform is necessary, and only the axle loads are weighed while one pair of wheels are raised up quite a small distance h_1 (Fig. 5.27). The angle is measured by a clinometer or protractor, and then moments may be taken making sure the above rule is applied. Taking moments about point A (Fig. 5.27):

$$F_1(y_1 + x_1) = W_t \times y_1$$

now $y_1 + x_1 = b \cos \theta$

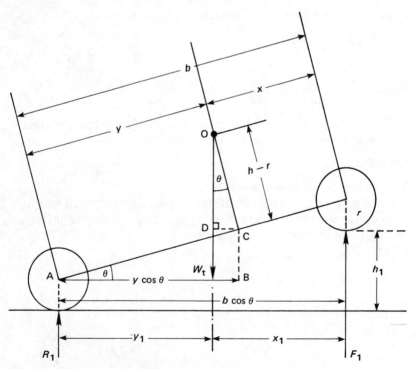

Fig. 5.27 Determination of the height of a vehicle's CG. Method 2.

and $\quad\quad y_1 = \text{Ab} - \text{CD} = y \cos \theta - (h - r) \sin \theta \quad$ (r is wheel radius)

therefore $\quad F_1 \times b \cos \theta = W_t \times y \cos \theta - W_t(h - r) \sin \theta$

and $\quad\quad W_t(h - r) \sin \theta = W_t y \cos \theta - F_1 b \cos \theta$

therefore $\quad (h - r) = \dfrac{W_t y \cos \theta - F_1 b \cos \theta}{W_t \sin \theta}$

If masses are given they can be used instead of weights, i.e. mass moments.

Worked example

A vehicle having a mass of 2000 kg has a wheelbase of 2.44 m and its centre of gravity lies 1.52 m from the rear axle. The front end of the vehicle is lifted 35 cm and gives a mass reading of 1150 kg. The wheel radius is 30.5 cm. Determine the height of the CG.

In this case mass moments will be taken about the rear wheels.

$$\sin \theta = \frac{h_1}{b} = \frac{0.35}{2.44} = 8.247°$$

$$\cos \theta = 0.9896 \text{ and } \sin \theta = 0.1434$$

$$h - r = \frac{m \cos \theta - F_1 b \cos \theta}{m \sin \theta}$$

$$= \frac{2000 \times 1.52 \times 0.9896 - 1150 \times 2.44 \times 0.9896}{2000 \times 0.1434}$$

$$h - r = \frac{3008 - 2776}{286.8}$$

$$= 0.8089 \text{ m}$$

thus $\quad\quad h = (h - r) + r$

$$= 0.8089 + 0.305$$

$$= 1.114 \text{ m} \quad\quad\quad\quad\quad \blacklozenge\blacklozenge\blacklozenge$$

Centre of gravity of thin plates and solid components

Thin plates

The centre of gravity or centroid of thin plates (termed laminae) can be determined by finding the centre of area of the figure. If the plate is a symmetrical rectangle, square, circular or elliptical shape the centre of area may be found as shown in the diagrams in Fig. 5.28.

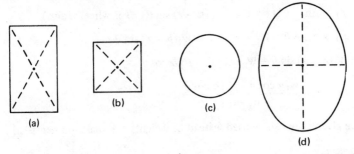

Fig. 5.28 Laminae shapes: (a) symmetrical rectangle, (b) square, (c) circle and (d) ellipse.

The centroid of an irregular shaped plate may be found by experiment. This consists of suspending the plate from two different points (more if necessary) and suspending a weighted line (plumb line) from the points and marking their direction on the plate. The intersection of the lines is the centre of area or gravity (see Fig. 5.29).

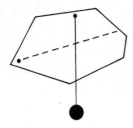

Fig. 5.29 CG of an irregularly-shaped thin plate.

Solid components

The centre of gravity of solid components may be determined by the principle of moments. Consider the machined shaft in Fig. 5.30. The centre of gravity of shaft A and B can be considered to lie on the axis xx and exactly at the linear centre of each shaft section. The weight of the sections A and B would be proportional to their volumes. Thus

$$\text{volume of shaft A} = V_a = \frac{\pi d^2}{4} \times L_a$$

$$= \frac{\pi \times 0.4^2}{4} \times 0.8 = 0.1 \text{ m}^3$$

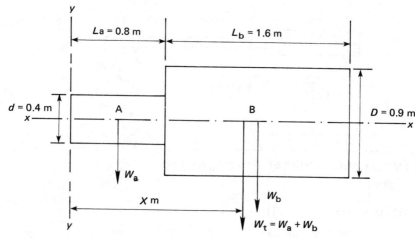

Fig. 5.30 Determination of CG for solid components.

volume of shaft B $= V_b = \dfrac{\pi D^2}{4} \times L_b$

$= \dfrac{\pi \times 0.9^2}{4} \times 1.6 = 1.0178 \text{ m}^3$

Taking moments about the vertical axis yy:

$$V_a \times 1/2 L_a + V_b \times (1/2 L_b + L_a) = (V_a + V_b) \times X$$

therefore $\dfrac{V_a \times 1/2 L_a + V_b \times (1/2 L_b + L_a)}{(V_a + V_b)} = X \text{ m}$

thus $\dfrac{0.1 \times 0.4 + 1.0178 \times 1.6}{1.1178} = 1.493 \text{ m}$

Thus the centre of gravity of the shaft component lies 1.493 m from the outer end of shaft section A.

With components such as connecting rods the centre of gravity may be found by balancing the rod on a knife edge or using the principle of moments. In the latter case the weight of one end of the rod is required while the other end is supported at its centre on a knife edge (see Fig. 5.31).

If $\quad W_t$ = total weight of the connecting rod

$\quad W_s$ = the weight at the small end

$\quad W_b$ = the weight at the big end

$\quad L$ = length between big and small end centres

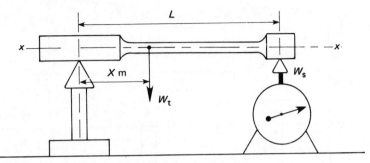

Fig. 5.31 Determination of connecting rod CG.

Taking moments (Fig. 5.31):

$$W_t \times X = W_s \times L$$

Worked example

A connecting rod has a total weight of 3.2 kg and a length between big and small-end centres of 26 cm. When supported on a knife edge at the big-end centre the small-end spring balance reading was 1.3 kg. Calculate the position of the rod's centre of gravity.

$$W_t \times X = W_s \times L$$

and $\quad X \text{ cm} = \dfrac{W_s \times L}{W_t} = \dfrac{1.3 \times 26}{3.2} = 10.56 \text{ cm}$

The centre of gravity of the connecting rod lies 10.56 cm from the big end centre and $26 - 10.56 = 15.44$ cm from the centre of the small end.

The above principles may be employed to determine the centre of gravity of other components.

◆◆◆

EXERCISES 5.2

Moments and centre of gravity (E14)

1. The centre of gravity of a single cylinder engine crankshaft having a mass of 5.6 kg acts at a distance of 5.2 cm from the shaft axis. At what radius must the balance mass of 2.6 kg be placed to counterbalance the crankpin?

2. A vehicle having a total mass of 2.5 tonne carries 58% on the front wheels when the vehicle is on a level surface. The wheelbase is 3.2 m and track 1.6 m. Find the position of the centre of gravity relative to the rear axle and its

height above the road surface if the point of balance on tilt test is at an angle of 46°.

3. A vehicle of total mass 5.6 tonne has a wheelbase of 4.3 m. On a level surface the centre of gravity lies 1.85 m from the rear axle at a height of 1.6 m. Determine the front and rear wheel reactions and the overturning angle if the centre of gravity is in the centre of the 2.2 m track.

4. Consider the machined shaft in Fig. 5.30 with the following dimensions: $d = 0.3$ m; $D = 0.7$ m, $L_a = 0.65$ m; $L_b = 1.2$ m. Determine the centre of gravity of the shaft from the axis yy.

5. Consider the connecting rod in Fig. 5.31 to have the following dimensions: Length $L = 30$ cm; small end balance reading 1.9 kg; the total mass of the connecting rod 4.7 kg. Determine the position of the rod's centre of gravity from the big-end centre.

6. A crankshaft, with flywheel fitted, has its centre of gravity 265 mm from the flywheel end. The total mass of flywheel and shaft is 109 kg, and the overall length 820 mm. Calculate the weight at the flywheel end in newtons.

7. A vehicle having a total mass of 2800 kg carries 56% of this mass on its front wheels. The track is 1.46 m and wheelbase 2.9 m. When on a tilt test the point of balance was reached at an angle of 47°. Calculate the position of the CG from the rear wheels and the height above the road surface.

5.8 REACTION OF BEAM SUPPORTS (E15)

An important application of the principle of moments is found in the determination of the upward thrust or reaction by the supports of horizontal beams with vertical loading.

Worked examples

An example is given in Fig. 5.32 which may be followed step by step.

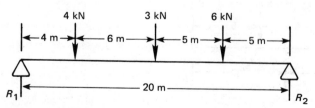

Fig. 5.32 Example of reaction of beam supports.

Consider the beam loaded as shown and find the reactions at the supports R_1 and R_2. The weight of the beam in this instance is to be neglected.

clockwise moments (CW moments) = anti-clockwise moments (ACW moments)

$$\text{CW moments about } R_1 = (4 \times 4) + (3 \times 10) + (6 \times 15)$$

$$= 16 + 30 + 90$$

$$= 136 \text{ kN}$$

$$\text{ACW moments about } R_1 = R_2 \times 20$$

and

$$\text{CW moments} = \text{ACW moments}$$

$$136 = R_2 \times 20$$

thus

$$\frac{136}{20} = 6.8 \text{ kN}$$

total vertical load $- R_2 = R_1$

thus

$$13 - 6.8 = 6.2 \text{ kN}$$

$$R_1 = 6.2 \text{ kN and } R_2 = 6.8 \text{ kN}$$

Moments could have been taken about R_2 to determine value of R_1:

thus

$$\text{CW moments} = \text{ACW moments}$$

$$R_1 \times 20 = (6 \times 5) + (3 \times 10) + (4 \times 16)$$

$$= 30 + 30 + 64$$

$$R_1 = \frac{124}{20} = 6.2 \text{ kN}$$

♦♦♦

A beam is loaded as shown in Fig. 5.33. The beam is of uniform section throughout its length and weighs 2 kN. Calculate the reactions at the supports.

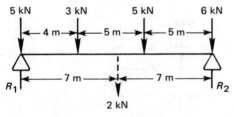

Fig. 5.33 Example of reaction of beam supports.

Two points must be noted with this type of problem. The beam is uniform in section so its total weight must lie at its centre of gravity which is 7 m from either end and is shown as a broken line. Moments are the product of force and perpendicular distance, therefore the 5 kN acting on R_1 has no moment about R_1, likewise the 6 kN load acting on R_2 has no moment about R_2.

Taking moments about R_1:

$$\text{CW moments} = \text{ACW moments}$$

$$(3 \times 4) + (2 \times 7) + (5 \times 9) + (6 \times 14) = R_2 \times 14$$

hence

$$\frac{12 + 14 + 45 + 84}{14} = 11.07 \text{ kN}$$

$$R_1 = \text{total load} - R_2 = 21 - 11.07 = 9.93 \text{ kN}$$

Check by taking moments about R_2:

$$R_1 \times 14 = (5 \times 5) + (2 \times 7) + (3 \times 10) + (5 \times 14)$$

$$= 25 + 14 + 30 + 70$$

$$R_1 = \frac{139}{14}$$

$$= 9.928 \text{ kN} \qquad\qquad \blacklozenge\blacklozenge\blacklozenge$$

An overhanging beam is now to be considered, but in this instance, Fig. 5.34, the weight of the beam is neglected.

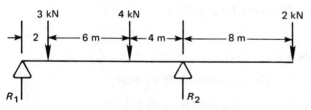

Fig. 5.34 Example with an overhanging beam.

Taking moments about R_1:

$$\text{CW moments} = \text{ACW moments}$$

$$(3 \times 2) + (4 \times 8) + (2 \times 20) = R_2 \times 12$$

and

$$\frac{6 + 32 + 40}{12} = 6.5 \text{ kN}$$

Taking moments about R_2 :

$$\text{CM moments = ACW moments}$$

$$(2 \times 8) + (R_1 \times 12) = (3 \times 10) + (4 \times 4)$$

and

$$R_1 \times 12 = (3 \times 10) + (4 \times 4) - (2 \times 8)$$

$$= 30 + 16 - 16$$

thus

$$R_1 = \frac{30}{12}$$

$$= 2.5 \text{ kN}$$

Check: Total loads $= R_1 + R_2 = 2.5 + 6.5 = 9$ kN   ♦♦♦

Another example of an overhanging beam is shown Fig. 5.35. The beam is of uniform section and has a weight of 3 kN. Determine the reaction values R_1 and R_2. The weight of the beam acting at its centre of gravity is shown by broken line arrow.

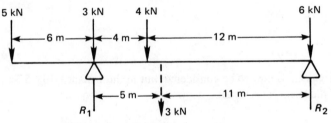

Fig. 5.35 Example with an overhanging beam.

Taking moments about R_1 :

$$\text{CW moments = ACW moments}$$

$$(4 \times 4) + (3 \times 5) + (6 \times 16) = R_2 \times 16 + (5 \times 6)$$

$$16 + 15 + 96 - 30 = R_2 \times 16$$

$$\frac{97}{16} = 6.063 \text{ kN}$$

Taking moments about R_2 :

$$\text{CW moments = ACW moments}$$

$$R_1 \times 16 = (3 \times 11) + (4 \times 12) + (3 \times 16) + (5 \times 22)$$

thus $$R_1 = \frac{239}{16}$$

$$= 14.937 \text{ kN}$$

Check: $R_1 + R_2$ = total load = 21 kN

$$= 6.063 + 14.937$$

$$= 21 \text{ kN}$$

◆◆◆

A loaded beam of uniform section weighs 3 kN and carries five point loads as shown in Fig. 5.36. Determine the reaction at the supports.

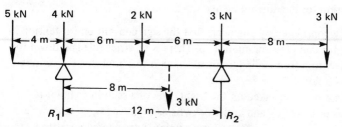

Fig. 5.36 Example of reaction of beam supports.

Taking moments about R_1:

CW moments = ACW moments

$$(2 \times 6) + (3 \times 8) + (3 \times 12) + (3 \times 20) = R_2 \times 12 + (5 \times 4)$$

$$12 + 24 + 36 + 60 - 20 = R_2 \times 12$$

$$\frac{132 - 20}{12} = 9.333 \text{ kN}$$

Taking moments about R_2:

CW moments = ACW moments

$$(3 \times 8) + R_1 \times 12 = (3 \times 4) + (2 \times 6) + (4 \times 12) + (5 \times 16)$$

$$R_1 \times 12 = 12 + 12 + 48 + 80 - 24$$

$$R_1 = \frac{152 - 24}{12}$$

$$= 10.666 \text{ kN}$$

Check: Total loading = 20 kN

$$R_1 + R_2 = 9.333 + 10.666$$

$$= 19.999 \text{ or } 20 \text{ kN}$$

◆◆◆

5.9 BENDING MOMENTS AND SHEARING FORCES

Beams with concentrated or point loads

Simple supported beams as shown Fig. 5.38(a) under concentrated or point load are to be considered, in the first instance, for bending moments. The bending moment (BM) at a cross-section of a beam is defined as the algebraic sum of the moments of all external forces taken on one side of the section under consideration. This may be on the left side, or on the right side of that section.

Sign convention for bending moments

It is generally considered by engineers that the sign convention for tension is plus (+) and for compression minus (−). There is no strict rule laid down for the sign convention for bending moments, and in this book the convention adopted is as follows:

A clockwise moment taken on the 'right' side of a section or point is considered as positive (+), and anti-clockwise as negative (−). A clockwise moment taken on the 'left' of a section or point is considered negative (−), and anti-clockwise as positive (+).

Fig. 5.37 explains the above rules.

Note: The sign only indicates the *direction* of the moment taken to the left or to the right of a section, and does *not* influence the magnitude of the moment. When the sign is a plus it is sometimes not shown.

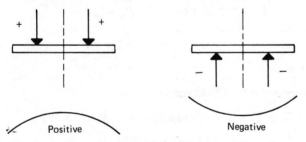

Fig. 5.37 Bending moments (sign convention)

To show the principle of moments and the sign convention used, a simply supported beam is considered having a single concentrated load of 6 kN (see Fig. 5.38(a)). The bending moments at sections *XX* and *YY* are to be calculated.

The reactions at the supports are to be found which in this case are $R_a = -3$ kN, and $R_b = -3$ kN.

BM at section XX = -3 kN x 5 m = -15 kN m. (In this case the sign is a minus one to the right, or left of section XX)

> BM at section YY = -3 kN x 8 m + (+6 kN x 3 m) (considered to
> right of section
> YY)
>
> = -24 kN m + (+18 kN m)
>
> = -6 kN m

The alternative method by considering moments to the left of section YY:

> BM at section YY = -3 kN x 2 m = -6 kN m

Bending moment and shear force diagrams

The BM diagram is drawn below the loading diagram, using the same scale for the dimensions. Negative ($-$) BM are plotted below the zero line and positive (+) above the zero line.

Shear force diagrams in this book follow the same sign rule. Minus ($-$) forces below the zero line and positive (+) shear forces above. Study Fig. 5.38(b) and (c).

Shearing force and shearing force diagrams

One of the forces set up in a beam which is under a bending moment is vertical shear stress, and the shearing force may be calculated for a system of loads. A shearing force diagram can then be drawn. When the loads and reactions are acting at right angles to the plane of the beam, the shearing force at any section can be defined as the algebraic sum of the forces acting upon one side of the section under consideration.

The sign convention employed for shear in this book is:

Left side of section	downward force positive	(+)
	upward force negative	($-$)
Right side of section	downward force negative	($-$)
	upward force positive	(+)

Fig. 5.39 explains the sign rule.

The following points should be considered when drawing shearing force diagrams:

(a) Where there is no loading the diagram is horizontal.

(b) Under a concentrated load or a reaction the diagram becomes vertical to the scale of the load.

(c) Where a uniformly distributed load is carried, the diagram is a straight

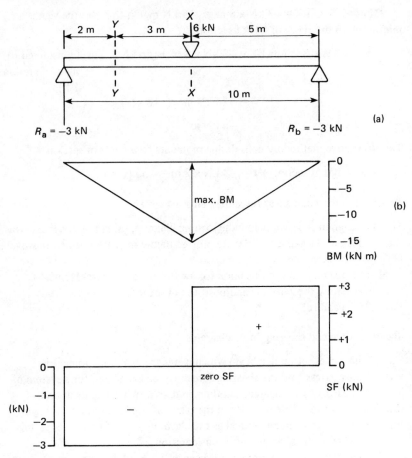

Fig. 5.38 Bending moments.

Fig. 5.39 Sign rule for shear force.

line slope, and the angle or magnitude of the slope depending upon the rate of the distributed uniform load (distributed loads are not asked for in the TEC syllabus).

(d) Where the bending moment is at zero or at its maximum the shear force in each case would be zero (Fig. 5.38(b) and (c)).

Consider the shearing forces for the beam in Fig. 5.38(a) with a concentrated load at the centre of the span.

shearing force between R_a and section $XX = -3$ kN

shearing force between R_b and section $XX = +3$ kN

(see sign convention)

From the shearing force diagram, Fig. 5.38(c), it can be seen that at the centre of the beam span the shear force is zero, and the bending moment is at a maximum.

Worked examples

Simple beam with point loads (Fig. 5.40(a))
The front beam axle of a truck carries a load of 40 kN and the centre of

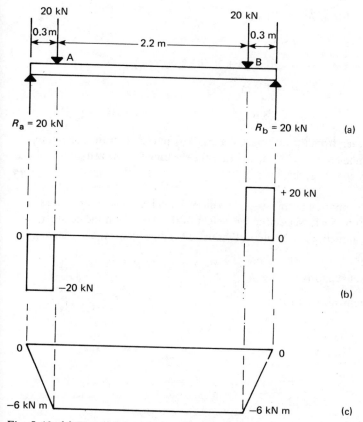

Fig. 5.40 (a) Simple beam with point loads, (b) shear force and (c) bending moment.

gravity is in the centre of the vehicle's 2.8 m track. The spring seats are at a 2.2 m displacement. Draw the BM and SF diagrams and state the maximum bending moment and the position where the shearing force is zero.

R_a and R_b each have a value of 20 kN.

SF between R_a and A = −20 kN

SF between A　and B = −20 +20

$$= 0 \text{ kN}$$

SF between B and R_b = −20 +20 +20

$$= +20 \text{ kN}$$

BM at R_a = 0 kN m

BM at A　= −20 × 0.3

$$= -6 \text{ kN m}$$

BM at B　= −20 × 2.5 + 20 × 2.2

$$= -6 \text{ kN m}$$

BM at R_b = 0 kN m

It can be seen from the diagrams, Fig. 5.40(b) and (c), that the maximum bending moment is −6 kN m, and that the shearing force is zero, both taking place between the spring seats.　　　　　　　　　　　　　　　◆◆◆

A simply supported beam has three concentrated loads placed upon it as shown in Fig. 5.41. Neglecting the weight of the beam, find the bending moments at sections A, B and C. Produce a bending moment and shearing force diagram.

Reaction at supports, R_1 and R_2.

Taking moments about R_2:

$$R_1 \times 10 = 1 \times 3 + 5 \times 5 + 3 \times 8$$

$$R_1 = 5.2 \text{ kN}$$

$$R_2 = 9 - 5.2$$

$$= 3.8 \text{ kN}$$

Bending moments at sections A, B and C

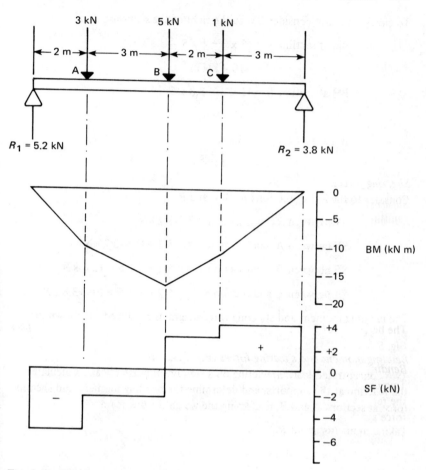

Fig. 5.41 Simply supported beam.

Consider to the left of sections:

BM at section A = $-5.2 \times 2 = -10.4$ kN m

BM at section B = $-5.2 \times 5 + 3 \times 3$

$= -17$ kN m

BM at section C = $-5.2 \times 7 + 3 \times 5 + 5 \times 2$

$= -11.4$ kN m

To check on above consider BM to the right of the sections:

$$\text{BM at section A} = +5 \times 3 + 1 \times 5 - 3.8 \times 8$$

$$= -10.4 \text{ kN m}$$

$$\text{BM at section B} = +1 \times 2 - 3.8 \times 5$$

$$= -17 \text{ kN m}$$

$$\text{BM at section C} = -3.8 \times 3$$

$$= -11.4 \text{ kN m}$$

Shearing forces.
Consider to the left of sections A, B, C and R_2

$$\text{SF between } R_1 \text{ and section A} = -5.2 \text{ kN}$$

$$\text{SF between A   and section B} = -5.2 + 3 = -2.2 \text{ kN}$$

$$\text{SF between B   and section C} = -5.2 + 3 + 5 = +2.8 \text{ kN}$$

$$\text{SF between C and section } R_2 = -5.2 + 3 + 5 + 1 = +3.8 \text{ kN}$$

The bending moment and shearing force diagrams produced are shown in
Fig. 5.41. ◆◆◆

Bending moment and shearing forces (Fig. 5.42(a))
Two concentrated loads are acting on a simply supported beam. Calculate
the reaction at the supports, and determine the bending moment and shearing
force at sections A and B, neglecting the weight of the beam.

Taking moments about R_2:

$$R_1 \times 12 = 4 \times 9 + 8 \times 6$$

$$R_1 = \frac{84}{12}$$

$$= 7 \text{ kN}$$

$$R_2 = 12 - 7 = 5 \text{ kN}$$

Reaction at supports: $R_1 = 7$ kN, $R_2 = 5$ kN.

Determine the bending moment at section A. Consider to the left of section
A:

$$R_1 \times 3 \quad \text{CW moment} (-) = 7 \times 3 = -21 \text{ kN m}$$

Bending the moment at section B. Consider to the left of section B:

$$R_1 \times 6 = -7 \times 6 = -42 \text{ (CW moments)}$$

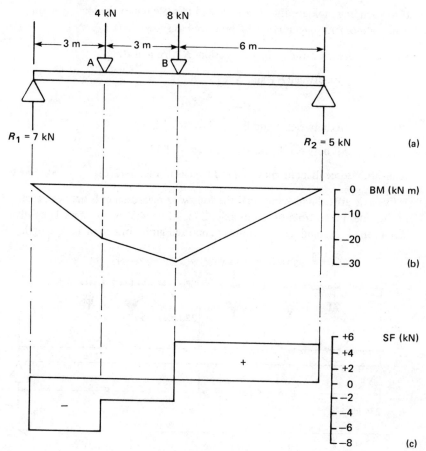

Fig. 5.42 Bending moment and shear force diagrams.

and $\qquad$ 4 × 3 = +12 kN m (ACW moments)

Bending moment at section B = −42 + 12

$$= -30 \text{ kN m}$$

Alternatively consider to the right of sections A and B:

$\qquad$ BM at A: 8 × 3 = +24 kN m (CW moments)

$\qquad$ and $\qquad$ 5 × 9 = −45 kN m (ACW moments)

$\qquad$ BM at A $\qquad$ = −21 kN m

$\qquad$ BM at B: 5 × 6 = −30 kN m (ACW moments)

If the bending moment figures are plotted to scale under the load diagram a bending moment diagram may be produced as shown in (b).

Shearing forces: Consider right of sections R_1, A, and B:

$$\text{SF between } R_1 \text{ and A} = +5 -8 -4$$

$$= -7 \text{ kN}$$

$$\text{SF between A and B} = +5 -8 = -3 \text{ kN}$$

$$\text{SF between B and } R_2 = +5 -0 = +5 \text{ kN}$$

A shearing force diagram may be produced as in Fig. 5.42(c). ♦♦♦

A five axle articulated vehicle has the following measurements between each of the axles taken from the front axle: 2 m, 2.5 m, 4.5 m, and 2 m. The fully laden vehicle is standing on a simply supported girder bridge of 16 m length

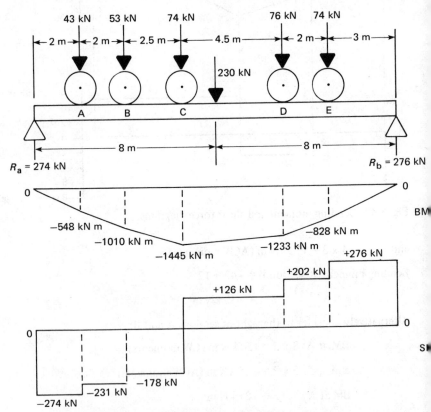

Fig. 5.43 Bending moment and shear force diagrams.

and the rear wheels are 3 m from the right hand support. The axle loads front to rear are: L_1 = 43 kN, L_2 = 53 kN, L_3 = 74 kN, L_4 = 76 kN and L_5 = 74 kN (Fig. 5.43). Determine:

(a) the position of the loaded vehicles centre of gravity from the front axle;
(b) the reaction at the bridge supports if the weight of the bridge is 230 kN;
(c) the bending moments at the wheel contact centres, and the shear forces between the axles.

(a) taking moments about the front axle R_F, to find position of CG.
$$53 \times 2 + 74 \times 4.5 + 76 \times 9 + 74 \times 11 = 320 \times Y \text{ m}$$

$$\frac{106 + 333 + 684 + 814}{320} = 6.053 \text{ m from the front axle}$$

Therefore   CG is 6.053 m from the front axle.

(b) Taking moments about the left supports, R_a

$$R_b \times 16 = 43 \times 2 + 53 \times 4 + 74 \times 6.5 + 230 \times 8 + 76 \times 11 + 74 \times 13$$

$$R_b = \frac{4417}{16} = 276 \text{ kN}$$

$$R_a = 550 - 276 = 274 \text{ kN}$$

Reactions at bridge supports: R_a = 274 kN, R_b = 276 kN.

(c) Consider BM to the left of sections:

$$\text{BM at section A} = -R_a \times 2 = -274 \times 2$$
$$= -548 \text{ kN m}$$

$$\text{BM at section B} = -274 \times 4 + 43 \times 2$$
$$= -1010 \text{ kN m}$$

$$\text{BM at section C} = -274 \times 6.5 + 53 \times 2.5 + 43 \times 4.5$$
$$= -1445 \text{ kN m}$$

$$\text{BM at section D} = -274 \times 11 + 230 \times 3 + 74 \times 4.5 + 53 \times 7 + 43 \times 9$$
$$= -1233 \text{ kN m}$$

$$\text{BM at section E} = -274 \times 13 + 76 \times 2 + 230 \times 5 + 74 \times 6.5 + 53 \times 9$$
$$+ 43 \times 11$$
$$= -828 \text{ kN m}$$

or to the right of section E $= -R_b \times 3 = -276 \times 3$

$$= -828 \text{ kN m}$$

Shearing forces: Consider left of sections:

SF between R_a and A $= -274$ kN

SF between A and B $= -274 + 43$

$$= -231 \text{ kN}$$

SF between B and C $= -274 + 43 + 53$

$$= -178 \text{ kN}$$

SF between C and D $= -274 + 43 + 53 + 74 + 230$

$$= +126 \text{ kN}$$

SF between D and E $= -274 + 43 + 53 + 74 + 230 + 76$

$$= +202 \text{ kN}$$

SF between E and $R_b = -274 + 43 + 53 + 74 + 230 + 76 + 74$

$$= +276 \text{ kN}$$

or $= R_b = +276$ kN

BM and SF diagrams for the above are shown in Fig. 5.43   ♦♦♦

Beam with overhang

A beam has concentrated loads placed upon it as shown in Fig. 5.44: Draw the bending moment and shearing force diagrams to a suitable scale.

BM at section A $= 0$ kN m

BM at section B $= +8 \times 3 = +24$ kN m

BM at section C $= +8 \times 4 - 17 \times 1 = +15$ kN m

BM at section D $= +8 \times 8 + 4 \times 4 - 17 \times 5 = -5$ kN m

BM at section E $= +8 \times 9 + 4 \times 6 + 6 \times 2 - 17 \times 7 = -11$ kN m

BM at section F $= 0$ kN m

SF between A and B $= +8$ kN

SF between B and C $= +8 - 17 = -9$ kN

SF between C and D $= +8 + 4 - 17 = -5$ kN

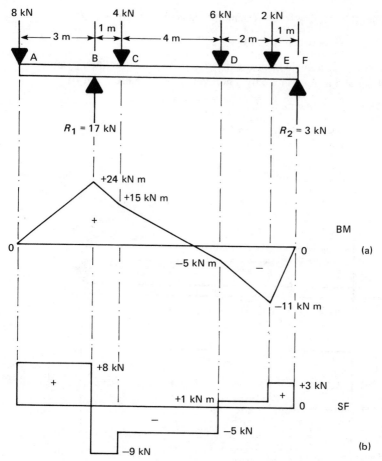

Fig. 5.44 Example of beam with overhang.

SF between D and E = +8 +4 +6 −17 = +1 kN

SF between E and F = +8 +4 +6 +2 −17 = +3 kN

Diagrams for BM and SF are shown in Fig. 5.44(a) and (b).

◆◆◆

Cantilever with single concentrated load at free end (Fig. 5.45)

The load acting on the cantilever is 2 kN 'downwards' which must be balanced by a 2 kN load or force acting 'upwards' at the support end. Taking moments about the supported or fixed end, 2 × 10 = 20 kN m, and this must also be balanced at the support end.

Consider the shearing forces. (using the sign convention)

SF between A and B = −2 kN

As there is only a single load, the shearing force is constant along the cantilever and is represented by a horizontal line (see Fig. 5.45(a)).

Consider the bending moments:

BM at section A = +2 × 10

= +20 kN m

BM at section XX = +2 × 7

= +14 kN m (see Fig. 5.45(b))

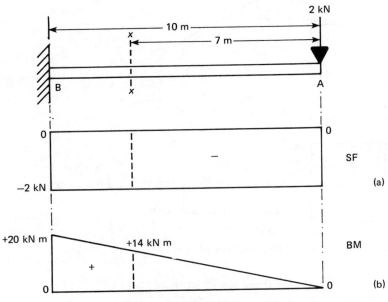

Fig. 5.45 Cantilever with single concentrated load. (a) Shear force diagram and (b) bending moment diagram.

Cantilever with several concentrated loads (Fig. 5.46)

SF between A and B = $-L_1$ = −2 kN

SF between B and C = $-L_1 - L_2$ = −(2 + 4)

= −6 kN

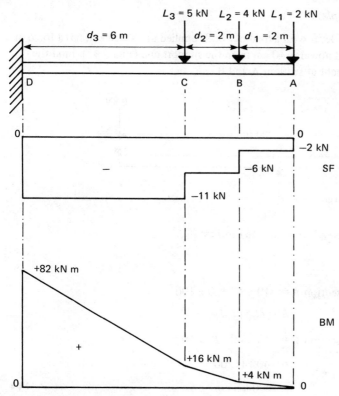

Fig. 5.46 Cantilever with several concentrated loads.

SF between C and D $= -L_1 - L_2 - L_3 = -(2 + 4 + 5)$

$$= -11 \text{ kN}$$

BM at section A $= 0$ kN m

BM at section B $= +L_1 \times d_1 = +2 \times 2$

$$= +4 \text{ kN m}$$

BM at section C $= +L_1 \times (d_1 + d_2) + L_2 \times d_2 = +2 \times 4 + 4 \times 2$

$$= +16 \text{ kN m}$$

BM at section D $= +L_1 \times (d_1 + d_2 + d_3) + L_2 \times (d_2 + d_3) + L_3 \times d_3$

$$= +2 \times 10 + 4 \times 8 + 5 \times 6$$

$$= +82 \text{ kN m}$$

Worked examples

A simple cantilever with a load of 20 kN applied at its free end has a force of 10 kN applied upwards 40 cm from the support end (Fig. 5.47). Find the bending moment at sections A and B.

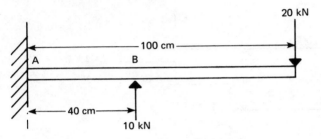

Fig. 5.47 Example with simple cantilever.

$$BM \text{ at section } A = -10 \times 40 + 20 \times 100$$
$$= +1600 \text{ kN cm}$$
$$BM \text{ at section } B = -10 \times 40 + 20 \times 60$$
$$= -400 + 1200$$
$$= +800 \text{ kN cm} \qquad \blacklozenge\blacklozenge\blacklozenge$$

A cantilever carrying two point loads of 4 kN and 6 kN has a force 4 kN acting upwards as shown in Fig. 5.48. Draw the bending moment and shearing force diagrams and determine the position along the cantilever from the fixed end D where the bending moment is zero.

$$SF \text{ between points } A \text{ and } B = +4 \text{ kN}$$
$$SF \text{ between points } B \text{ and } C = +4 - 6$$
$$= -2 \text{ kN}$$
$$SF \text{ between points } C \text{ and } D = +4 - (6 + 4)$$
$$= -6 \text{ kN} \qquad \text{Fig. 5.48(a)}$$

$$BM \text{ at section } A = 0 \text{ kN m}$$
$$BM \text{ at section } B = -4 \times 2$$
$$= -8 \text{ kN m}$$

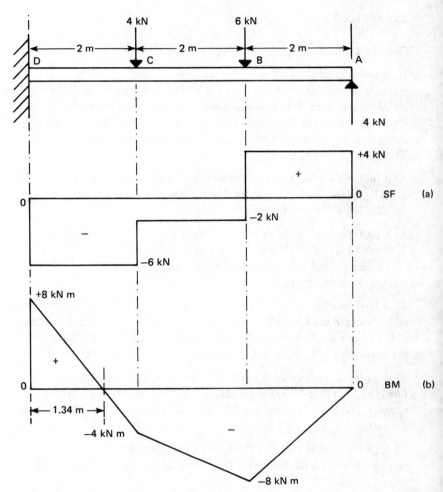

Fig. 5.48 Example of cantilever with two point loads.

$$\text{BM at section C} = -4 \times 4 + 6 \times 2$$

$$= -4 \text{ kN m}$$

$$\text{BM at section D} = -4 \times 6 + 6 \times 4 + 4 \times 2$$

$$= +8 \text{ kN m} \qquad \text{Fig. 5.48(b)}$$

Bending moment is zero at 1.34 m from the fixed end D.   ◆◆◆

EXERCISES 5.3

Shear force and bending moment diagrams and cantilevers (E15)

1. A four-wheeled truck having axle loads of 2.35 Mg at front and 5.41 Mg at rear axle, is crossing a simply supported bridge. The bridge is of uniform girder construction 20 m in length between supports and has a mass of 7.646 Mg. Determine the reaction at the bridge supports when the vehicle's rear wheels are 8.2 m from the bridge support if the vehicle's wheelbase is 3.6 m.

2. A uniform section girder of 7 m length between supports has a weight of 150 kN. A load of 90 kN is placed 3 m from the left-hand support. Calculate the reaction at the two supports.

3. A uniform beam having a mass of 2 Mg is 4 m in length and supported at its ends. A load of 14 kN is applied 1.2 m from the left-hand end, and a 16 kN load applied directly over the right-hand support. Determine the reaction at the supports.

4. A 10 m beam is supported at its left-hand end and 4 m from the right-hand end. Concentrated loads of 20 kN, 12 kN, and 18 kN are carried at distances of 0 m, 2 m and 10 m, respectively, from the left-hand support. Neglecting the beam mass of 15.3 Mg, calculate the reaction at the girder supports.

5. A girder of uniform section 6 m in length is simply supported at its ends. Loads of 500 kN and 700 kN are placed 1 m and 5 m from the left-hand support. The beam has a mass of 15.3 Mg. Calculate the reaction at the girder supports.

6. A vehicle having a mass of 15 Mg and a wheelbase of 5 m has its centre of gravity 2.8 m from the front axle. Find the load carried by the front and rear axles.

7. A four-wheeled truck is standing on a simply supported level part of a ramp 12 m in length. The vehicle's wheelbase is 5 m and the front wheels are 3 m from one end of the ramp. Calculate the reactions at the ramp supports if the ramp weight is 260 N per m run, and the vehicle's weight is 90 kN with its centre of gravity 3.3 m from its front axle.

8. A four-axle articulated truck has the following dimensions between axles taken from the front axle: 2.8 m, 6.2 m, and 1.2 m. The gross laden weight is 300 kN. The load carried by the axles are: front 56 kN, second axle 112 kN, third axle 70 kN, and the fourth axle 62 kN. Determine: (a) the position of the centre of gravity of the tractor and trailer unit, and (b) if the vehicle is standing on a bridge which is 15 m between supports, calculate the reaction

at the supports when the vehicles front wheels are 4 m from the left-hand support.

9. From the diagram (Fig. 5.49) calculate the bending moments at points A, B, C and D together with the shearing forces between these points.

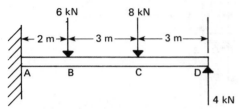

Fig. 5.49 Question 9.

10. The rear axle of a truck has a track of 2.6 m and the supporting leaf springs have a displacement of 2 m. The load on the springs is near-side 20 kN and off-side 22 kN. Determine the bending moment at the spring platforms.

11. A uniform beam of 6 m span between supports weighs 6 kN and carries a fuel tank across its length weighing 36 kN. Calculate the bending moment and shearing force at the centre of the span.

12. A six-wheeled loaded vehicle is standing on a level girder-type bridge as shown in diagram Fig. 5.50. Determine the bending moments at points B, C and D and the shearing forces between A and B, B and C, C and D, and D and E.

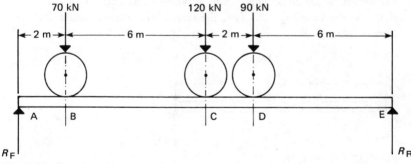

Fig. 5.50 Question 12.

13. A girder projects 6 m from a garage wall and weighs 12 kN. An engine weighing 21 kN is being lifted at a point 5 m from the fixed end of the girder. A screw jack is adjusted to support the free end giving an upward thrust of 8 kN. Calculate the bending moments 5 m and 3 m from the fixed end, and the shearing forces between free end and load, and load and fixed end.

14. A four-wheeled trailer is loaded with a large casting which may be considered as three concentrated loads as shown in diagram Fig. 5.51. Draw the bending moment and shearing force diagrams.

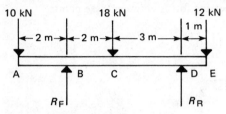

Fig. 5.51 Question 14.

15. A cantilever carries 3 concentrated loads as shown in Fig. 5.52. Determine the bending moments at points A, B, C and D and the shearing forces between these points.

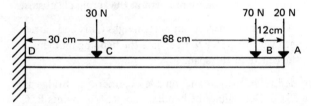

Fig. 5.52 Question 15.

16. Determine the bending moments at points A, B, C and D for the cantilever shown in Fig. 5.53. Give the value of the shearing forces between these points.

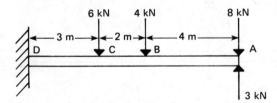

Fig. 5.53 Question 16.

5.10 SPRINGS AND TORSION BARS (E16)

Springs

A spring is a device which can cope with a large degree of strain without permanent deformation. When deflected or strained by an external force or load the spring absorbs energy, most of which is given up when the force is removed. Springs are often referred to as 'soft', 'hard' or 'stiff' springs, but the technical term is the *rate of the spring* or *spring rate*, and represents the force or loading required to produce unit deflection. N/mm or kN/mm are examples of units.

A loaded spring oscillates at a certain 'natural' frequency. Without any form of damping, which includes any friction such as the interleaf friction inherent with laminated leaf springs, the spring would oscillate with a simple harmonic motion, and the time for one complete oscillation is *t* seconds given by

$$t = 2\pi \sqrt{\left(\frac{d}{a}\right)}$$

where *d* is the initial displacement (m) under static load *N* (N), and *a* is the maximum acceleration (m/s^2) which occurs at the upper and lower limits of travel.

Vehicle suspension springs are necessary to isolate the driver and passengers or load from very violent vertical accelerations of several *g* magnitude when, for instance, the roadwheels pass over steps or ledges which cause abrupt vertical accelerations even with a normal spring and damper system.

Laminated road springs

These springs are subjected to bending and some torsional stresses. Driving conditions impose forces which tend to distort the spring. The surface stress should be the same throughout the spring. When supported at each end the bending moment at any point is proportional to the distance of that point from the nearest support.

If the spring leaves are of constant thickness, a constant bending stress can only be achieved by varying the width in proportion to the bending moment. Thus in theory the width should increase from nothing at the supports to a maximum in the centre.

The plan view of the 'beam' should be diamond shaped (Fig. 5.54). The Latin word for this shape is 'rhombus'. A single plate of this shape would be impracticable, so a modern spring is made up of leaves which are similar in length but cut into strips from one single rhombus spring as shown in the diagram.

The spring rate is slightly variable due to interleaf friction. As the spring frequently has to cope with driving and braking forces, the leaves have to be rigid which entails a high rate and this can provide rough or unpleasant ride characteristics.

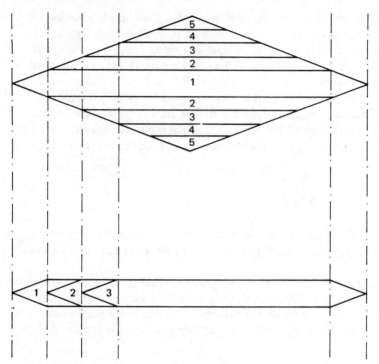

Fig. 5.54 Laminated spring, 'rhomboid plan'.

Dual or variable rate springs

A semi-elliptic road spring behaves as a simply supported beam whose modulus of section decreases linearly from the centre out to the spring eyes, and is, therefore, proportional to the bending moment, as was seen in the previous section.

Under load the leaf road spring will behave similarly to the helical open coiled compression spring whose reduction in length is proportional to the applied axial load. In simple form, the leaf spring has a single rate throughout its normal elastic range of deflection except for the small variation due to interleaf friction. If a secondary spring consisting of a few leaves which are comparatively flat, or with a slight reverse camber, are fitted beneath the main spring assembly (Fig. 5.55(a)) under heavy loads the resistance to deflection is increased thus the spring rate changes as seen graphically (Fig. 5.56). The transition from one rate to the new rate would not in practice be so abrupt as shown in the diagram.

This change in rate enables an unloaded truck or public service vehicle to provide a better ride at a lower spring rate and still provide the necessary

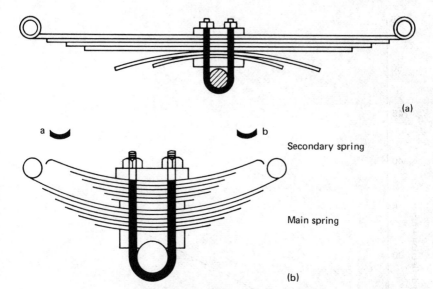

Fig. 5.55 (a) Variable rate road spring. (b) Dual or variable rate spring assembly. Under heavy load conditions in (b) the top leaf of the secondary spring engages the stops 'a' and 'b' which are attached to the chassis frame. The stiffness or rate of the whole spring assembly is thus increased.

stiffness when fully loaded. Such a spring is termed a dual or variable rate combination. Certain conical helical springs of flat and round section are designed to give dual rate characteristics. Another dual rate system is shown in Fig. 5.55(b). The graph shows an initial spring rate of 25 kN/mm deflection, which changes to one of 50 kN/mm. The figures were chosen to enable the principle to be followed easily.

Open coiled helical springs

An open coiled helical spring under a compressive force which produces a reduction in length or a tensional force which increases the spring length will, in each case, have created an alteration in length which is proportional to the applied axial force, providing the elastic limit has not been exceeded (Hooke's Law). The graph will be a straight line.

Fig. 5.57 shows the load/compression graph for an engine valve spring. A diagrammatic sketch of the test rig (Fig. 5.58) is given where a 'loaded' dial indicator (not shown) would be applied to the top plate to record the reduction in spring length.

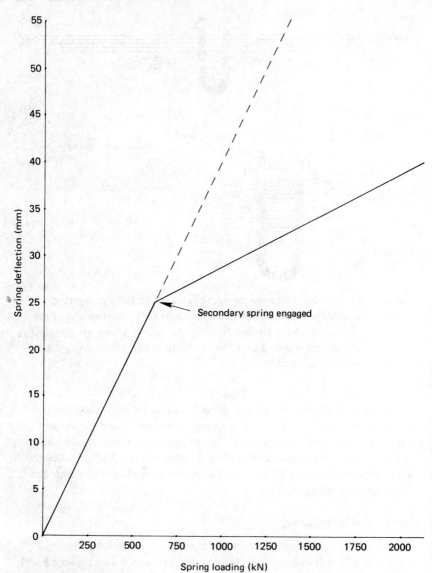

Fig. 5.56 Load versus deflection graph for dual or variable rate leaf spring
(diagrammatic representation).

The slope or angle of the graph which indicates the spring stiffness or rate
can be ascertained by:

$$\frac{\text{value } x}{\text{value } y} = \frac{40}{16} = 2.5 \text{ N/mm}$$

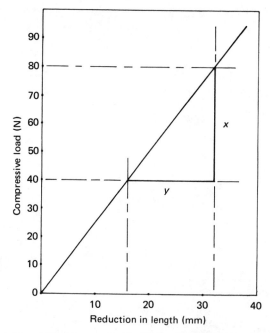

Fig. 5.57 Open coiled helical valve spring (compressive load test).

Torsion bars

When a turning moment or torque is applied to a shaft as shown in Fig. 5.59 the shaft would be in pure torsion. Torsional stress and angle of twist are dealt with in Part 2.

A torsion bar such as used in a car suspension system is shown Fig. 5.60(a) and (b). Such a bar is used instead of a laminated leaf or helical open coiled suspension spring. The serrated end of the bar is anchored to the chassis or subframe and a system of adjusting the torsion bar tension is employed. The other serrated end is connected to the lower link of the suspension system (5.60(b)). Rise and fall of the roadwheel twists or untwists the torsion bar. If such a bar was tested on a torsion testing rig it would be found that the angle of twist is proportional to the applied torque. The results plotted would produce a straight line graph as for helical or leaf springs. Thus again Hooke's Law applies, providing the twisting or winding up of the shaft is within the elastic limit of the torsion bar material.

Worked example

A torsion bar twists 1.5° when a torque of 1250 N m is applied. Draw a graph

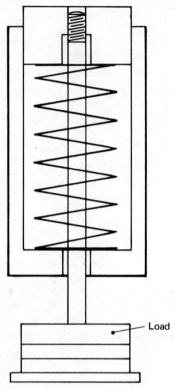

Fig. 5.58 Spring compression rig.

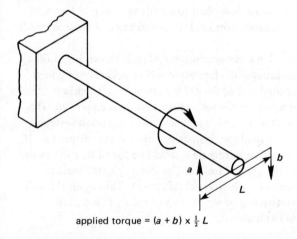

applied torque = $(a + b) \times \frac{1}{2} L$

Fig. 5.59 Steel bar under torsion.

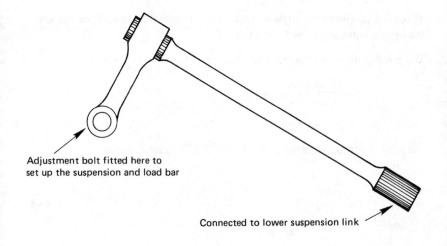

Adjustment bolt fitted here to
set up the suspension and load bar

Connected to lower suspension link

(a)

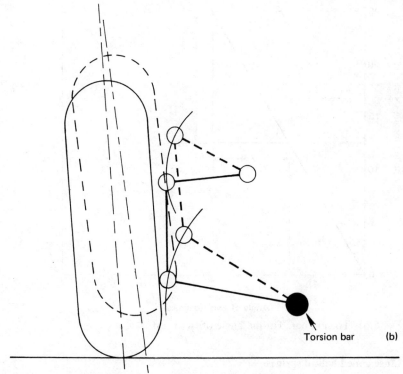

Torsion bar

(b)

Fig. 5.60 (a) Torsion bar. (b) Front independent suspension with torsion bar
springing.

of applied torque versus angle of twist and determine the rate of the bar and the torque required to twist the shaft 2.75°.

The graph is drawn in Fig. 5.61 and from the slope of the graph:

$$\frac{x}{y} = \frac{1250}{1.5}$$

$= 833.33$ N m per degree of twist

torque required to twist shaft $2.75°$ = rate x degrees

$= 833.33 \times 2.75$

$= 2291.6$ N m ♦♦♦

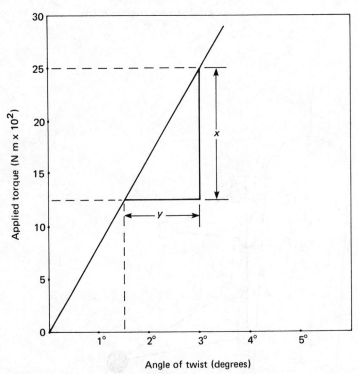

Fig. 5.61 Torsion bar. Torque/angle of twist test.

Close coiled helical springs

This type of spring behaves under stress almost as if it was a straight rod of the same diameter wire under torsional stress. For absolute true torsion, the plane of the coils would have to be at right angles to the spring axis. This type of spring is used for pull-off springs for brake shoes.

Worked examples

A spring is required which will have a reduction in length of 8 mm for an axial load of 16 N. Calculate the stiffness or spring rate.

$$\text{stiffness or spring rate (N/mm)} = \frac{\text{load (N)}}{\text{extension (mm)}} = \frac{16}{8} = 2 \text{ N/mm}$$

◆◆◆

The spring of a centrifugal governor fitted to an automatic transmission unit has a spring rate of 28 N/mm. Calculate the deflection of the governor sleeve in mm if the force supplied by the sleeve is 63 N.

$$\text{spring rate} = \frac{\text{load}}{\text{deflection}}$$

thus

$$\text{deflection (mm)} = \frac{\text{load (N)}}{\text{rate (N/mm)}}$$

$$= \frac{63}{28}$$

$$= 2.25 \text{ mm deflection}$$

◆◆◆

A suspension torsion bar is found to be twisted through an angle of 4° 30'. If the torsional spring rate of the bar is 0.56 kN m/degree twist, what torque was applied?

$$\text{torsional rate of bar} = 0.56 \text{ kN m/degree}$$

therefore torque required to twist bar $4.5° = 0.56 \times 4.5$

$$= 2.52 \text{ kN m}$$

◆◆◆

A torsion bar under torsional test twisted 1.2° for an applied torque of 0.6 kN m, and 7° twist when 4.2 kN m torque was applied. Determine the torsional spring rate of the bar, and the degree of twist when 2.7 kN m is applied.

$$\text{slope of graph or torsional spring rate} = \frac{x}{y} = \frac{\text{torque}}{\text{angle of twist}}$$

$$= \frac{4.2 - 0.6}{7 - 1.2} = \frac{3.6}{5.8} = 0.62 \text{ kN m/twist degree}$$

$$\text{degrees twist} = \frac{\text{torque}}{\text{torsional rate}} = \frac{2.7}{0.62} = 4.35° \text{ twist}$$

◆◆◆

EXERCISES 5.4

Springs and torsion bars (E16)

1. A helical open coiled suspension spring having a free length of 28 cm has this length reduced to 26.4 cm when an axial load of 3.8 kN is applied. What is the spring rate and what reduction in length would a load of 5.6 kN create?

2. An engine valve spring with a rate of 45 N/mm has an opening force of 387 N. How far will the valve open?

3. A drum brake pull-off spring is 8 cm in free length which becomes 10 cm when a load of 0.4 kN is applied: (a) what force or load is required to stretch the spring 1 cm?; (b) what force must be applied to make the spring become 12.5 cm in overall length?

4. A front suspension torsion bar has sustained a 2.7° twist when a torque of 0.56 kN m was applied. This was increased to 2.9 kN m and the twist became 4°. Determine the torsional stiffness of the bar and the angle of twist if the torque was again increased to a figure of 3.6 kN m.

5. A valve spring having a spring rate of 8.5 N/mm lifts the valve 6.5 mm. Calculate the force operating the valve.

6. A helical open coiled spring measures 12 cm when carrying a load of 8 kN and 13.25 cm when the load was increased to 13 kN. What is the stiffness of the spring and its 'free' length?

7. A torsion bar has a 5° angle of twist. The torsional stiffness of the bar is 0.7 kN m/degree twist. What torque was necessary to give the above angle of twist?

5.11 TRANSMISSION AND STEERING COMPONENTS (E17)

Machines (mechanical)

The modern automobile engineering workshop will contain a number of machines, some working by purely mechanical means consisting of a series of levers and pinions, and others having the addition of electrical and/or hydraulic power. A little revision of the principles on which machines operate may not come amiss, and the necessary formulae can be studied and reduced to their simplest terms. Hydraulic machines are dealt with in part 2.

A machine is a device which receives work from an outside source to be modified into work which is more suitable for some desired purpose. Due to friction there must be some losses in the system.

All machines have an input side and an output side. Input is where the external effort is applied, and the output side is where the work is to be completed or load is dealt with. The relationship between the load and the effort gives an indication of the force ratio (FR) (mechanical advantage) the machine is capable of giving.

$$\text{force ratio (FR)} = \frac{\text{load}}{\text{effort}} = \frac{W}{E}$$

This is a ratio and has no units.

Movement ratio (MR) (velocity ratio)

The ratio between the distance moved by the effort in relation to that moved by the load is termed the movement ratio (MR).

The simple lever, Fig. 5.62, has a movement ratio of 2:1. If the effort which is applied at a distance of 2 m from the pivot or fulcrum point is moved through 10 cm in a circular path, the load will also follow a circular path, but of 1 m radius and only moving through 5 cm, thus the machine has a movement or velocity ratio of 2:1. If there were no friction losses the machine would lift exactly twice the value of the applied effort. In other words the load W would equal MR times the effort. The effort in such a case is known as the 'ideal' effort.

$$\text{movement ratio} = \text{MR} = \frac{\text{movement of effort}}{\text{movement of load}} = \frac{\text{movement of input}}{\text{movement of output}}$$

$$= \frac{\text{radius, or diameter, or circumference, or no. of teeth of driven pinion}}{\text{radius, or diameter, or circumference, or no. of teeth of driver pinion}}$$

$$= \frac{\text{rev/min of driver}}{\text{rev/min of driven}} = \text{gear or reduction ratio}$$

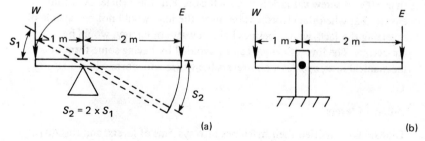

Fig. 5.62 Movement ratio.

Force ratio (FR), (mechanical advantage)

Force ratio (FR) is the relationship between the effort and the load that it deals with

$$FR = \frac{\text{load } (W)}{\text{effort } (E)}$$

If the simple lever on a fulcrum is modified, Fig. 5.62(b), to make it more stable by fitting a clamp at the pivot point friction will be created and the effort of 100 N would not lift a load of 200 N. This is because some part of the 100 N effort has been lost in overcoming the friction at the clamped pivot. If friction is neglected then load = ideal effort x MR and

$$\text{ideal effort} = \frac{\text{load}}{\text{MR}}$$

When friction is taken into account then:

$$\text{actual effort} = \frac{\text{load}}{\text{FR}}$$

Mechanical efficiency

Mechanical efficiency (ME) implies how efficiently the machine can convert the effort applied into useful work, and is the ratio between the mechanical advantage and the velocity ratio. See the graphs in Fig. 5.63.

$$ME = \frac{FR}{MR} = \frac{\text{load}}{\text{effort x MR}} = \frac{\text{ideal effort}}{\text{actual effort}} = \frac{\text{work done on load}}{\text{work done by effort}}$$

$$= \frac{\text{load x distance moved}}{\text{effort x distance moved}} = \frac{\text{actual load}}{\text{ideal load}}$$

Certain simple machines are designed with a mechanical efficiency of less than 50%. A screw car jack is one such case. This low efficiency would ensure that when the effort was removed the load would not be capable of reversing the jack, which, besides being a waste of energy, would be dangerous. The low efficiency can be avoided by having some form of mechanical lock, such as a non-reversible worm and worm-wheel.

Orders of levers

The Greeks classified their machines into systems of levers, and this division still persists to this day.

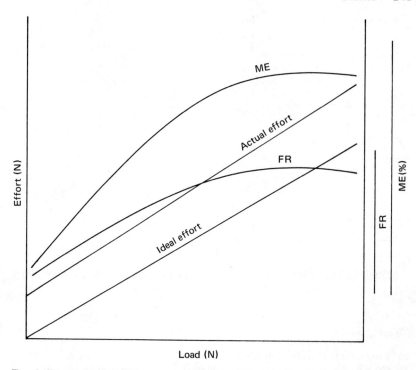

Load (N)

Fig. 5.63 A set of performance graphs for a garage hoist.

Levers of the first order

Fig. 5.64(a), the turning point or fulcrum is situated between the load and the effort. Tongs, pliers and pinch bars are of the first order.

Levers of the second order (Fig. 5.64(b))

The load is applied between the fulcrum and the effort. Wheelbarrows, nutcrackers and a boat oar in rollocks are of the second order of levers.

Levers of the third order (Fig. 5.64(c))

In this order the effort is between the fulcrum and point where the load is applied. The arm is an example of this system where the effort is greater than the load raised. Fire tongs are of this order.

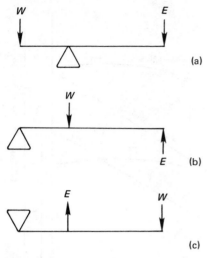

Fig. 5.64 Orders of levers: (a) first order, (b) second order and (c) third order.

Steering boxes

Steering boxes, besides reducing the drivers effort at the steering wheel rim by providing a reduction ratio between steering and drop arm, also convert the purely rotary movement of the steering wheel to an angular movement of the drop arm through a suitable arc, perhaps 75° total movement. Reduction ratios vary considerably and are approximately 9:1 for cars and much higher for trucks – 20 to 28:1. The fitting of power steering has enabled higher ratios to be used where steering is 'heavy'. Some small measure of irreversibility is common practice to avoid repercussions of the more severe road shocks at the steering wheel, but this introduces a lowering of the overall efficiency of the steering box, especially in the reverse phase.

$$\text{steering torque (N m)} = F \times d \times n_s \times e$$

where F = the steering wheel rim force (one side of rim only) (N)

　　　d = diameter of steering wheel rim (m)

　　　n_s = reduction ratio of steering box

　　　e = mechanical efficiency of the unit (this will be lower in the reverse movement, i.e. from roadwheels to steering wheel)

Worked examples

The diameter of a truck steering wheel is 64 cm and the reduction ratio is 17.5. Calculate the steering torque if the efficiency is 67% and the total applied force at the wheel rim is 48 N.

$$\text{steering torque (N m)} = F \times d \times n_s \times e$$
$$= 1/2 \times 48 \times 0.64 \times 17.5 \times 0.67$$
$$= 180 \text{ N m} \qquad \blacklozenge\blacklozenge\blacklozenge$$

A vehicle's steering wheel is 0.47 m in diameter and the overall reduction between steering wheel and roadwheels is 21.75. Due to road irregularity the roadwheels apply momentarily a reverse torque of 385 N m. If the efficiency in reverse phase is 57%, what total force will the driver have to apply to maintain the direction of motion?

$$F = \frac{N m}{d \times n_s \times e} = \frac{385}{0.47 \times 21.75 \times 0.57}$$
$$= 66 \text{ N}$$

If, under the driver's control, the same torque was applied but the efficiency was now 81%, how much force would the driver have to apply?

$$F = \frac{385}{0.47 \times 21.75 \times 0.81}$$
$$= 46.4 \text{ N} \qquad \blacklozenge\blacklozenge\blacklozenge$$

Gears and pinions

Many years after the wheel was invented, power was transmitted very inefficiently by having two wheels or cylinders pressed together, and each cylinder attached to a shaft. To reduce slip between the two cylindrical surfaces, material such as hide was employed. At a later date slots and pegs were used which formed the basis for gear teeth production.

Pitch circle (PC)

The pitch circle of a pair of pinions is equivalent to two cylinders or circles rotating in contact. The working radius or leverage is taken from the pitch circle and termed the pitch radius. This is the contact point where the force is applied from one pinion to another (see Fig. 5.65).

Circular pitch (CP)

This is the distance between two consecutive gear teeth, and is measured on the arc of the pitch circle.

$$\text{circular pitch CP} = \frac{\pi d}{T}$$

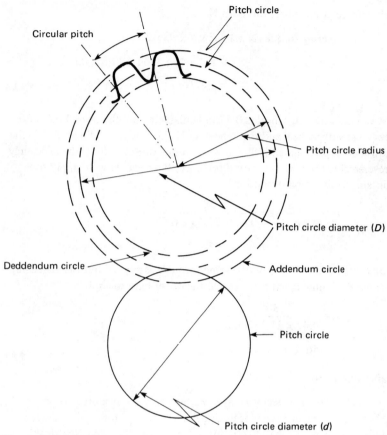

Fig. 5.65 Pitch circle.

where d is the pinion pitch circle diameter (PCD) and T the number of teeth.

thus $$T = \frac{\pi d}{\text{CP}}$$

Diametrical pitch (DP)

The number of teeth per metre of the pitch circle diameter. This is now generally used instead of teeth per circular pitch.

$$\text{DP} = \frac{T}{d}$$

Module pitch (MP)

Module pitch is the reciprocal of the diametrical pitch.

$$MP = \frac{d \text{ in millimetres}}{T}$$

The addendum circle

This is the circle which passes through the top or crest of the teeth, and is measured radially from the pitch circle.

The deddendum circle

This circle passes through the bottom or roots of the teeth and is measured radially below the pitch circle.

The base circle

This circle is used for the tooth design, and the tooth profile is evolved from it.

Simple train of gears or pinions

A simple train of gears or pinions would all lie in the same plane. Where shafts have to rotate in the same direction, i.e. input and output shafts, an idler is interposed between the two shafts and gears (Fig. 5.66). The idler pinion does not affect the gear or movement ratio between the driver and driven shafts.

$$\text{gear ratio} = MR = \frac{\text{no. of teeth of driven}}{\text{no. of teeth of driver}} = \frac{\text{rev/min of driver}}{\text{rev/min of driven}}$$

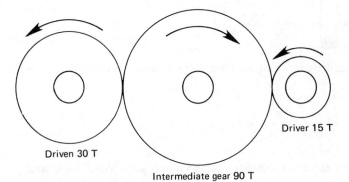

Driver 15 T

Driven 30 T

Intermediate gear 90 T

Fig. 5.66 Gear drive for single plane. MR = 2:1.

Compound trains

These consist of two or more trains of pinions in series, i.e. not in the same plane (Fig. 5.67)

$$\text{gear ratio or MR} = \frac{\text{product of no. teeth of driven pinions}}{\text{product of no. teeth of driver pinions}}$$

$$= \frac{DVN_1 \times DVN_2 \times DVN_3}{DVR_1 \times DVR_2 \times DVR_3} \text{ or } \frac{\text{rev/min of driver (input)}}{\text{rev/min of driven (output)}}$$

Crownwheel and pinion (Bevelwheel and pinion)

$$\text{gear ratio or MR} = \frac{\text{no of teeth on crownwheel}}{\text{no. of teeth on pinion}} = \frac{\text{rev/min of pinion}}{\text{rev/min of crownwheel}}$$

Most cars and many trucks fit crownwheel and pinion final drives. It is not always realized that the crownwheel always has an odd number of teeth and the pinion an even number. This arrangement gives uniform wear and ensures that a pair of teeth only engage once in so many revolutions. For instance, if a crownwheel has 57 teeth, a certain tooth on the pinion will only engage a certain tooth on the crownwheel once every 57 revolutions of the roadwheels. In final drive fault diagnosis the above frequency must be borne in mind. So often some noise from the brake shoes or another source is attributed to the final drive. A chipped tooth on the crown wheel and pinion will have a very low frequency knock compared to the revolutions of the roadwheels.

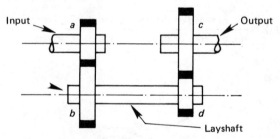

Fig. 5.67 Gear drive for compound plane. MR = driven/driver = $(b \times c)/(a \times d)$.

The gearbox

Function

The overall resistance to a vehicle's motion varies considerably. The internal combustion engine develops its maximum torque and power within a very limited engine revolution range. A gear box and its ratios, together with some help from the clutch, enable a range of torque and tractive effort values to be available to deal with the overall resistance to the vehicle's motion and at the same time keeping the engine revolutions within the limits of maximum torque and maximum power.

Efficiency

The overall efficiency of a gearbox:

$$ME = \frac{\text{output torque}}{\text{input torque} \times GR}$$

where GR is the gear ratio or movement ratio MR.

Worked example

A gearbox in second gear has a ratio of 2.31:1. The engine torque is 126 N m and the output torque to the propellor shaft is 287 N m. Calculate the mechanical efficiency of the gearbox in second gear.

$$ME \% = \frac{\text{output torque}}{\text{input torque} \times GR} \times 100$$

$$= \frac{287}{126 \times 2.31} \times 100$$

$$= 98.6\%$$

♦♦♦

The efficiency of a gearbox may be found by experiment. Brief details are given below (see Fig. 5.68).

Movement or gear ratio

Place chalk marks on the input and output pulleys. Count the number of revolutions of the input pulley needed to complete one revolution of output pulley. Repeat for each gear ratio.

$$GR \text{ or } MR = \frac{\text{revolutions of input pulley}}{1 \text{ revolution of output pulley}}$$

Force ratio (FR)

Load the output pulley and apply loads to the input pulley until a steady movement or rotation takes place without acceleration.

$$FR = \frac{\text{load (output)}}{\text{effort (input)}} \text{ or } \frac{\text{output torque}}{\text{input torque}}$$

$$ME = \frac{FR}{GR} = \frac{\text{output torque}}{\text{input torque} \times GR}$$

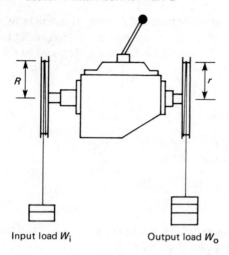

Input load W_i Output load W_o

Gear ration = GR = $\dfrac{\text{revolutions of input shaft}}{1 \text{ revolution of output shaft}}$

Efficiency = ME = $\dfrac{\text{FR}}{\text{GR}} = \dfrac{\text{output torque}}{\text{input torque} \times \text{GR}} = \dfrac{W_o \times r}{W_i \times R \times \text{GR}}$

Fig. 5.68   Efficiency of a gearbox.

Final drive unit

Function

This unit changes the drive through a right angle and at the same time gives a reduction ratio to multiply the torque from the gearbox and through the medium of a differential ensures each half shaft is delivered with identical torque under all normal road conditions.

Efficiency

The efficiency of a final drive unit or rear axle complete, may be found by experiment in a similar manner to the gearbox. Fig. 5.69 shows the principles.

$$f = \dfrac{\text{revolutions of input or effort pulley}}{\text{revolutions by output pulleys}}$$

$$\text{ME} = \dfrac{\text{FR}}{f} = \dfrac{\text{output torque}}{\text{input torque} \times f} \quad \text{where } f \text{ is the final drive ratio}$$

Determination of vehicle's overall reduction ratio

A simple experiment may be carried out to determine a vehicles final drive

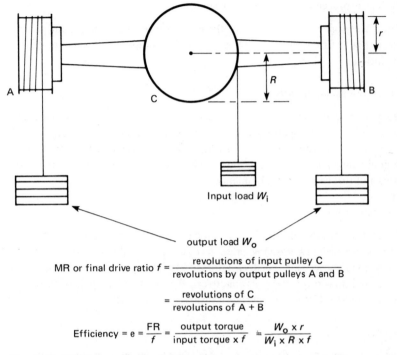

$$\text{MR or final drive ratio } f = \frac{\text{revolutions of input pulley C}}{\text{revolutions by output pulleys A and B}}$$

$$= \frac{\text{revolutions of C}}{\text{revolutions of A + B}}$$

$$\text{Efficiency} = e = \frac{FR}{f} = \frac{\text{output torque}}{\text{input torque} \times f} \fallingdotseq \frac{W_o \times r}{W_i \times R \times f}$$

Fig. 5.69 Efficiency of a final drive unit.

ratio and the gearbox ratios. If a starting handle is not available, a spanner may be used on the nut fitted at the nose of the crankshaft and fan pulley.

Procedure

1. Chock the front wheels and jack up one rear wheel. Mark tyre and floor surface.
2. Select top gear. Rotate engine crankshaft until rear wheel has made exactly two revolutions. Note revolutions given to crankshaft.

final drive ratio (f) = number of turns of crankshaft

3. Select and engage first gear and repeat above procedure (2) and again note exact revolutions of crankshaft.

overall reduction ratio = $n_1 \times f$

where n_1 = 1st gear ratio and f = final drive ratio

therefore   1st gear ratio = $n_1 = \dfrac{\text{number of crankshaft revolutions}}{\text{final drive ratio}}$

4. Repeat procedure for the other gears.

Note: When one wheel is raised off the road surface, and a standard type differential is fitted, the raised wheel will make double the normal number of revolutions.

Special transmission units

Heavy duty trucks and specialist vehicles are fitted with certain transmission units not found on the average automobile or light truck. Full descriptions of these units are beyond the scope of this book and the syllabus it covers, but no doubt they are dealt with in motor vehicle technology. However, the gear ratios and torque ratios can be mentioned.

The transfer box

This unit divides the drive from the main gearbox (without any change in ratio) between the two driving axles. A third differential may be fitted to accommodate inter-axle speed variation and transmission wind-up. Some torque and power loss takes place between the input and outputs of the unit and must influence the overall transmission efficiency.

Two-speed axles

This is a convenient method of providing a large number of gear ratios and retaining a light gearbox. The torque applied to the final drive unit is also moderate as the extra reduction and the increased torque are made after the crownwheel and pinion.

$$\text{Available torque at the roadwheels} = T_R$$

$$T_R \text{ at 1st speed} = Tnf_1 e$$

$$T_R \text{ at 2nd speed} = Tnf_2 e$$

where T = engine torque;

n = gearbox ratio;

f_1 = 1st axle speed;

f_2 = 2nd axle speed; and

e = transmission efficiency.

Double reduction axles

A single large step reduction ratio can only be attained by having a very large crown- or worm-wheel, both in diameter and depth, to ensure sufficient strength to cope with the bending moment and high torque. Such a unit would be bulky and very heavy, thus two reductions within the same unit add little, if anything, to the weight, and overcome the bending and torque problems.

$$\text{torque at the roadwheels } T_R = Tnf_a \times f_b \times e$$

where f_a and f_b are the first and second reductions. The other symbols are as above.

Hub reduction

A reduction made at the wheel hub reduces the stresses which would be applied to the final drive unit having a large reduction ratio. For example if a 2:1 hub reduction is made this halves the torque to be transmitted to the axle shafts, differential, crownwheel and pinion, propellor shaft and gearbox.

$$T_R = Tnfhe$$

where h = hub reduction ratio.

Third differentials

The advantages of fitting a differential between two driving axles is as follows:

1. Avoids 'drag' set up by unequal tyre radii and tracking, thus reducing transmission 'wind-up'.
2. Equalizes the driving forces at the roadwheels and minimizes tyre wear.
3. Permits smaller and lighter final drive units and axles.

Note: A differential lock is fitted to vehicles having to negotiate muddy sites, etc., as if one wheel slips or lifts, the drive would be lost.

Tractive effort

To initiate motion to a wheeled vehicle, a force has to be applied to the vehicle. This is termed the propelling force or tractive effort (TE). This force is obtained through the torque supplied to the driving roadwheels (T_R).

$$T_R = \text{force} \times \text{leverage} = \text{tractive effort} \times \text{rolling radius of roadwheels}$$

$$= \text{TE} \times r \, \text{N m}$$

therefore $\quad \text{TE} = \dfrac{T_R}{r}$

and as $T_R = Tnfe$

then $\quad \text{TE} = \dfrac{Tnfe}{r} \, \text{N}$

where T = engine torque

     n = gearbox reduction ratio

     f = final drive ratio

     e = transmission efficiency

     r = effective radius of roadwheels.

With the information now available some interesting problems concerning the transmission units and the propelling or tractive force can be accomplished. Some fully worked examples follow.

   Note: The power developed at the roadwheels = engine power x efficiency of the transmission. Therefore

$$\text{kW at roadwheels} = \text{kW (engine)} \times e$$

Worked examples

Tractive effort, gear ratios, etc.
An engine is developing 63 kW power at an engine speed of 2900 rev/min. Third gear of ratio 1.9:1 is engaged, and the final drive ratio is 4.53:1. If the rolling radius of the roadwheels is 0.34 m, determine the tractive effort available if the transmission efficiency is 87%.

$$kW = \frac{T2\pi N}{60 \times 10^3}$$

where T is in N m

Thus
$$T\,\text{N m} = \frac{kW \times 10^3 \times 60}{2 \times \pi \times N}$$

$$= \frac{63 \times 10^3 \times 60}{2 \times \pi \times 2900}$$

$$= 207.45 \text{ N m}$$

tractive effort (TE) N $= \dfrac{Tnfe}{r}$

$$= \frac{207.45 \times 1.9 \times 4.53 \times 0.87}{0.34}$$

$$= 4568 \text{ N or } 4.568 \text{ kN} \qquad \blacklozenge\blacklozenge\blacklozenge$$

A vehicle in second gear, which has a ratio 2.68:1, is producing a torque of 1260 N m at the half-shafts. The two litre four-stroke engine is developing a bmep of 790 kN/m². Assuming a transmission efficiency of 79%, determine the final drive reduction ratio.

$$\text{work done in one revolution} = T2\pi = \frac{\text{bmep } LAn}{2}$$

therefore

$$T \text{ N m} = \frac{\text{bmep} \times LAn}{4 \times \pi}$$

$$= \frac{790 \times 10^3 \times 0.002}{4 \times \pi}$$

$$= 125.7 \text{ N m}$$

torque at the half-shafts $T_R = Tnfe$

therefore

$$f = \frac{T_R}{Tne} = \frac{1260}{125.7 \times 2.68 \times 0.79}$$

$$f = 4.73:1 \qquad \blacklozenge\blacklozenge\blacklozenge$$

A vehicle in first gear is set in motion by a tractive effort of 3.6 kN applied by the driving roadwheels which have a rolling diameter of 0.72 m. The final drive and gearbox ratios are 4.56:1 and 3.41:1, respectively. The engine was developing 47 kW power and the overall transmission efficiency was 89%. Calculate the running speed of the engine in rev/min.

$$\text{TE (kN)} = \frac{T \times n \times f \times e}{10^3 \times r}$$

and

$$T \text{ N m} = \frac{\text{TE} \times 10^3 \times r}{n \times f \times e}$$

$$= \frac{3.6 \times 10^3 \times 0.36}{3.41 \times 4.56 \times 0.89}$$

$$= 93.64 \text{ Nm}$$

$$\text{kW} = \frac{T2\pi N}{10^3 \times 60}$$

and

$$N \text{ rev/min} = \frac{\text{kW} \times 10^3 \times 60}{T2\pi}$$

$$= \frac{47 \times 10^3 \times 60}{93.64 \times 2 \times \pi}$$

$$= 4793 \text{ rev/min} \qquad \blacklozenge\blacklozenge\blacklozenge$$

The differential unit

When a torque T_R (N m) is applied to the wormwheel or crownwheel as they are bolted to the differential housing, it is applied to the housing and transmitted to the planet pinions of the differential. Each planet pinion may be regarded as a lever between the sun pinions which divides the input torque evenly at all times between the two sun pinions and half-shafts. This torque distribution can be modfieid by the fitting of a limited-slip differential.

Taking moments about A (see Fig. 5.70):

$$B \times 2X = T_R \times X$$

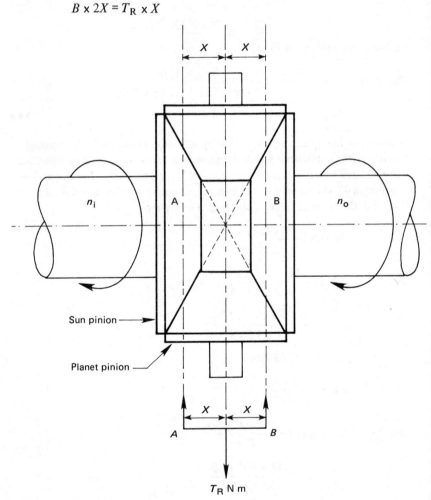

Fig. 5.70 The differential unit.

and $\qquad B = \dfrac{T_R X}{2X} = \dfrac{T_R}{2}$

This proves that the torque is equally divided between the two sun pinions.

Let N_c = rev/min of crownwheel or differential unit, n_i = rev/min of inner wheels, and n_o = rev/min of outer wheels. Then

$$N_c = \frac{n_i + n_o}{2}$$

and $\qquad N_c \times 2 - n_i = n_o$ rev/min

or $\qquad N_c \times 2 - n_o = n_i$

Power developed at a single roadwheel:

$$W_R = \frac{T_R 2\pi n_i (\text{or } n_o)}{2 \times 60} = \frac{T_R \times n_i (\text{or } n_o)}{19} \text{ W}$$

where T_R is in N m.

Although the torque delivered to the normal type of differential is equally divided between the two sun pinions and half-shafts, the power to each wheel will vary according to their revolutions per second. Power is the *rate* of doing work.

Worked examples

The torque developed by an engine is 82 N m at 2000 rev/min. The final drive ratio is 4.73:1. In top gear the inside roadwheel is making 60 rev/min. Calculate the torque and power at the inner and outer driving roadwheels.

$$\text{power at the crankshaft (kW)} = \frac{T 2\pi N}{10^3 \times 60}$$

$$= \frac{82 \times 2 \times \pi \times 2000}{10^3 \times 60}$$

$$= 17.17 \text{ kW}$$

torque at differential housing and roadwheels

$$T_R \text{ (N m)} = T \times f$$

where $\qquad T$ = engine torque and

$\qquad f$ = final drive ratio.

$$= 82 \times 4.73$$

$$= 387.86 \text{ N m}$$

torque at each half-shaft = 387.86 ÷ 2 = 193.93 N m

$$\text{rev/min of differential} = N_c = \frac{N}{f} = \frac{2000}{4.73} = 422.8$$

$$N_c = \frac{n_i + n_o}{2}$$

and $n_o = N_c \times 2 - n_i = 422.8 \times 2 - 60 = 785.6 \text{ rev/min}$

$$\text{power at outer wheel (kW)} = \frac{T_R 2\pi n_o}{10^3 \times 60} = \frac{193.93 \times 2 \times \pi \times 785.6}{10^3 \times 60}$$

$$= 15.95 \text{ kW}$$

$$\text{power at the inner wheel (kW)} = \frac{193.93 \times 2 \times \pi \times 60}{10^3 \times 60}$$

$$= 1.2 \text{ kW} \qquad \blacklozenge\blacklozenge\blacklozenge$$

Torque and power at the roadwheels

(a) A six cylinder four-stroke cycle engine with a capacity of 2130 cm^3 is operating at 4500 rev/min and developing 560 kN/m^2 bmep. If the final drive ratio is 5.2:1 and the transmission efficiency in top gear is 90%, determine the power at the roadwheels when top gear is engaged.

(b) If this vehicle is negotiating a road bend and the inside roadwheels are making 230 rev/min, calculate the rev/min of the outer wheels and the torque and power at both the outer and inner driving wheels.

(a) power at roadwheels = engine power x transmission efficiency

$$= \text{kW} \times e$$

$$= \frac{\text{bmep} \times LAn \times N}{60 \times 2 \times 10^6} \times e \; (note \; \text{cm}^3/10^6 = \text{m}^3)$$

$$= \frac{560 \times 2130 \times 4500}{60 \times 2 \times 10^6} \times 0.9$$

$$= 40.2 \text{ kW power at the roadwheels}$$

(b) Rev/min of crownwheel $= N_c = \dfrac{N}{f} = \dfrac{4500}{5.2} = 865.38 \text{ rev/min}$

and $N_c = \dfrac{n_i + n_o}{2}$

where n_i and n_o are the rev/min of the inner and outer wheels, respectively. Therefore

$$N_c \times 2 - n_i = n_o$$

thus $n_o = 865.38 \times 2 - 230 = 1500.76$ rev/min

power at the roadwheels $(kW_R) = \dfrac{T_R 2\pi N_c}{10^3 \times 60}$

where T_R = roadwheel torque N m and N_c = rev/min of crown wheel.
Therefore

$$\text{torque at roadwheels } T_R = \frac{kW_R \times 10^3 \times 60}{2 \times \pi \times N_c}$$

$$= \frac{40.2 \times 10^3 \times 60}{2 \times \pi \times 865.38}$$

$$= 443.6 \text{ N m}$$

thus torque at either driving wheel = 443.6 ÷ 2 = 221.8 N m

power at outer driving wheel (kW) $= \dfrac{T_R 2\pi n_o}{10^3 \times 60}$

$$= \frac{221.8 \times 2\pi \times 1500.76}{10^3 \times 60}$$

$$= 34.85 \text{ kW}$$

power at inner wheel $= \dfrac{221.8 \times 2 \times \pi \times 230}{10^3 \times 60}$

$$= 5.342 \text{ kW}$$

♦♦♦

The limited slip differential (LSD)

In addition to the loss of driving torque due to bad and slippery roads, there is the problem of the transferred vertical loading from one of the driving wheels. When a normal bevel pinion turns its crownwheel it also tries to turn the whole axle unit in the same direction in which the propellor shaft is rotating.

During high acceleration, weight is transferred from the off-side wheel to the near-side, and the off-side may slip or spin. This effect is not expected in vehicles which have their crankshafts parallel to the axle as there is no bevel pinion to create this lifting torque to the axle.

Fig. 5.71 shows the useful percentage of torque available at a slipping wheel (horizontal axis) and the vertical axis shows the sum total percentage

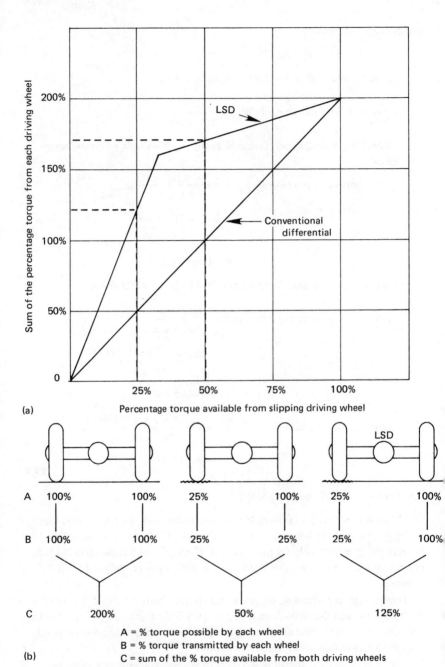

Fig. 5.71 The sum total of the percentage torque for each driving wheel versus that available from the slipping driving wheel.

of torque available to both driving wheels. Thus, with a normal differential, if the slipping wheel is providing 25% useful traction torque, the other wheel on the good road surface is also restricted to 25% traction torque, giving a sum total percentage for both driving wheels of 50%.

If an LSD had been fitted the sum total percentage traction torque for both driving wheels would have been 125%, when the slipping wheel is providing 50% traction torque, instead of the sum total being only 100%, it is in fact 170%. The area between the two graphs represents the percentage of useful torque gained.

The epicyclic gear train

An epicyclic gear train (Fig. 5.72) consists of pinions which rotate about their own axis, but may at the same time rotate bodily about the axis of another pinion or set of pinions; hence the name sun and planet pinions.

If the annulus is held (Fig. 5.72(a)) and the sun is moved one tooth, the teeth of the planet pinion will act as a lever pivoting at point X, and the axis of the planet gear will move from point 1 to point 2 which is a smaller linear distance than from point S1 to S2, hence a reduction ratio:

$$\frac{A+S}{S} = \frac{A}{S} + 1$$

If the annulus, which is the fulcrum for the planets, is moved from X to Y at the same time as the sun is rotating, the planet axis will have moved a greater distance to point 4 (instead of point 3) which produces a decrease in the reduction ratio, giving a higher gear or velocity ratio. This is one method of altering the gear ratio by varying the rev/min imparted to the annulus.

Epicyclic gear ratios

Three gear ratios are possible with a train of gears as shown in Fig. 5.72(b)
Number of teeth of $A = S + 2P$

Ratio 1: $A = 0$ $S + 1$ $C = \dfrac{A+S}{S} = \dfrac{A}{S} + 1$ (annulus held)

Ratio 2: $S = 0$ $A + 1$ $C = \dfrac{A+S}{A} = \dfrac{S}{A} + 1$ (sun held)

Ratio 3: $S = 0$ $C + 1$ $A = \dfrac{A}{A+S}$ is an overdrive (sun held)

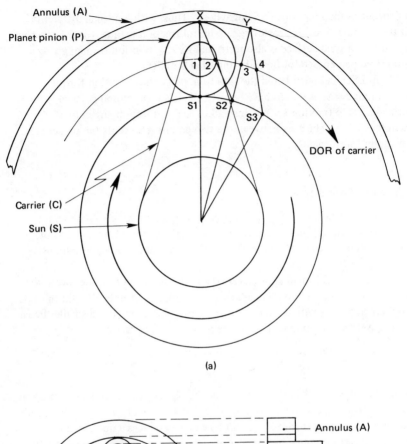

(a)

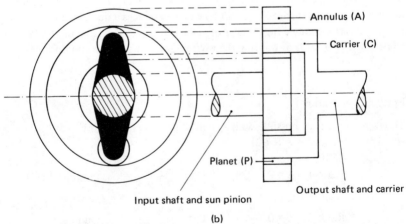

(b)

Fig. 5.72 An epicyclic gear train.

Worked examples

Epicyclic gearing

A double-reduction final drive unit has one of the reduction steps by epicyclic gearing.

$$\text{The ratio} = \frac{A + S}{S}$$

where A is the annulus which has 66 teeth, and S is the sun pinion which has 22 teeth and is driven at 208 rev/min. How many teeth have the planet pinions and at what speed was the planet carrier driven?

It will be seen from the text that

$$A = S + 2P$$

and $$P = \frac{A - S}{2} = \frac{66 - 22}{2}$$

$$= 22 \text{ teeth}$$

$$\text{reduction ratio} = \frac{A + S}{S} = \frac{A}{S} + 1 = \frac{66}{22} + 1 = 4{:}1$$

$$\text{movement ratio MR} = \frac{\text{rev/min of driver}}{\text{rev/min of driven}} = \frac{\text{sun rev/min}}{\text{carrier rev/min}}$$

therefore $$\text{carrier C rev/min} = \frac{\text{S rev/min}}{\text{MR}} = \frac{208}{4} = 52 \text{ rev/min}$$ ◆◆◆

An epicyclic geared overdrive has a step-up ratio equal to:

$$\frac{A}{A + S}$$

The planet pinions have 13 teeth and the sun 29 teeth. Determine the step-up ratio of the overdrive.

$$A = S + 2P$$

therefore $$A = 29 + 2 \times 13 = 55 \text{ teeth}$$

$$\text{step-up ratio is equal to} \frac{A}{A + S} = \frac{55}{55 + 29} = \frac{55}{84} = 0.654{:}1$$ ◆◆◆

A hub reduction unit consists of epicyclic gearing as shown in Fig. 5.73. The sun pinion has 23 teeth and the planets 11 teeth each. The planet carrier

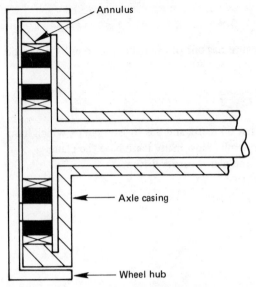

Fig. 5.73 Hub reduction unit. MR = (A + S)/S = (A/S) + 1.

drives the hub and roadwheel. If the sun is making 162 rev/min, at what speed are the roadwheels being driven if the vehicle is moving in a straight path?

$$A = S + 2P = 23 + 2 \times 11 = 45 \text{ teeth}$$

$$\text{reduction ratio} = \frac{A}{S} + 1 = \frac{45}{23} + 1$$

$$= 2.956:1$$

$$\text{movement ratio MR} = \frac{\text{rev/min of driver}}{\text{rev/min of driven}} = \frac{\text{rev/min of sun}}{\text{rev/min of carrier}}$$

therefore   roadwheel and carrier rev/min $= \dfrac{\text{rev/min of sun}}{\text{MR}}$

$$= \frac{162}{2.956}$$

$$= 54.8 \text{ rev/min}$$ ◆◆◆

EXERCISES 5.5

Transmission and steering components (E17)

1. A vehicle has a hub reduction in which the annulus is attached to the axle

casing. If the annulus has 60 teeth and the planet pinions 16 and the sun pinion is making 50 rev/min, at what speed is the roadwheel driven?

2. A two-start worm drives a worm-wheel with 40 teeth which drives a recovery vehicle's winch drum of 15 cm diameter. The effort handle in the form of a cranked lever has an effective length of 33 cm. If the effort applied is 168 N and the efficiency 67%, what load may be lifted?

3. The rev/min of the output shaft of the train of gears shown Fig. 5.74 is to be 120 when the input shaft is making 1600 rev/min. How many teeth has pinion D?

Fig. 5.74 Question 3.

4. The reduction gear for a recovery vehicle winch consists of a series of pinions as shown in Fig. 5.75. The number of teeth on the pinions are: A = 16, B = 31, C = 54, D = 18, and E = 68. The input rev/min at A are 800 in a clockwise direction. Calculate the rev/min at output E and the direction of rotation, viewing in the direction of the arrow.

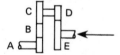

Fig. 5.75 Question 4.

5. A vehicle is being propelled in second gear by a tractive effort of 2.86 kN. The effective diameter of the roadwheels is 0.62 m. Second gear ratio is 2.75:1 and final drive 4.37:1. The roadwheels are making 167 rev/min. Determine the power being produced by the engine if the transmission losses amount to 23%.

6. An engine producing 36 kW power at 2560 rev/min is the power unit for a car which is in third gear of 1.26:1 ratio, Final drive ratio is 4.79:1. The rolling radius of the roadwheels is 0.26 m. Find the tractive effort when the transmission efficiency is 74%.

7. A complete rear axle was under an efficiency test in a college laboratory. The input pulley diameter was 350 mm and the external diameter of the wheel hubs 246 mm. The following data were recorded: revolutions of input pulley = 14.25, input load 21 N, revolutions of both wheel hubs = 3, output load 134 N. Determine the overall efficiency of the axle.

8. The total force applied to the rim of a steering wheel was 62 N which produced an output torque of 201 N m. The reduction ratio was 16.6:1 and the efficiency 72%. Calculate the steering wheel diameter.

9. A vehicle in second gear of 2.33:1 ratio is developing a torque of 1150 N m at the final drive crownwheel. The 2 litre four-stroke engine is developing a bmep of 630 kN/m^2. Assuming a transmission efficiency of 84%, find the final drive reduction ratio.

10. A steering wheel is 62 cm in diameter and the reduction ratio 22.3:1. The overall efficiency is 69% and the effort applied to the steering wheel is 42 N. Calculate the steering torque.

11. The engine of a truck is making 2340 rev/min when a gearbox ratio of 2.78:1 and final drive ratio 5.36:1 are employed. If the near-side wheel is making 26 rev/min, at what speed is the outer wheel rotating?

12. An effort of 67 N is applied by a driver to the 650 mm diameter steering wheel. The overall efficiency of the steering unit is 73%. What ratio is used in the system if the steering torque is 268 N m?

13. A vehicle is negotiating a road curve. The inner wheel is making 156 rev/min and the outer wheel 198 rev/min. The final drive ratio is 5.74:1, and gearbox ratio engaged 2.76:1. The engine torque at this moment is 132 N m. Determine the power the engine is developing in kW.

6
Electricity (F18)

6.1 THE SECONDARY CELL

A secondary cell, unlike a primary cell, does not convert chemical energy into electrical energy by destroying itself. The electrical energy supplied from an external source is converted and stored in the cell as chemical energy. When required this energy may be converted into direct electric current (d.c.).

Construction of a lead–acid cell

A casing is required to hold the plates, separators and electrolyte. It must be a sound insulator, acid-proof, and able to withstand some degree of vibration, knocks and abrasions during its service life. Ribs are moulded into the bottom of the container for the separators to rest on, leaving a space between the bottom of the plates and container to allow for the sediment displaced from the plates during service life and so prevent internal short circuits. Inside the case, each cell will have positive and negative plates made up of grids of lead into which the active material, lead oxide, is pressed. Capacity and current output are very dependent on the plate area, thus a number of thin plates are used to obtain the maximum active area in a given space. The positive and negative grids are kept apart by separators. These can be made of wood, but porous rubber, plastic and fibreglass are in use to-day.

Charging process

When connected to a suitable d.c. supply, current passes from the positive (+) to the negative (−) plate. The lead sulphate of the + plate is being converted to lead peroxide, while at the − plate lead sulphate is being converted to porous spongy lead by the flowing current. When in good condition and normally charged, the positive plate (if it can be seen) would appear a chocolate brown colour, and the negative plate a slate grey. The electrolyte water content diminishes as the acid content increases, thus relative density is on the increase, and when fully charged reaches 1.27–1.29.

Cell discharging

When the cell is connected to an external circuit the above process reverses (Fig. 6.1). Current flows from the positive plate through the external circuit and returns via the negative plate. Both plates are being converted back to lead sulphate and water is produced in the process. Hence the relative density of the electrolyte falls due to the loss of the acid content. When fully discharged the relative density will be 1.11–1.13.

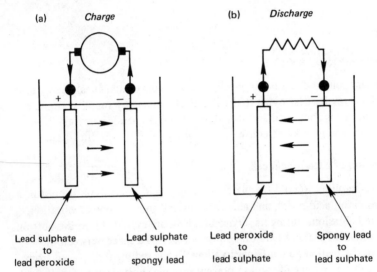

Fig. 6.1 Lead–acid battery. (a) Charge and (b) discharge.

Overcharging

Overcharging causes overheating and excessive gasing of the electrolyte, and weakening and the buckling of plate and separators. This can cause the active material to be forced from the positive plates and the formation of sediment could lead to short circuiting and possibly plate disintegration.

Undercharging

Insufficient charging will lead to excessive sulphation, increased internal resistance and loss of capacity.

Sulphation

As a lead–acid cell becomes discharged lead sulphate is formed on the plates. If recharging takes place normally, the sulphate is converted. Lead sulphate is a hard white substance which forms in crystals and can cause distortion of the grids and separators. A battery left in a discharged condition will build up sulphate at a rapid rate, increasing the internal resistance of the battery and reducing the battery's ability to provide a high current flow (low capacity) under starter motor action. The relative density of the electrolyte being too high or too low increases sulphation. A series of charge and discharge, carefully regulated, reduces the formation of hard sulphate and helps to maintain a healthy active material on which the acid can operate.

The electrolyte

This is a solution of sulphuric acid and distilled water and the relative density of the mixture is checked by a hydrometer.

	Relative densities
fully charged cell	1.270–1.290
half charged	1.190–1.210
discharged	1.110–1.130

Voltages during charge and discharge

Voltages are best recorded when the charge or discharge is being made at the normal rate for that particular battery capacity. When a battery is taken off charge its PD may be in the region of 2.3 to 2.4 volts, but when left for the electrolyte to cool the cell voltage will be about 2.1 volts. If it is now connected to an external load circuit and discharged at the normal rate (see *Cell and battery capacity*) the voltage will remain fairly constant for some hours (see Fig. 6.2) and then fall more quickly to 1.8 volts. On further discharge the fall is steeper and should be avoided to prevent sulphation.

Heavy discharge for short periods can be made for not more than 8 seconds such as for starter motor loads of 190–320 amperes. On charging at the normal rate from a cell voltage of 1.8, the voltage will rise to approximately 2.1 volts per cell in one to two hours then rise more slowly between 2.1 volts and 2.25 volts over a period of four hours and finally rise to 2.6 volts within a three-hour period.

Use of a hydrometer

Hydrometers are manufactured especially for testing the state of a cell by the relative density of the electrolyte. Calibrations are usually from 1.100 to 1.350 and sections may be coloured to show full charge, half-charge and discharged.

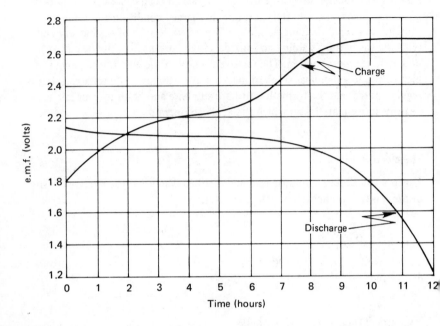

Fig. 6.2 Voltage variation with time.

Cell and battery capacity

Capacity is the ability to supply an electric current over a given period of time expressed in hours with the current in amperes, hence ampere hours or A h. A vehicle battery with a certain ampere hour rating should be able to supply a given current over a certain number of hours.

The ten-hour rating

The ten-hour rating is used in this country and represents the number of A h obtainable in a uniform and continuous discharge lasting 10 hours, commencing from a fully charged condition of 2.1 volts per cell and finishing when 1.8 volts per cell is reached. Thus the test is over the useful output range of the battery.

Some typical battery ratings are: 120 A h capacity = 12 A discharge for 10 hours; 72 A h capacity = 7.2 A discharge for 10 hours. Voltage range per cell, 2.1 volts to 1.8 volts.

Temperature and battery output

Low temperatures lower the current output and effective capacity. At the same time the engine's resistance to torque is higher and a sufficient safety factor regarding capacity should be allowed for.

Example taken from a fully charged battery.

Temperature	Voltage	Discharge current (amperes)
26°C	10	218
5°C	10	178
−10°C	10	150

6.2 BATTERY DEVELOPMENTS

The main problem with the lead—acid battery is its deterioration during normal service or when unused. This deterioration is mainly due to the addition of antimony to the grid plate lead thereby improving their robustness and service life, but reducing internal conductivity and increasing self-discharge. Some 4% to 7% antimony is used in the normal lead—acid battery.

The alkaline or nickel—cadmium battery has been used for many years where long life, robustness and the ability to accept considerably high charging and discharging rates together with long periods of inactivity are required. Unfortunately, the nickel—cadmium cell voltage is only 1.2 volts, thus the battery requires more cells than its lead—acid counterpart, making it heavier and bulkier, and also very expensive.

Long life maintenance-free batteries

Coming onto the market now are a new series of lead—acid batteries having a maintenance-free life of some 450 000 km fitted to commercial transport vehicles.

The internal conductivity of the cells has been improved by using lead—calcium grids instead of lead—antimony, and a denser paste which not only lowers the internal resistance of the cells but also withstands very heavy and frequent discharges without buckling.

New vehicles are fitted with alternators which have the characteristic of supplying high charging rates at low rotational speeds. This makes it more important for a battery to supply the necessary high torque and power which is required for cold starts when battery efficiency is low. The improved robustness and the lower internal resistance has improved the cold-start function.

Battery cases are moulded in reinforced polypropylene for good strength/weight ratio and in some cases stainless steel is used for the terminal posts.

The lids are sealed onto the main casing and incorporate a liquid/gas separator and flame arrestor in each cell and a form of hydrometer indicator to show when charging becomes necessary. The 'fleet' price of these models is very reasonable indeed and they will no doubt replace the ordinary lead—acid batteries for heavy duty service.

EXERCISES 6.1

1. The relative density of the electrolyte for a fully charged lead acid cell should be in the region of (a) 1.62, (b) 1.12, (c) 1.35, (d) 1.28.

2. A lead acid cell fully charged will have a voltage of (a) 2.5 V, (b) 1.12 V, (c) 1.8 V, (d) 2.1 V.

3. A lead acid battery of 40 amp hour capacity would be capable of a 10 hour discharge at the rate of (a) 4 amp, (b) 40 amp, (c) 0.04 amp, (d) 8 amp.

4. The relative density of the electrolyte of a fully discharged lead acid cell should be (a) 1.11, (b) 1.19, (c) 1.03, (d) 1.38.

5. Briefly describe sulphation and its causes.

6. Give a brief account of the charging and discharging process for a lead acid cell.

7
Miscellaneous exercises

7.1 MATERIALS

1. A steel rod of 7 mm diameter is to be made into a brake rod which will operate under tensile loads. In a test on an effective length of one metre, a tensile load of 236 N was applied. A safety factor of five is required which gives a safe working stress of 68 MN/m². Young's Modulus for the material is 198 GN/m². Determine the tensile strength of the material; the maximum safe tensile load; and the extension on the one metre length.

2. Sketch a load–extension graph which would apply to the tensile testing of a piece of mild steel, and explain the following terms:
(a) the limit of proportionality,
(b) the elastic limit,
(c) the yield stress,
(d) the maximum load,
(e) the tensile strength,
(f) the percentage elongation
(g) the percentage reduction in area.

3. A 650 mm length of 21 mm diameter steel rod with a Young's Modulus of 205 GN/m² extended 1.365 mm over the 650 mm length under tensile test. Determine the tensile load that was applied in kN.

4. An open coiled throttle return spring is stretched 4.3 cm when full throttle is applied and the tensional force is 2.5 N. By how much would it stretch for a tensile force of 0.32 N, assuming both forces are within the spring's elastic limit?

5. An aluminium alloy connecting rod has an average cross-sectional area of 126 mm², and is 23 cm between small- and big-end centres. The peak cylinder pressure developed in the CI engine cylinder of 130 mm diameter was 6620 kN/m². Young's Modulus for the material is 73 GN/m². Calculate the reduction in length between the connecting rod centres due to the peak gas pressure.

6. Tick what you consider is the correct answer:

Does Young's Modulus
(a) indicate the strength of the material?
(b) indicates the stress in a material?
(c) indicates the degree of elasticity a material possesses?
(d) indicates the strain in a material?

Limit of proportionality. Does this indicate:
(a) the curved portion of the load–extension graph?
(b) the strength of the material?
(c) the end of the elastic limit range?
(d) the plastic deformation range?

7. A tensile test on an 11.284 mm diameter steel test specimen of 50 mm gauge length produced the following results: final length on point of fracture, 64.2 mm; diameter at point of fracture, 7.35 mm; load at yield point 48.6 kN; maximum load 86.6 kN. Calculate: (a) the percentage reduction in area, (b) the percentage elongation, (c) the stress at yield point, and (d) the tensile strength.

7.2 HEAT

1. A CI engine piston of aluminium alloy has a diameter of 110 mm when the temperature is 16°C. Calculate the increase in diameter when the piston temperature has risen to 410°C. Coefficient of linear expansion for the alloy 0.000 022 °C.

2. An engine sump contains 7.2 l of oil. The oil temperature undergoes a temperature rise of 62°C. The relative density of the oil is 0.9 and specific heat 1668 J/(kg K). What amount of heat did the oil gain?

3. A cylinder bore of a CI engine is 112 mm diameter and the top of the aluminium alloy piston has a clearance of 2 mm when at a temperature of 16°C. What clearance will be available when the piston reaches a working temperature of 330°C?

4. The clearance between a steel gudgeon pin of 8 mm diameter and the aluminium alloy piston is 0.012 mm when both are at a temperature of 26°C. The coefficient of linear expansion of the piston material is 0.000 0221. Assuming piston and pin reach a working temperature of 278°C, what is the working clearance between pin and piston?

5. A vacuum gauge connected to the induction manifold reads 686 mm of mercury. What is the absolute pressure within the manifold?

6. A six cylinder four-stroke engine of 65 mm bore and stroke develops an imep of 970 kN/m^2 at 2800 rev/min. If the engine torque at this speed is 87 N m, determine the power lost to friction, etc., and the mechanical efficiency.

7. Air in a car tyre is found to be at a pressure of 201 kN/m^2 and 30°C temperature. Later when re-tested the temperature had fallen to 20°C. What would be the new tyre pressure assuming the volume remains constant?

8. A four cylinder engine of 3000 cm^3 total swept capacity has a clearance volume of 55 cm^3 per cylinder. The pressure of the charge before compression is 108 kN/m^2 abs and temperature 17°C. At the end of compression the temperature has increased to 612°C, calculate the final pressure.

9. A compressor has an air pressure of 103 kN/m^2 abs at 18°C at the commencement of its compression stroke. At the end of this stroke the pressure and temperature have become 1760 kN/m^2 abs and 132°C respectively. Determine the volume ratio of the machine.

10. If a quantity of gas at a pressure of 717 mm of mercury and temperature 16°C occupies a volume of 360 ml, what volume would it occupy at standard temperature and pressure?

11. The air pressure in a CI engine cylinder is 1.22 bar and temperature 23°C. The compression ratio is 19:1. At the end of compression the pressure becomes 73 bars. Calculate the air temperature.

12. A single cylinder motorcycle engine has a cylinder bore diameter of 82 mm and stroke of 86 mm. When the bmep is 806 kN/m^2, what average work is completed on the power stroke?

13. An engine having a compression ratio of 9.5:1 has a clearance volume of 58 cm^3 and stroke 102 mm. If the bmep is 796 kN/m^2, determine the average work done per power stroke.

14. Determine the bmep and brake thermal efficiency when a four cylinder four-stroke engine of 80 mm bore and 100 mm stroke consumes 6.9 l of fuel per hour, developing 16.5 kW power at 2000 rev/min. Relative density of the fuel 0.72 and CV 45 MJ/kg.

15. A six cylinder two-stroke engine of 3000 cm^3 swept capacity on test gave a specific fuel consumption of 0.35 kg/(kW h) when developing a bmep of 638 kN/m^2 at 1600 rev/min. If the CV of the fuel used was 45 MJ/kg, calculate the brake thermal efficiency.

16. An engine having four cylinders operating on the four-stroke cycle has a total swept volume of 2500 cm^3. At 3800 rev/min it develops a bmep of

750 kN/m² while consuming 20.6 kg of fuel per hour. CV of the fuel 45 MJ/kg. Determine the brake thermal efficiency and the power available in the fuel consumed.

17. A single cylinder two-stroke engine of 89 mm bore diameter has a power output of 23.6 kW at a mean piston speed of 920 m/min. What bmep is being developed?

18. An eight cylinder four-stroke cycle CI engine having a swept capacity of 0.003 m³ is producing a torque of 130 N m. Determine the bmep.

19. A six cylinder four stroke CI engine has a swept capacity of 8 litres and develops a torque of 420 Nm. The mechanical efficiency is 78.2%. Calculate the imep and the brake thermal efficiency if the specific fuel consumption is 0.29 kg/(kW h) and calorific value of the fuel 45 MJ/kg.

20. During a Morse test at 4000 rev/min a four cylinder four-stroke engine developed 27.7 kW brake power and 35.6 kW indicated power. Determine the engines mechanical efficiency and give a brief account of the method used to obtain these results.

7.3 DYNAMICS

1. The dwell angle of the ignition contact points was 60° when the four cylinder four-stroke engine was making 4600 rev/min. For what period of time were the contact points closed?

2. An engine crankshaft has an angular velocity of 272 rad/s. The engine stroke is 85 mm. Calculate the mean piston speed in metres per second.

3. The test dwell-angle of the distributor points for a four cylinder four-stroke engine was 61 degrees and this period was observed to take 0.006 seconds. At what speed was the test made?

4. A single plate clutch of 70 mm mean radius has a spring force of 3.2 kN acting at right angles to the frictional surfaces which have a coefficient of friction of 0.32. Maximum engine torque occurs at 2300 rev/min, and maximum power at 5750 rev/min. Determine the power the clutch is capable of transmitting at maximum engine power and state whether this clutch is suitable for the engine characteristics.

5. The power lost to friction at a bearing of 70 mm diameter rotating at 3600 rev/min is 0.3 kW. The coefficient of friction is 0.004. What mass load was the journal subjected to and how much heat was generated per min?

6. The clutch lining of a single driven plate has a total face area of 724 mm².

The mean radius is 11.5 cm and the coefficient of friction 0.35 between linings and driving surfaces. The spring pressure is limited to a maximum of 4 N/(mm^2 of the lining area). Calculate the power that could be transmitted by this clutch at 4800 rev/min and the heat generated if it developed a 3% slip.

7. A crankshaft having three main bearings of 65 mm diameter is rotating at 5200 rev/min and the coefficient of friction is 0.008. Calculate the power lost due to friction and the total heat generated at the bearings per minute if the average load is 3.65 kN per bearing.

8. A multi-plate clutch has six driven plates each of which carries a pair of annular friction linings having an outside diameter of 16 cm and inside diameter 10 cm. The spring pressure is to be limited to 2 N/(cm^2 of lining area). The coefficient of friction between linings and driven members is 0.3. If the effective mean radius of the clutch is 13 cm, what power can this clutch safely transmit at 4200 rev/min? If the clutch develops a 2% slip at this power, how much heat would be generated in one minute?

9. The front wheels of a vehicle are fitted with two caliper disc units per wheel. The pads operate at a radius of 145 mm and have a coefficient of friction of 0.45. The opposed pistons in each unit are of 30 mm diameter. The drivers pedal effort raises a brake line pressure of 2960 kN/m^2 and combined with the assistance of the brake servo a total line pressure of 4876 kN/m^2 is developed. The rear drum brakes account for 35% of the front brakes retarding torque. Determine the total braking torque during the retardation.

10. A stone thrown up at an angle of 43° by the rear tyre of a car is moving with a velocity of 20 m/s. What height will it reach in its flight and what horizontal distance is travelled before it reaches the height at which it left the tyre?

11. An engine flywheel is rotating at 3500 rev/min. Its diameter is 40 cm. Determine its angular velocity in rad/s and the linear velocity of a point on the flywheel rim.

12. If the flywheel in question 11 was accelerated from 3500 rev/min to 5000 rev/min in 0.5 s determine the angular acceleration of the flywheel and the linear acceleration of a point on the flywheel rim.

13. A truck is moving at a velocity of 4 m/s and then accelerated at the rate of 2.3 m/s^2 until it reaches a velocity of 14 m/s. Calculate the distance travelled during the acceleration.

14. A vehicle is being propelled in second gear by a tractive effort of 3.20

kN. The effective radius of the roadwheels is 0.35 m. Second gear ratio is 2.33:1 and final drive 4.53:1. The pair of driven roadwheels were making 186 rev/min. Determine the engine power if the transmission efficiency is 83%.

15. A mass is projected vertically with a velocity of 26 m/s. To what height will it rise and how long will it take to reach the height at which it was projected?

16. The engine of a truck is making 2650 rev/min when a gearbox ratio of 2.35:1 is engaged. The final drive ratio is 5.73:1. If the nearside wheel is making 152 rev/min, at what speed is the outer driven wheel rotating?

17. An engine crankshaft is making 3680 rev/min. The stroke is 80 mm. Determine the mean piston velocity m/s and the angular velocity of the crankshaft rad/s.

18. The phase angle of an in-line diesel fuel injection pump is 90°. If injection commences at intervals of 0.008 s at what speed was the four stroke CI engine running and how many cylinders to have injections?

7.4 STATICS

1. The force pressing a roadwheel to the road surface is 1.7 kN and the lateral force when cornering is 0.85 kN. Determine the resultant force and its direction in relation to the road surface.

2. The force on a piston is 3.5 kN and the connecting rod is placed at an angle of 7° to the cylinder bore axis. Friction between piston and cylinder amounts to 146 N. Calculate the force in the connecting rod and the reaction at the cylinder wall.

3. Determine the force acting parallel to the surface of a smooth inclined plane of 35° angle that would support a weight of 1000 N resting on the plane. What is the value of the resultant of the supporting force and the weight?

4. A force making an angle of 40° with the vertical and has a horizontal component of 10 N. Find the magnitude of the force.

5. An engine crankshaft has moved through an angle of 26° from TDC which displaces the connecting rod 7.5° from the cylinder axis. The force on the piston is 3540 N. The engine stroke is 110 mm. Determine the torque being delivered to the crankshaft.

6. A torsion bar undergoes a torsion test and twists 1.6° for an applied torque of 0.75 kN m. This increases to 5.4° twist when the torque is 3.6 kN m.

Calculate the torsional spring rate and the degree of twist when 1.8 kN m torque is applied.

7. A single cylinder engine crankshaft has an unbalanced mass of 7.3 kg acting at 62 mm distance from the shaft axis. What is the value of a balance mass which is to be placed at 5.56 cm from the shaft axis?

8. A connecting rod, 28 cm between centres, is weighed at the big-end centre and gave a reading of 2.8 kg, and 0.86 kg at the small-end centre. Find the position of the centre of gravity from the small-end centre.

9. A four-wheeled truck having a front axle loading of 3.62 Mg and rear axle loading of 6.58 Mg is standing on a simply supported level girder ramp of uniform section, 16 m in length. The ramp has a mass of 8.4 Mg. The vehicle's wheelbase is 4.2 m and is exactly in the centre of the ramp. Determine the reaction at the ramp supports.

10. An engine has a mass of 118 kg and is 1.45 m in length. When the front end was weighed the reading was 69.5 kg. Find the position at which a lifting eye may be fitted to enable the engine to be lifted and remain horizontal.

11. Two balance masses acting in the same plane balance a wheel. Mass A of 15.3 g is placed 17° from the tube valve and mass B of 37 g 56° from mass A. These two masses are to be replaced by a single mass. Find the value and position in relation to the valve.

12. The face-plate of a lathe carries masses A at 10 cm, B at 12 cm, and C at 9 cm from the axis of rotation. The angle between A and B is 60°, and 150° between masses B and C. Mass A = 5 kg, B = 7 kg and C = 10 kg. The face-plate is to be balanced by attaching a mass at 105 mm radius. Find the angular position from A and value of the balance mass.

13. A girder 8 m in length is supported at each end and has the following point loads: A = 8 kN at 2 m, B = 9 kN at 3 m, and C = 5 kN at 7 m from the left-hand support (R_a). The uniform beam weighs 10 kN. Determine the bending moments and shear forces at the supports and load positions A, B and C and at the beam centre.

14. A six-wheeled vehicle has a displacement of 6 m between the front axle and the leading rear axle, and 3 m between the two driving axles. The vehicle is on a girder type lift which has a support at the left-hand end and another support 3 m from the right-hand end of the 13 m length lift.

The front wheels of the vehicle are 2 m from the left-hand support. The 13 m lift platform weighs 70 kN. The vehicle axle loadings are: front axle 32 kN; leading rear axle 43 kN; and the trailing axle 47 kN. Find the reaction at the two lift supports.

Answers to Exercises

CHAPTER 1

Exercises 1.1 (p. 19)

1. 0.4 cm
2. 10.5 cm, 12.3 cm
3. (Descriptive)
4. 1.65 mm
5. 48.25 N, 11.97 cm
6. 4.8 kN, 0.743 mm
7. 200 GN/m^2
8. 38.4 kN
9. 12.15 cm; 1.2 kN/cm
10. 5.625 N/mm^2; 0.000 04, 140 GN/m^2
11. (a) 60.41%, (b) 32%, (c) 520 MN/m^2, (d) 880 MN/m^2
12. 187.5 MN/m^2, 197.5 MN/m^2
13. (a) 485 MN/m^2, (b) 186.5 MN/m^2, (c) 62.18%, (d) 29%, (e) 786 MN/m^2

CHAPTER 2

Exercises 2.1 (p. 27)

1. 33.52°C
2. 3.24 mm
3. 36.8 mm
4. 44.27 mm
5. 1.24 mm
6. 3.168 cm^2
7. 86.19 mm
8. 0.169 mm
9. 0.882 mm
10. 8.364 mm^3

Exercises 2.2 (p. 34)

1. 22 kW
2. 14.17°C
3. 174.9°C
4. 10.38 l/min
5. 77.865 kJ

Exercises 2.3 (p. 42)

1. 256°C
2. 33.7°C
3. 666°C
4. 4821 kN/m² abs
5. 12.27:1
6. 0.32 l
7. 659°C
8. 30 m³
9. 201.8°C
10. 23.89 kN/m² abs
11. 182.3 kN/m²

Exercises 2.4 (p. 48)

1. 129 mm
2. 9:1, 6.63:1
3. 8:1
4. 14.95:1
5. 10:1, 6.42:1
6. 70 mm
7. (a) 12:1, (b) 10.83:1
8. 12.32:1, 99 mm

Exercises 2.5 (p. 52)

1. 3.2 times
2. 14 bhp, 3.025 RAC hp rating
3. (a) 158.6 lbf/in², (b) 147 lbf/in², (c) 4.79 in³, (d) 6.37 in, (e) 57.62

Exercises 2.6 (p. 61)

1. 127 mm, 158.75 mm
2. 6.6 bar
3. 6.56 kW
4. 346 kN/m²
5. 999 N, 150 J
6. 327.24 J

Exercises 2.7 (p. 69)

1. 27.54%, 34.42%
2. 7.5 km/l

8. 22.2%, 779.2 kN/m²
9. 20.45%, 800 cm³

3. 36.83 kW
4. 38.38 kW
5. 32.310 MJ
6. 11.3 kW
7. 27.9%

10. 26.41 kW
11. (a) 40 kW, (b) 78.4%, (c) 0.27 kg/(kW h)
     (d) 29.62%
12. 20.39%

Exercises 2.8 (p. 77)

1. P_i = 22.05 kW, 85.8%   2. 89.6%   3. 82.85%

Exercises 2.9 (p. 79)

1. 47.11 kW, 77.26%   2. 84%, 0.6 m

Exercises 2.10 (p. 95)

1. 20.85%
2. 25 kW, 32.46 kW
3. 562 kN/m^2, 26.66%
4. (a) 63 kW, (b) 82.9%, (c) 0.286 kg/(kW h), (d) 28.6%
5. 26.1%
6. 1052 N m, 4.22 tonnes
7. 25%, 492 kN/m^2
8. P_b 20.12%, cooling 17.258%, exhaust, radiation, etc. 62.62%
9. 4.36 kN
10. 20.45%, 931 cm^3
11. bmep 826.8 kN/m^2, imep 1033.5 kN/m^2
12. P_b 26.52%, cooling 33.97%, exhaust, radiation, etc. 39.51%.
13. 24.86%, P_b 22.38%, cooling 35.4%, friction 2.48%, exhaust and radiation 39.7%

CHAPTER 3

Exercises 3.1 (p. 110)

1. 6.44s, 87.6 m, 2.6 m/s^2
2. 494.8 m, first gear – 0.444 m/s^2, 2nd gear – 0.507 m/s^2
3. 0.694 m/s^2, 138.9 m
4. 44.5 m/s, 1534 m
5. 39.13 m
6. 24 m/s, 22.7 m

Exercises 3.2 (p. 121)

1. 13.32 m/s, 3.277 m, 17.7 J
2. 26.71 s, 262 m/s
3. 7.34 m, 2.446 s
4. 15.99 m/s
5. 8.074 m, 2.02 m
6. 4.405 m, 37.8 m
7. 2.452 m/s, 14.12 m, 1.354 s, 13.28 m/s
8. 0.644 m, 3.68 m

Exercises 3.3 (p. 126)

1. (a) 48.6 rad/s, (b) 2242 rev/min
2. 415.18 rev/min, 43.47 rad/s
3. 0.5 m
4. 2.094 rad/s, 0.795 m/s
5. 21.3 rad/s, 8.094 m/s, 29.13 km/h
6. 10.92 m/s, 439.8 rad/s
7. 3500 rev/min, 366.5 rad/s
8. 4132 rev/min
9. (a) 10.55°, (b) 29.55°, (c) 31.36°, (d) 21.7°
10. 0.0036 s
11. 655.74 m/s
12. 1000 rev/min, 6 cylinders
13. 3332 rev/min, 174.5 rad/s
14. 0.68 m

Exercises 3.4 (p. 133)

1. 5.12 kW, 18.45 MJ/h
2. Shaft A — 586 W, 2.10 MJ/h. Shaft B — 100.5 W, 362 kJ/h
3. 0.014
4. 590 W, 35.4 kJ/min
5. 1.38 W, 83 J/min

Exercises 3.5 (p. 138)

1. 45.7%
2. 35°
3. 0.372
4. 196.4 N m, 116.2 kW
5. 0.476 m or 476 mm diameter
6. 60 kW

Exercises 3.6 (p. 153)

1. (a) 231.7 N m, (b) 15.77 kW, (c) 946 kJ/min
2. 0.35
3. 29%
4. 145.9 kN
5. 7.91 kN
6. 2623 N m

CHAPTER 5

Exercises 5.1 (p. 188)

1. 29.43 kN, 50.97 kN
2. 21.1 kN, 4.38 kN
3. 2.743 kN, 10.23 kN
4. 5.97 kN, 28.6°
5. 3.67 kN
6. 4 kN, 12° south of East
7. 1.39 kN, 59.74°
8. 1880 N, 65.8°, 20.2°
9. 32.5 g, 31.5° from X, 8.55 N
10. 2.72 kN, 72.9°
11. 701 N, 1438 N
12. 68.7 g, 51° from A
13. 4.78 kN, 1.46 kN
14. 0.215 kg each, 4758 N
15. 5.2 kN, 18.25°
16. 1995 N, 346.4 N
17. 14.5 kN m
18. 16.88 kN m

Exercises 5.2 (p. 204)

1. 112 mm
2. 1.856 m, 0.772 m
3. R_F = 2.4 tonne, R_R = 3.19 tonne, 34.5°
4. 1.167 m from axis yy
5. 12.127 cm
6. 723.68 N
7. 1.624 m, 0.68 m

Exercises 5.3 (p. 226)

1. R_a = 72.8 kN, R_b = 78.2 kN
2. R_a = 126.43 kN; R_b = 113.57 kN
3. R_a = 19.6 kN, R_b = 30 kN
4. 16 kN left, 34 kN right
5. R_L = 608.4 kN, R_R = 741.6 kN
6. R_F = 82.4 kN, R_R = 64.74 kN
7. R_a = 44.3 kN; R_b = 48.8 kN
8. (a) 5.253 m from front axle, (b) R_a = 115 kN, R_b = 185 kN
9. BM at A = + 20 kN m, SF between AB = + 10 kN
   BM at B =   0 kN m, SF between BC = + 4 kN
   BM at C = − 12 kN m, SF between CD = − 4 kN
10. Nearside BM = −6.07 kN m, offside BM = −6.35 kN m
11. BM at centre = 63 kN m,
    SF at centre = 0 kN
12. BM at B = − 310 kN m, SF between AB = − 155 kN
    BM at C = − 820 kN m, SF between BC = − 85 kN
    BM at D = − 750 kN m, SF between CD = + 35 kN
                          SF between DE = + 125 kN
13. BM = −8 kN m, BM = + 18 kN m
    SF = +8 kN, SF = − 25 kN
14. R_F = 22.4 kN R_R = 17.6 kN
    BM at B = +20 kN m   SF between AB = +10 kN
    BM at C = −4.8 kN m   SF between BC = −12.4 kN
    BM at D = +12 kN m   SF between CD = +5.6 kN
    BM at E = 0   SF between DE = −12 kN
15. BM at A = 0 N cm   16. BM at A = 0
    BM at B = 240 N cm   BM at B = +20 kN m
    BM at C = 6360 N cm   BM at C = +38 kN m
    BM at D = 9960 N cm   BM at D = +83 kN m
    SF between A and B = 20 N   SF between D and C = −15 kN
    SF between B and C = 90 N   SF between C and B = − 9 kN
    SF between C and D = 120 N   SF between B and A = −5 kN

Exercises 5.4 (p. 238)

1. 237.5 N/mm, 23.578 mm
2. 8.6 mm
3. (a) 0.2 kN/cm or 200 N/cm, (b) 0.9 kN or 900 N
4. 1.3 kN m/degree, 2°
5. 55.25 N.
6. 0.4 kN/mm, 10 cm
7. 3.5 kN

Exercises 5.5 (p. 262)

1. 15.9 rev/min
2. 4.952 kN
3. 150
4. 75 rev/min, anti-clockwise
5. 20.13 kW
6. 2.3 kN
7. 94.4%
8. 0.542 m
9. 5.86:1
10. 200.3 N m
11. 188 rev/min
12. 16.85:1
13. 38.76 kW

CHAPTER 6

Exercises 6.1 (p. 270)

1. (d) 1.28
2. (d) 2.1 v
3. (a) 4 amp
4. (a) 1.11

CHAPTER 7

7.1 Materials

1. 340 MN/m^2, 2.616 kN, 0.343 mm
3. 149 kN
4. 5.5 mm
5. 2.19 mm
7. (a) 57.57%, (b) 28.4%, (c) 486 N/mm^2 or MN/m^2, (d) 866 N/mm^2 or MN/m^2.

7.2 Heat

1. 0.943 mm
2. 670 kJ
3. 1.24 mm
4. 0.0324 mm
5. 9.872 kN/m^2 abs
6. 3.8 kW, 87%
7. 192 kN/m^2

8. 4812 kN/m² abs
9. 12.27:1
10. 320.8 ml
11. 659°C
12. 366 N m or J
13. 392 N m or J
14. 492 kN/m², 26.5%
15. 22.85%
16. 23%, 257.5 kW
17. 494.8 kN/m²
18. 544.5 kN/m²
19. 843.6 kN/m², 27.58%
20. 77.8%

7.3 Dynamics

1. 0.004 34 s
2. 441.5 m/s
3. 1694 rev/min
4. 86.32 kW. Clutch is capable of transmitting 13.3 N m torque above the maximum engine torque.
5. 579 kg, 18 kJ/min
6. 117 kW, 210.6 kJ/min
7. 1.565 kW, 93.9 kJ/min
8. 605 kW, 726 kJ/min
9. 1213 N m
10. 9.48 m, 40.67 m
11. 366.5 rad/s, 73.3 m/s
12. 314.2 rad/s², 62.84 m/s²
13. 39.13 m
14. 26.26 kW
15. 34.45 m, 5.3 s
16. 241.6 rev/min
17. 9.81 m/s, 385.3 rad/s
18. 3748 rev/min, four cylinders

7.4 Statics

1. 1.9 kN, 63.4°
2. 3.379 kN, 414 N
3. 573.5 N, 819 N
4. 15.56 N
5. 107.7 N m

6. 0.75 kN m/degree twist, 2.4°
7. 8.14 kg
8. 8.6 cm
9. R_a = 87.44 kN, R_b = 95 kN
10. 0.854 m from rear end
11. 47.2 g placed 32.56° from valve
12. 263.2°, 11.3 kg
13. BM at R_a = 0, BM at A = −34.5 kN m, BM at B = −43.75 kN m, BM at centre of beam = −44 kN m, BM at C = −14.75 kN m. Shear force (SF) between R_a and A = −17.25 kN, SF between A and B = −9.25 kN, SF between B and centre of beam = −0.25 kN, SF between centre and C = +9.75 kN, SF between C and R_b = +14.75 kN
14. R_a = 54 kN, R_b = 138 kN

Index

Absolute pressure, 35, 36
Absolute temperature, 38
Absolute zero of temperature, 36
Acceleration
  gravitational, 111
  relative, 113
  uniform, 107
Adiabatic compression of a gas,
  39, 40
Adiabatic expansion of a gas, 39,
  40
Air blast injection, 54
Air−fuel ratio, 103
Air standard efficiency, 53
Ampere-hour, 268
Angle of friction, 129
Angle of twist, 236, 237
Angular displacement, 121, 122
Angular velocity, 123
Annealing, 9
Annulus, 259−62
Anti-corrosive, 166, 168
Anti-scuffing, 166
Area projected, 156, 157
Atmospheric pressure, 35
Average velocity, 106
Axles
  double reduction, 250
  two-speed, 250

Balancing of roadwheel, 181
Bar, 35
Battery developments, 269
Beam, reaction of supports, 205
Bearings
  ball, 157, 158

lead−bronze, 156
materials, 155
needle roller, 163
plain, 155
pre-lubricated, 156
projected area, 156, 157
roller, 157, 161,162, 163
tapered roller 161, 163
white-metal shell, 155
Bending, 2
Bending moment of beams,
  210−25
  sign convention of, 210
Bodies projected at an angle, 117,
  118
Boiling point
  of fuels, 98, 99
  of liquids, 33
Boyle's Law, 36, 39
Bore/stroke ratio, 59, 60
Bow's notation, 170
Brake mean effective pressure, 56,
  58, 59, 60, 61
Brake power, 58, 59, 60, 61
Brake thermal efficiency, 66, 67,
  68, 69
Brakes, 139
  disc, 148
  drum, 139
  leading and trailing shoe, 145,
    146, 147
  pedal travel, 141
  servo action, 141
  shoe factor, 141
Braking efficiency and stopping
    distance, 142, 143

Braking effort, 139
Braking force, 139
Braking torque, 139
Breaking stress, 11, 13

Calorific value, 97
Calorimeter, 97
Cantilever, 221−5
Cell or battery capacity, 268
Centre of gravity, 195−204
Cetane number, 101
Characteristic engine curves, 72
Charles' Law, 37, 38, 39
Clutch, 133
  axial spring force, 135
  cone, 134
  plate, 133, 136
  power transmitted, 134, 135
  slip, 136
  torque transmitted by, 134, 135
Coefficient of friction, 128, 129
Coefficient of linear expansion,
  22
Combustion cycle, dual, 54
Combustion of hydrocarbon fuels,
  101
Compression
  adiabatic, 32, 40
  isothermal, 39, 40
  ratio, 43−8
  stroke, 45, 53
Compressive strain, 1, 2, 3
Compressive stress, 1, 2
Connecting rod
  angular displacement, 175, 176
  force or thrust in, 175
Conservation of energy, 74
Constant pressure cycle, 53, 54
Constant volume cycle, 53
Consumption
  fuel, 65
  loop, 73, 86
Crankshaft, torque at, 176, 177
Curves
  brake mean effective pressure,
    67, 86, 88

  brake power, 67, 72, 80, 85
  brake thermal efficiency, 67,
    84, 85
  engine characteristics, 72
  frictional power, 80
  fuel power, 85
  indicated mean effective
    pressure, 67
  indicated power, 67, 80
  indicated thermal efficiency, 67
  mechanical efficiency, 80
  performance, 67
  specific fuel consumption, 72,
    80, 84, 85, 86
  torque, engine, 72, 80
Cycle
  constant pressure, 53, 54
  constant volume, 53
  dual, combustion, 54, 55

Density, relative, 65, 66
Detonation, 98, 102
Diagrams
  bending moment of beams,
    212, 213, 215, 217, 221,
    222, 223, 225
  force, 169, 170
  indicator, engine, 56
  pressure−volume, 56
  space, 169, 170
Diesel cycle, 54, 55
Diesel index number, 101
Differential, 254
  limited slip, 257
  third, 251
DIN, 63
Direct burning period, 54
Disc brakes, 148
Displacement
  angular, 121, 122
  of connecting rod, 175, 176
  of piston, 179
Double reduction axle, 250
Double shear, 2
Dual combustion cycle, 54, 55
Dynamic balance, 181

Effective pressure
  brake mean, 58
  indicated mean, 56
Efficiency
  air standard, 53
  brake thermal, 66, 67, 68, 69,
    84, 85
  braking, 139, 142, 143
  final drive, 248, 249
  gearbox, 247
  indicated thermal, 67, 68
  mechanical, 57, 58, 59, 74, 75,
    76, 77, 78, 79, 80
  rear axle, 248, 249
  thermal, 66, 85
  transmission, 252
  volumetric, 73
Effort
  braking, 139
  ideal, 240
  tractive, 251
Elastic limit, 4, 11
Elasticity, 3
  modulus of, 56
Electricity, 265
Electrolyte, 267
Elementary thermodynamics, 35,
  42
Energy
  conservation of, 74
  change of, 74
Engine
  characteristics and curves, 71, 72
  cycles, 52
  efficiency, 49
  performance curves, 67
  pistons, 26
  power, 49
  testing, 71
  torque, 61, 63, 64, 65, 73
Epicyclic gearing, 259–62
Equations
  gas, 39
  of free falling bodies, 111
  of linear motion, 108
Equilibrium, 196, 197

Exhaust gases, percentage of, 103
Expansion, 22
  cubical, 24, 25, 27
  linear, 22, 23, 27
  superficial, 24, 25, 26
  thermal, 24
Extension, 1, 3, 4, 6, 7, 8, 9, 10,
  12, 13

Falling bodies
  acceleration of, 111
  equations of, 111
  free, 111
  having horizontal motion, 113,
    114, 115, 116
Flash point, 100
Final drive unit, 248
Forces
  braking, 143
  cylinder wall, 175
  gravitational, 111
  in connecting rod, 175
  on piston, 175
  propelling, 251
Free falling bodies, 111
Friction, 128
  angle of, 129
  bearing, 128, 129
  clutch, 133
  coefficient of, 128, 129
  force of, 128, 129
  heat generated by, 131
  laws of, 128, 129
  static, 128
Frictional forces, 128
Frictional torque, 130
Fuel consumption, 65, 85
  curves, of, 84, 85
  loop, 73, 86
  specific, 65, 66, 67, 72, 73
Fuels
  hydrocarbon, 97
  in IC engines, 97
  liquid, 97
  non-volatile, 101
  thermal efficiency of, 98

Fuel power, 66, 68, 69, 85

Gas
    absolute pressure, 35
    equation, 39
    laws, 36, 37, 38
Gears and pinions, 243
Gearbox, 246
    efficiency, 247
    ratio, 247
Graphs, scale of, 74
Gravitational force, 111
Gravity
    acceleration due to, 111
    force of, 111

Heat
    balance tests, 89, 90, 91, 92
    energy, 74
    energy loss, 89, 90
    latent, 28
    sensible, 28
    transfer, 31
Hooke's Law, 4, 7
Hydrometer, 267

Ideal effort, 240
Ignition
    curves, 88
    tests, 86
    timing, 86, 87, 88
Indicated mean effective pressure,
        56, 57, 58
Indicated power, 57, 58, 59, 74
Indicator diagram, engine, 56
Isothermal expansion and
        compression, 39, 40

Kilowatt, 65, 66, 67, 68, 69
Kilowatt-hour, 66, 67, 68, 69
Kinetic friction, 128

Latent heat
    of fusion, 28, 29, 30
    of vaporization, 28, 98

Laws
    Boyle's, 36, 39
    Charles', 37, 38, 39
    gas, 36, 37, 38
    Hooke's, 47
    of friction, 128, 129
Lead—acid cell, 265
Levers, order of, 240, 241
Limit
    elastic, 4, 11
    of proportionality, 5, 12
Linear displacement, 121, 122
Linear expansion, 22
Linear motion, equations of, 108
Linear velocity, 123
Load—extension graph, 8, 12
Loop, fuel consumption, 73
Lubrication, 155
    oils, properties of, 164

Machine, mechanical, 230
Materials, 1
Maximum bending moment, 212
Mean effective pressure
    brake, 58
    indicated, 56
Mechanical efficiency, 57, 74,
        240
    curves of, 80
Mid-ordinate rule, 56
Mixture ratio, 98, 99
Modulus of elasticity, 5, 6, 11, 12
Moment, bending, 210
    diagrams, 212
    sign convention for, 210
Moments, principle of, 190, 191
Motion, equations of, 108
Morse test, 74, 75, 76, 77

Natural frequency of oscillation,
        229
Normal temperature and pressure,
        40

Pascal, 35
Percentage elongation, 15, 16, 17

Percentage reduction in area, 17
Performance, engine curves, 67, 72
Permanent elongation, 14
Pistons
    displacement, 179
    expansion, 26
    force on, 175
    side thrust of, 175, 176
    slap, 26
    speed, mean, 50, 81
    work done on, 55
Planet carrier, 259, 260, 261
Planet pinions, 259, 260, 261
Power
    at crankshaft, 62, 63
    at driving roadwheels, 252
    brake, 58, 59, 62, 63, 72
    lost to friction, 75, 78, 79, 80
    transmitted by clutch, 134, 136, 137
    transmitted by engine, 49, 50
Pressure, 35, 40
Projected bearing area, 156
Proof load, 18
Proof stress, 11, 13, 14, 15, 18
Properties of lubricating oils, 164
Proportionality, limit of, 5, 12, 13, 14, 15, 16, 17
Pumping and frictional losses, 90

RAC treasury hp rating, 50, 51, 52
Radiation losses, 89, 91, 92, 93, 94, 95
Ratios
    air–fuel, 103
    compression, 43–8
    final drive, 248
    gearbox, 247
    movement, 239
    overall, reduction, 248
Reduction, hub, 251, 262
Reduction in area, 11
Repose, angle of, 129
Retarded ignition, 87
Roadwheel balancing, 181

SAE, 63
Scalar quantity, 104
Shear
    double, 1, 2
    single, 1, 2
    stress, 1, 2
Shearing force and shearing force diagrams, 211–25
Side thrust of piston, 175, 176
Specific fuel consumption, 65, 73
Specific heat capacity, 30, 31, 34
Speed, 104
Springs
    period of oscillation, 229
    rate, 229
    variable rate, 230
Standard efficiency, air, 53
Standard temperature and pressure, 40
Standard test specimen, 11
Static balance, roadwheel, 181
Strain, 1
    compressive, 2, 3
    tensile, 13
Strength, tensile, 13
Stress, 1
    bending, 2, 3
    breaking, 11, 13
    compressive, 1, 2
    proof, 11, 13
    tensile, 1
    torsional, 2

Tangential force, 186
Temperature, 35
    absolute, 38
    absolute zero, 36
    normal, 40
Tensile
    strain, 3
    strength, 6
    stress, 1
    test piece, 11, 12
    tests, 11
Test, Morse, 74, 75, 76, 77
Test specimen, 11, 12

Testing of materials, 8, 11
Thermal efficiency, 66
   brake, 66, 67, 68, 69
   curves of, 67, 85
   of fuels, 98
   indicated, 67, 68
Thermodynamics, elementary, 35,
   42
Thermal expansion, 22
Thrust
   between piston and cylinder
     wall, 175, 176
   in connecting rod, 175
   race or bearing, 160
Torque, 62, 73
   braking, 139
   crankshaft, 63, 176, 177, 178
   engine, 61, 63, 64, 65, 73
   frictional, 139
   input, 247
   output, 247
   roadwheels, 250, 251
   transmitted by clutch, 134,
     135
   transmitted by gearbox, 248
   unit of, 61
   work done by, 63
Torsion bars, 233–6
Torsional stress, 2

Tractive effort, 251
Transmission and steering
   components, 238
Transmission efficiency, 252
Triangle and polygon of forces,
   169–73, 184
Twist, angle of, 236, 237

Velocity
   average, 104, 105, 106
   uniform, 104
Viscometer, Redwood no. 1, 167,
   168
Viscosity, index, 164, 165
Volume, 35
Volumetric efficiency, 73

Wheel balance, 181–4
   dynamic, 181
   static, 181
Work done, 55, 56, 58, 59, 61, 62
   in an engine cylinder, 55
   on power stroke, 59, 60, 61

Yield point, 12, 13, 14
Young's modulus, 5, 6, 11, 12

Zero temperature, absolute, 36